Shinggel

THE PLOT OF SATIRE

THE PLOT OF SATIRE

ALVIN B. KERNAN

New Haven and London: Yale University Press

Copyright © 1965 by Yale University.
Third printing, February 1971.
Designed by John O. C. McCrillis,
set in Linotype Garamond,
and printed in the United States of America by
The Carl Purington Rollins Printing-Office of
the Yale University Press, New Haven, Connecticut.

Distributed in Great Britain, Europe, and Africa by
Yale University Press, Ltd., London; in Canada by
McGill-Queen's University Press, Montreal; in Mexico
by Centro Interamericano de Libros Académicos,
Mexico City; in Central and South America by
Kaiman & Polon, Inc., New York City; in Australasia
by Australia and New Zealand Book Co., Pty., Ltd.,
Artarmon, New South Wales; in India by UBS
Publishers' Distributors Pvt., Ltd., Delhi; in Japan by
John Weatherhill, Inc., Tokyo.

Library of Congress catalog card number: 65–22327
ISBN: 0–300–00621–7

Published with assistance from the
Kingsley Trust Association Publication Fund
established by the Scroll and Key Society of
Yale College.

Preface

Few books are written without the aid of a great many people, and *The Plot of Satire* is no exception to the general rule. The book was conceived and writing begun during 1957–58 while on a Morse Fellowship, continued during several years of teaching a seminar in comedy and satire, and the bulk of the writing done in a year (1961–62) free of teaching financed by an American Council of Learned Societies Fellowship and Yale University. During this time several of the chapters were published in a modified form —"*The Dunciad* and the Plot of Satire," *SEL,* II, 1962; "The Wall and the Jungle: The Early Novels of Evelyn Waugh," *Yale Review,* LIII, 1964; "The Mob Tendency in Satire: *The Day of the Locust,*" *Satire Newsletter,* I, 1963; while the chapter on *Volpone* appeared in an extended form as the introduction to the edition of that play in the Yale Ben Jonson. I am most grateful for the efforts made over these sections by the various editors involved and for their permission to reprint. At the same time I should like to thank a number of friends and colleagues who looked at portions of the manuscript and suggested changes; most particularly my thanks are due Maynard Mack, Louis L. Martz, Eugene Waith, Adam Parry, and Aubrey Williams.

A word is necessary about citations. In a book in which the emphasis is critical, I have assumed that readers will be more concerned with following the direction of the argument than with being told the exact location of every line and word quoted. In order to improve the appearance of the page and facilitate reading, I have provided no precise citations for brief excerpts; instead, when the work from which they are taken is first referred to, a covering citation is provided, giving the range of pages or sections from which quotations are drawn. In the case of longer

passages, however, and some short ones crucial to the argument, I have provided exact references in as unobtrusive a manner as possible.

A.B.K.

New Haven, Connecticut
June 1965

Acknowledgments

My thanks are due the following publishers and literary agents for permission to quote copyrighted material from the listed works:

> *The Satyricon of Petronius,* trans. William Arrowsmith, University of Michigan Press. Copyright © by William Arrowsmith 1959.
>
> George Orwell, *Down and Out in Paris and London,* Harcourt, Brace and World. Copyright 1933 by George Orwell. Reprinted by permission of Brandt and Brandt and Martin Secker and Warburg Ltd.
>
> George Orwell, "Such, Such, Were the Joys," Harcourt, Brace and World; and Martin Secker and Warburg.
>
> Nathanael West, *Miss Lonelyhearts and The Day of the Locust.* Copyright 1936 by the Estate of Nathanael West. Copyright 1939 by Nathanael West. Copyright © 1962 by New Directions. Reprinted by permission of the publishers, New Directions.
>
> Evelyn Waugh, *Decline and Fall, Vile Bodies, Black Mischief, Handful of Dust, Helena, Brideshead Revisited, When the Going Was Good,* Little, Brown and Company; and A. D. Peters and Company.

Contents

I

THE CRITICAL SETTING

1. The Two Poles of Satire

After a good deal of bloodshed and strong coercion, the Christian community was at last made to understand that evil and its personification, the Devil, are not positive forces existing in their own right, but are rather negatives properly defined only as the absence of good. Satire has most often been regarded from the same orthodox perspective and treated as a negative literary genre which shows not the action of some essential force—as comedy, tragedy, and epic do—but rather the bumbling confusion which occurs in the absence of good sense and with the loss of traditional values. The better authors of satire, however, have been literary Manichees who have shown an ancient and powerful force operating constantly and expressing its own nature through all lands and times. Pope makes this view clear and takes the necessary step when he erects the force as a goddess, and gives it a name, The Mighty Mother, Dulness:

> In eldest time e'er mortals writ or read.
> E'er Pallas issu'd from the Thund'rer's head,
> Dulness o'er all posses'd her ancient right,
> Daughter of Chaos and eternal Night:
> Fate in their dotage this fair Ideot gave,
> Gross as her sire, and as her mother grave,
> Laborious, heavy, busy, bold, and blind,
> She rul'd in native Anarchy, the mind.
>   Still her old Empire to restore she tries,
> For, born a Goddess, Dulness never dies.
>   (*The Dunciad*, I, 9–18)[1]

1. The Twickenham Edition of the Poems of Alexander Pope, 5, ed. James Sutherland (London and New Haven, 1953).

To the modern ear the word "dullness" suggests nothing more sinister than torpidity and doltishness; but in the course of *The Dunciad* Pope expands the meaning of the term by showing that, while his duncesmay be "blind," they are still endlessly "Laborious . . . busy, bold." Broad-faced and smiling, they may work at random and never know what they are doing, but their activity is ceaseless, and as it accumulates, it becomes gradually more vicious and more frightening. What begins as the mere clumsy attempts of a few hack writers to win fame and fortune moves in the space of four books to universal darkness, chaos, and uncreation. Before Pope is finished with the words "dullness" and "dunce," they have become broad enough to cover the wide range of idiocy and viciousness portrayed in all satire and thus to provide us with generic names for the perennial subject of satire, that primal energy which drives the world toward the strange grotesque shapes it assumes in this type of writing.

It would appear that to understand satire and make sense of its incredible variety of forms and techniques, we must concentrate on its central fact, the energy of dullness. But such a view has been prohibited for a long time by both the tendency to regard it as a "negative" genre and a related critical perspective that looks at satire through the author. Noticing the tendency of satiric authors to speak in the first person, to flaunt their literary personalities, to attack their personal enemies by name, and to manipulate their material in a most obvious fashion, readers and critics have marked satire down as a form of skillful attack which uses any method at hand to discredit whatever the author fears or hates. This view makes of satire a type of propaganda originating in the author's prejudices and shaped to persuade us to share those prejudices. In its crudest form, this theory has led critics to explain satire by tracing its peculiarities back to the physical illnesses, the psychic disorders, and the social difficulties of the poet: Swift's "madness," Pope's hunchback, Ben Jonson's toilet training,[2] Byron's ostracism and family medical history,

2. This remarkable explanation of Jonson's work is Edmund Wilson's, "Morose Ben Jonson," *The Triple Thinkers* (New York, 1948), pp. 213–32.

and Orwell's painful childhood. Hand in hand with the biograph-
ical approach we always get the historical approach, which examines the picture of society constructed in a given satire, compares
it with other nonsatiric views of the same society, and then concludes that the satirist is at best exaggerating, at worst lying,
for some sinister reason. Juvenal's Rome, this method will inform
us, could not possibly have been as debauched and dirty as he
paints it, and therefore there must have been something wrong
with the man who constructed this grotesque version of the Rome
of the Caesars. More sophisticated critics have avoided such crude
methods as these but have retained the view of satire as persua-
sive rhetoric. These critics are willing to grant the sanity, even
the genius, of certain authors of satire in perceiving what is
wrong with their world and ours, and their moral intention to
cure it, but these critics have continued to regard the actual
satire as only a series of loosely related illustrations of stupidity
and a variety of strategies designed to show the dangers of certain practices and views.

The authors of satire, on the other hand, have always insisted
in their works and occasional writings, that their satire originates
in the dullness of men, not in their own malice. "Fools rush into
my head, and so I write," is the way Pope puts it. The scenes of
idiocy and greed which they construct are not, they have argued,
the products of misanthropy, but the work of serious artists trying
to catch the grotesque shapes toward which the human form and
the world are being forced under the weight of stupidity. Their
works, they state again and again, are not the reflections of a dis-
torting, crazy-house mirror, but rather images of a crazy world reflected in a "steele glass," a perfectly ground and uncompromising-
ly honest mirror. In one satire the mirror is perfect but we have to
step through the looking-glass and look at its back side to see the
true images it catches. In short, the authors of satire have insisted
that their works are literature, symbolic worlds and plots constructed to reveal the nature and workings of dullness, not com-
plexes of devices aimed at disabling particular men or practices
by ridicule. Enough work has been done by critics to support the

satirists' claims for their art, but as yet we have only a very limited amount of criticism which helps us to locate the true nature of dullness, the forms it takes, the patterns it follows.

Dryden's "A Discourse Concerning the Original and Progress of Satire" (1693)[3] summarizes the attempts of Renaissance scholars to provide satire with a history and a definition, and it is the last serious attempt to understand satire before this century. It would be useless to pretend that the "Essay on Satire" is a subtle and complete description of satire which stands to this literary kind as Aristotle's *Poetics* stands to tragedy: a complete formal definition and a generator of further definitions. The "Essay on Satire" is fragmentary, poorly organized, frequently ambiguous, and conventional in the extreme. But with patience its parts can be sorted out and a large framework discerned which will contain most serious criticism of satire before and since Dryden's time. The task Dryden sets for himself is a large one: "to give . . . from the best authors, the origin, the antiquity, the growth, the change, and the completement of Satire among the Romans; to describe, if not define, the nature of that poem, with its several qualifications and virtues, together with the several sorts of it; to compare the excellencies of Horace, Persius, and Juvenal, and show the particular manners of their satires; and, lastly, to give an account of this new way of version, which is attempted in our performance." Satire then is to be defined in four ways: (1) by tracing its historical development from primitive forms to its "completement" by the Romans, (2) by formal description of its "nature," (3) by comparison of the work of the three most important Roman satirists, and (4) by a description of the new kind of satire Dryden is offering—the "Essay" was written as an introduction to Dryden's translation of Juvenal and Persius.

The first three of these methods are still standard critical techniques, and by using all of them Dryden achieves a remarkable effect of universality for his conclusions, since each method leads him to exactly the same point. In his study of the historical

3. All citations of the "Essay on Satire" are to *Essays of John Dryden,* ed. W. P. Ker (2 vols. Oxford, 1926), 2, 15–114.

development of satire, he begins at the beginning: "After God had cursed Adam and Eve in Paradise, the husband and wife excused themselves, by laying the blame on one another; and gave a beginning to those conjugal dialogues in prose, which the poets have perfected in verse." Facetious as these lines are, they still contain Dryden's major premise, that satire originated in some sort of rude curse which manifests no more than the ill will of the speaker. He then turns from myth to history and, relying on the writings of various humanist scholars, Scaliger, Dacier, Heinsius, and Casaubon, traces the development of satire from its crude beginnings in invective and curses—"scoffs and revilings are of the growth of all nations"—through such rough satiric forms as Greek old comedy, *silloi,* Fescennine verses, and Atellan fables to the ultimate stabilization and perfection of the form in the work of Horace, Juvenal, and Persius. The passage is from "nature, and that depraved," to "art," where the invective impulse "bore better fruit." Dryden notes, however, that certain atavistic forms of crude invective still occur and offers as examples the commedia dell'arte and certain contemporary political lampoons and libels which are, he says, "as free from the imputation of wit as of morality."[4] The historical movement of satire is, then, from crude scoffs and revilings to polished literary forms which have as their distinguishing marks the qualities of "wit and morality."

Dryden is not so impressive in his attempt "to describe, if not define, the nature" of satire. He relies principally on a Aristotelian definition quoted from Heinsius: "Satire is a kind of poetry, without a series of action, invented for the purging of our minds; in which human vices . . . are severely reprehended; partly dramatically, partly simply, and sometimes in both kinds of speaking . . . consisting in a low familiar way . . . in a sharp and pungent

4. Dryden is doubtless referring here to the bitter and usually scurrilous "Poems on Affairs of State," the political satires written and circulated in great numbers in the last thirty years or so of the seventeenth century and the early years of the eighteenth. See *Poems on Affairs of State, 1,* ed. George de F. Lord (New Haven, 1964).

manner of speech . . . by which either hatred or laughter, or indignation is moved." Heinsius isolates a number of the permanent qualities of satire: the peculiarly fragmented plot, the mixture of direct denunciation and the dramatization of vice, and the crude, harsh language found so often in the form. But Dryden refers to this as an "obscure and perplexed definition, or rather description." His own description, a great deal more general and lucid, is stated in a variety of ways throughout the "Essay," but emerges most clearly in the statement, "There can be no pleasantry where there is no wit; no impression can be made where there is no truth for the foundation." The terms of this formula vary: "truth" becomes "profit," the "rules of a virtuous life," and "justice"; while "wit" becomes "delight," "pleasure," "art."

True satire exists for Dryden only within these two poles of morality and wit, and it is with these touchstones that he examines the respective merits of Horace, Persius, and Juvenal: "Moral doctrine . . . and urbanity, or well-mannered wit, are the two things which constitute Roman satire."[5] Persius and Horace are "discovered" to be more profitable and instructive than Juvenal, but the latter is declared their superior in his "vigorous and masculine wit." With the curious judgment that Horace is more didactic than Juvenal and is inferior in wit or style, we need not quarrel, since we are concerned only with Dryden's critical theories.

The satirist, then, must first be a responsible critic of men and manners who gives "the rules of a happy and virtuous life." He cannot be an irresponsible railer lashing out at anyone or anything which displeases him. But his criticism must be witty as well as moral, it must be phrased in such a way as to make its point with some elegance and sting: "there is still a vast difference betwixt the slovenly butchering of a man, and the fineness of a stroke that separates the head from the body, and leaves it standing in its place." In this famous passage, Dryden is apparently admiring satiric wit simply for its own sake, as a craftsman in any art admires the technical skill with which a piece of work is done.

---

5. Dryden is here drawing, as he admits, on Isaac Casaubon.

But elsewhere he offers a variety of reasons why wit is necessary. Wit safeguards the satirist from reprisals by his victims and avoids ill will: "The character of Zimri in my *Absalom* is, in my opinion, worth the whole poem . . . and he, for whom it was intended, was too witty to resent it as an injury." Elsewhere he offers in several forms other varieties of the affective argument that wit or art is the sugar coating for the moral pill. Only in one place in the "Essay" does Dryden suggest that wit or art is a functional part of satire, that it is used in such a way as to render exactly the man and action satirized: "To spare the grossness of the names [fool, blockhead, knave] and to do the thing yet more severely, is to draw a full face, and to make the nose and cheeks stand out, and yet not to employ any depth of shadowing." But having broken through in this passage to an understanding that truth and art may be one in great satire—a condition which his own satires so perfectly mainifest—Dryden abandoned his insight. Having done so much to clarify the history of satire and describe its nature, the great satirist leaves us with a picture of two unrelated halves: on one hand, a rigid moral system consistently used as a standard of judgment and, on the other, a graceful style with the attributes so prized by his age—smoothness, ease, clarity, vigor, graceful turns, and unity of subject matter.

The attempt to understand satire by tracing its development from its most primitive forms to its "completement" in literary satire was not picked up again until this century. But in the years since Dryden wrote, knowledge of parts of the history of the genre has increased greatly, and in a recent book, *The Power of Satire: Magic, Ritual, Art*,[6] R. C. Elliott gathers all the diverse new materials together to construct a new and revealing history of the form. He begins, as Dryden does, by tracing the development of the genre from various primitive satiric activities to sophisticated forms of literary satire written in Rome and western Europe. But where Dryden relied on the *Bible* and on the literary history

6. *The Power of Satire* (Princeton, 1960), pp. 222–54.

worked out by the humanist scholars, Elliott turns to folklore, to
ancient myths, and to the anthropologists' descriptions of the
social customs of primitive tribes. He describes the flytings of the
Eskimos, the curses hurled like spears against the enemies of the
tribe by the Arabian satirist riding in the van of the army, and
the magical blasting spells employed by Irish satirists such as
Bricriu Poison-Tongue and Aithirne the Importunate. Out of this
material emerges a picture of a primitive satirist who used words
and ritual phrases in a magical fashion, relying on shame, sympathetic magic, and belief in darker powers to blast and destroy
the honor, the wealth, and even the health and lives of his victims.
This type of satiric activity, Elliott shows, still flourishes in primitive cultures and has never quite died out in our civilization. The
"hard attacker" first appears in the legendary Greek satirist
Archilochus who made verses against Lycambes and his daughter,
when her betrothal to him was broken, and caused them to hang
themselves. The tradition continues in such literary figures as
Timon, Loki, the Elizabethan malcontent, and Shakespeare's
Thersites who, in the good old manner, calls down on Patroclus,
"the rotten diseases of the South, the guts-griping, ruptures,
catarrhs, loads o' gravel i' th' back, lethargies, cold palsies," etc.,
etc. Today, once again, Elliott argues, the magical satirist, who had
disappeared into myth and literature, but not from consciousness,
has reappeared in such modern satirists as Roy Campbell, who in
Talking Bronco can compare himself to "a lion ensconced on the
breaking spine of a giraffe, raking the beast's side with his claws,
forcing him headlong to the ground in a pool of blood."

This is the magic and ritual of satire. The art, according to
Elliott, grows out of a recognition of both the social value and
the dangerous powers of satire, which fearful societies sought to
control by laws against the practice of magic, by legislation against
libel, by the prohibition of satires which attacked actual persons,
and by the development of beliefs that the blow of the satirist
recoiled on him if he did not speak the truth. In this way the vital
and socially necessary power of satire to attack corrupt men and
the institutions which defy ordinary controls is preserved, and

at the same time the malignant potential of satire is curbed. The attempt to balance the positive and negative forces of satire led to the creation of new types of literary satire and to the emergence of the form as "art." The "hard attacker" continued to appear in satire: Alceste in *Le Misanthrope,* Timon in *Timon of Athens,* and Gulliver in the conclusion of *Gulliver's Travels* are all still recognizable, Elliott argues, as the old railer of primitive magical satire—and they are useful, indeed inevitable, instruments employed by Molière, Shakespeare, and Swift to ferret out and denounce the dullness of the world. But the authors, Elliott demonstrates, are now aware of the moral crudeness, the viciousness, inherent in the making of satire, and they detach themselves from their satiric spokesmen by treating them ironically. The satirist is used to do the dirty work of exposing and castigating dullness and viciousness, but he in turn is satirized. The art of satire then becomes in Elliott's theory the distancing of the writer from his satiric spokesman, the removal of the author by one step at least from his satire, and the conversion of his speaker or his chief character from a *personal* voice invoking magical powers to a *dramatic* figure functioning in a poem. "It is a measure," Elliott remarks, "of the greatest satirists . . . that they recognize their own involvement in the folly of human life and willingly see themselves as victims, in obscure ways, of their own art." The art of satire thus becomes a thoroughly self-conscious stance and the expression of a far-ranging moral honesty.

The Power of Satire is a remarkable book, but it seems likely that it will be a number of years before its full meaning is absorbed into the standard ways of thinking about satire. For the present we can, however, see a number of its implications. First, and most obviously, it provides the crucial linkage between certain kinds of primitive satiric activities, which have long been known, and the literary satire which begins with Aristophanes and runs to the present day. As a result, satire now has a continuous history, and we can trace it back to its origins in magic and ancient rites. This helps to account for some of the powers of satire and a number of the persistent social attitudes toward it. At the same

time, the establishment of the dividing line between magical satiric activities and literary satire allows us to make more certainly that always necessary and always difficult distinction between satire proper and mere invective, diatribe, or lampoon— between a satirist like Evelyn Waugh and a denouncer like Philip Wylie. Second, by demonstrating that the *art* of satire is at least in part the distancing of the author from his satiric spokesman, Elliott helps to make further untenable that persistent identification of the writer of satire with his creature, a view which has vitiated so much criticism of satire and led to so much hopeless writing about why Swift hates mankind or Byron rejects society. But of even more consequence is the establishment of the fact that in great satire there is more than one point of view, that the narrow moral focus and the limited perceptions of the "hard attacker" busily concentrating on exposing particular kinds of foolishness need not set the boundaries of the satiric vision.[7]

Though the treatment of satire occupies only a small portion of *Anatomy of Criticism,*[8] Northrop Frye too has explained the genre in a way which helps to raise it to a position of importance it has never before enjoyed in critical schemes. By explaining genres, or myths, as major organizational patterns which men have traditionally used to order experience, and by making satire one of his four major myths, he has provided at the very least a working hypothesis which points future investigations in the right

7. Basil Willey expresses perfectly the generally held view of the crippling limitations of the satiric view. After discussing the way in which the satirist strips "the object satirized of the film of familiarity," Willey goes on to point out that the satirist misses the truth in received opinions and that "he must ignore the *explanation* of the thing satirized—how it came to be, its history. It is a fact of experience that *tout comprendre c'est tout pardonner,* and the satirist ex officio cannot pardon, so he must decline to understand all and explain all. Satire is by nature nonconstructive, since to construct effectively— to educate, for example, to reform, or to evangelize—one must study actual situations and actual persons in their historical setting, and this kind of study destroys the satiric approach." *The Eighteenth Century Background* (London, 1940), pp. 106–07.

8. (Princeton, 1957), pp. 223–39, 309–14.

direction.[9] And he has further clarified matters by isolating the characteristic images of satire and providing a rough chart of the standards by which satirists have judged human activity.

Frye first provides a *provisional*—the stress is his—scheme of all literature within which the major genres can be located and defined and then, as one small part of his work, describes satire. Despite enormous differences in vocabulary and frame of reference, the scheme Frye sets up is essentially Dryden's: "Satire demands at least a token fantasy, a content which the reader recognizes as grotesque, and at least an implicit moral standard, the latter being essential in a militant attitude to experience." Dryden's wit has here become fantasy, but fantasy has a highly specialized meaning for Frye. It is still what wit—by an expansion of the term—was for Dryden, the shape or form which art gives in various ways to the world and characters which satire serves up. But where Dryden obviously believed that these well-constructed images were the product of the poet's conscious skill, Frye conceives of them as being archetypal forms which originate in the human imagination. Where comedy and romance project "the forms of human desire"—the city, the sheepfold, the garden,

9. My indebtedness to Frye is apparent and continuing, but in some cases I have tried to preserve what I take to be the more traditional critical terms— what he calls "myths," I refer to as "genres," and what I call "modes" he terms "genres." I have also ventured to disagree silently with Frye at several places where his systematic scheme seems to override the actual evidence of the literature. One small example which bears on the subject of this book: Frye makes his four myths, Comedy, Romance, Tragedy, and Satire-Irony, correspond in that order to the four seasons of the year, and thus assigns satire to winter. If he is right, we could reasonably expect that whenever a season of the year is mentioned or used as setting in a particular work, then that season ought to be the one assigned to the *myth* (genre) in which the work falls. This is the case in comedy where spring predominates. But satire does not fit the scheme. Since satire is usually set in the city, not in nature, references to seasons are rare, but the predominant season is the sultry, close part of summer from July to early September; specifically the days when Sirius looms over the horizon, men go mad, and "poets recite all through the dog days of August" (Juvenal, Satire III, line 9). For other references to the dog days in satire, see *Absalom and Achitophel,* line 334; "Epistle to Dr. Arbuthnot," line 3; *The Dunciad,* Book IV, line 9; and *Don Juan,* Dedication, Stanza 4.

gathered together in an "apocalyptic" oneness and all parts of
a mystical body—satire (and tragedy) project "the world that
desire rejects"—Frye's "demonic" imagery. In the world of satire
the universal oneness of the apocalyptic vision is fragmented, the
gods become either brutal or distant and impersonal, society is
transformed into a mob ruled only by strength and cunning, the
city becomes a wasteland, the sheep changes to the wolf and the
vulture, while the garden reverts to jungle. In actual satires these
archetypal images provide the shapes which are "reduced" in
content or rendered in more plausible or realistic terms. The
society become mob is, for example, rendered as the aimless
ramblings of Pope's Dunces through the city of London in *The
Dunciad;* the animals of this demonic world assume the "realistic"
appearance of Volpone the fox, Mosca the fly, Voltore the vulture,
and Corvino the crow in Jonson's play; the garden become jungle
is "reduced" to the transition of Tony Last in Waugh's *A Handful
of Dust* from the ordered English estate of Hetton to the jungles
of Brazil in which he seeks a lost city but finds only a mad old
man who forces him to read the works of Dickens over and over
again. The total satire, or myth, with its many incidents and
scenes, is an arrangement of this demonic imagery "in movement."

Frye has described with great precision the master images which
appear in satire with astonishing regularity, though with a
variety of local habitations and names. He has thus brought us
a long way forward from Dryden's rather vague prescription of
"wit" for satire. And he has performed an equal service in locating
the other pole of satire, the moral basis for the criticism of human
activities. Dryden was content to make the point that true satire,
as distinct from lampoon and libel, must grow not from personal
animus but from a perception of a moral failing, and must not
be directed toward an individual but toward vice and folly. Swift,
describing his own satiric practice, puts the matter succinctly,

> Yet, Malice never was his Aim;
> He lash'd the Vice but spar'd the Name.
> ("Verses on the Death of Dr. Swift,"
> lines 459–60)

From his historical perspective on the full range of Western satire, Frye has been able to see that frequently one satirist's vice is another's wisdom, and while he agrees that a moral bias—or attitude toward experience—is necessary in satire, he is at the same time aware that the satirists of our tradition have criticized from a number of different value systems. In the main, he distinguishes three major attitudes. In the first, which Frye calls "satire of the low norm," convention is the standard by which foolishness is judged. The satirist attacks all behavior and all ways of thought which have not been tested by experience and sanctioned by the majority of men. The "plain, common-sense, conventional person," such as Horace of the *Sermones,* Piers Plowman of medieval and early Renaissance satire, or some of Fielding's booby heroes, serves as a perfect standard bearer of the low norm and stands in contrast to a world of cranks and dreamers. But since, as Frye points out, "social convention is mainly fossilized dogma, and the standard appealed to by low-norm satire is a set of conventions largely invented by dead cranks . . . the logic of satire itself drives it on . . . to a second phase in which the sources and values of conventions themselves are objects of ridicule." On this level the satirist attacks any systematic view of life—any science, philosophy, or habitual way of doing things. "Insofar as the satirist has a 'position' of his own, it is the preference of practice to theory, experience to metaphysics." Frye's prime example of this type of satire is Lucian's *Sale of Lives,* in which the various philosophers of antiquity are auctioned off to the highest bidder, their price being decided by the usefulness of their philosophies in life. All are ultimately useless. In English satire—though Frye does not mention it—the best instance of this type of satire is *Don Juan* with its unremitting vision of the eternal flux which mocks all patterns imposed on the living creature. Satire of this kind tends to disintegrate the forms and patterns which men see in life and to reflect this disintegration by the chaotic form of the satire. This stand in turn leads on to Frye's third phase of satire, where even common sense and the reality of immediate perceptions, which is taken for granted in the second phase, are called into doubt. Man and his world,

which the dunces take as sure and certain, are fragmented and
shown in grotesque, strange, and frightening shapes, such as the
world of darkness and sleep at the end of *The Dunciad,* the Lil-
liputian and Brobdingnagian figures in *Gulliver's Travels,* and the
mad circular dreams of Earwicker in *Finnegans Wake.* Frye goes
on to distinguish three other phases of satire and thus round out
his system, but these, as he says, "move around to the ironic aspect
of tragedy, and satire begins to recede."

We have come a long way toward a proper understanding of
satire in the last ten years, but the critical gap between morality
and wit which Dryden was unable to close still exists. It exists
between Frye's patterns of demonic imagery and the norms by
which the satirist criticizes his world; it exists between the body
of the works which Elliott discusses and the complex moral stances
in which he believes the art of satire to be located. It is true that
the morality-wit polarity suits satire in a way that it never does
comedy or tragedy. In successful instances of the latter kind it
would be nonsense to try to separate out the moral kernel, the
way of life the poet is espousing and recommending, from the
style and the composite parts. Ideas, forms, styles blend together
to form the quality of a moment and are then swept forward by
the pressure they have created to form a new moment. There is
no certainty, no rest, no possibility of stating immutable rules
and laws of existence. When moral pronouncements are made by
the characters, they are nearly always wrong, or at least inadequate.
But satire always contains either an implicit or explicit set of
values, which frequently takes specific form in judgments on such
matters as what kind of food to eat, how to manage your wife
and your household, how to dress, how to choose your friends
and treat your guests, what kind of plays to frequent and what
kind of books to read, how to conduct political life. If a system
of values tends to stand out in satire, so does the style—so much
so, in fact, that it is regularly referred to as rhetoric, a term
ordinarily applied only to style which calls attention to itself or
which is *obviously* designed to persuade. The set piece, the verbal
device, the outrageous appeal to the emotions, the tricky arrange-

ment of the argument, the enormously inflated or deflated image seem always to pop out of satire. If *ars est celare artem,* even the greatest satirists have consistently been failures.

Yet in great satire, though we may remain aware of the two components, art and morality, they become interrelated and create that oneness characteristic of great writing. In *Absalom and Achitophel,* for example, it is perfectly clear that the standard by which Dryden is measuring his objects of attack is harmony, balance, and order in society, government, and the individual character. His *art* or management of effects lies in the skill with which he portrays such politicians as Shaftesbury and Buckingham, and in the general ease with which he manages the heroic couplet. But moral standard and art become one in the poem—as, for example, in the brilliant portrait of Zimri (Buckingham), which Dryden himself praised because its wit prevented the anger of its victim:

> A man so various, that he seem'd to be
> Not one, but all Mankinds Epitome.
> Stiff in Opinions, always in the wrong;
> Was every thing by starts, and nothing long:
> But, in the course of one revolving Moon,
> Was Chymist, fidler, States-Man, and Buffoon:
> Then all for Women, Painting, Rhiming, Drinking;
> Besides ten thousand freaks that dy'd in thinking.
>
>   .   .   .
>
> So over Violent, or over Civil,
> That every man, with him, was God or Devil.
>
>   (lines 545–58)

A few terms of contempt like "buffoon" and "freaks" establish the attitude toward Zimri, but the standard by which he is tried and found deserving of such contempt is located in the form of the couplets themselves. The evenness of their rhythms, the regularity of rhyme, the balance of half-line against half-line and line against line, and the orderly march of couplet after couplet,

each neatly rounded off, establishes in poetic terms the harmonic order which Dryden is setting up as the ideal pattern in the state and in the individual life. The wit involved in the depiction of Zimri, far from being an isolated effect, is organically related in turn to the order of the verse. We laugh at this portrait not because its details are in themselves funny but because the man so imaged is so ludicrously out of step with the order which verse and rhetoric insist politely but relentlessly is the natural rhythm of existence. Where the verse coheres, Zimri is "various" and "not one." Where rhetorically one part of the poetic line balances and complements another part, Zimri's enthusiasms pull him apart. Where the couplets march evenly along the same seemly level, Zimri's frantic activities lead him down to bathos— "Chymist, fidler, States-Man, and Buffoon." And where the couplets do not depart too far from their regular pace—only enough to provide suitable variety—Zimri is excessive in all he does, "over Violent, or over Civil."

Here satire is no longer made up of two great lumps, art on one hand and moral or value judgment on the other. Instead, both components are dramatized, given a vitality which manifests itself in movement and sweeps onward to seek the forms proper to its nature. Art and morality, dunce and the reality he opposes, are locked together in an intricate and continuing conflict which generates the plot of satire. It is in these terms that the following pages approach satire, and the first step will be to isolate the peculiar energies of dullness as they appear in various works. When this is done, it will be possible to turn to more elaborate studies of satire and show how the full plot of satire is constructed from the interaction of the primal energy of dullness and the powers which oppose its "progress."

II

THE ENERGIES OF DULLNESS

2.   The Rhetoric of Satire: *Peri Bathous*

> I find there are certain Bounds set even to the Irregularities
> of Human Thought, and those a great deal narrower than is
> commonly apprehended. (JONATHAN SWIFT, *A Discourse
> Concerning the Mechanical Operation of the Spirit*)

Theoretically, there is no reason why satirists cannot attack any
person, attitude, or way of life which happens to amuse or dis-
please them. The range of actual satire supports this conclusion:
Aristophanes attacks the demagogue Cleon and the Athenian
war party; Juvenal the corrupting influences of Asiatic customs
and luxury on the sturdy, simple virtues of old Republican Rome;
Swift the Age of Reason's simpleminded optimism about human
nature and progress; Byron the Lake Poets, the politicians of the
Holy Alliance, and the beginnings of Victorian prudery; Aldous
Huxley modern science and sociology. The range of satiric attack
extends even further, for satirists, proud with indignation, have
gone on to rail against the very nature of man—Rochester's
Satyre Against Mankind—against the arrangement of life—
Hardy's *Satires of Circumstance*—and against the gods themselves
—Lucian's *Dialogues of the Gods*. So great is the range of satire
that it is not uncommon for one satirist to attack bitterly what
another satirist defends stoutly. Byron attacks the social order
and self-control which Pope and Swift defend and defends that
freedom of action and emotionalism which they attack. George
Orwell mauls the political and social conservatism which Evelyn
Waugh espouses.

Satirists do locate the causes of corruption in different persons
and institutions, but the differences are only nominal. Swift
understood that the "Irregularities of Human Thought,"[1] the

1. In *A Tale of a Tub With Other Early Works, 1696–1707*, ed. Herbert
Davis (Oxford, 1957), p. 188.

objects of satire, are strangely limited in number and kind, and
the history of satire bears him out. However various the accents
spoken by the men and women who inhabit satire, however
different the clothing they wear, the streets they walk, and the
cities they dirty, they exert the same kind of pressure on society
and nature, and create the same kind of world. Northrop Frye,
as we have seen, describes this typical satiric world as a conglom-
erate of recurring symbolic forms, a "world . . . of perverted or
wasted work, ruins and catacombs, instruments of torture and
monuments of folly." It is a world where man is at war with
mankind, where the gods or natural powers are brutal and distant;
a world of cannibalism, torture, mutilation; a world where love
corrupts to lust and sexual deviation. Its presiding animals are
the wolf, the tiger, and the dragon; its landscape is the jungle and
the wasteland; its buildings are labyrinths, dungeons, and Towers
of Babel.[2]

These are the characteristic shapes man and nature assume in
satire, but to think of satire (or any other kind of literary work)
as composed of a group of tonally related symbols is to conceive
of it as a mural, as a series of still parts or scenes, each elaborating
a central theme of waste and futility. Literature, however, is not
static but dynamic. It does not offer us set qualities and fixed scenes
but life in movement, or tense with the effort to move. Forces
pull and push in some direction; antagonisms are created, resolved,
and re-created in new forms; even as life takes one shape it begins
to shimmer and break up in order to seek more adequate realiza-
tions of its nature in some new shape. To use the Aristotelian
figure, life as presented in literature is like the growing plant:

2. This is, of course, too dark a picture to be literally true of lighter, more
laughing satires, such as those of Horace, Gay, or Molière, where the approach
is, as Horace puts it, *ridentem dicere verum,* to speak truth laughingly. These
satirists, and others like them, tend toward the comic, while the bitterer, more
pessimistic satirists—Juvenal, Pope, Swift—tend toward the tragic. The degree
of gloomy intensity varies considerably in satire, but within the great spectrum
of satire, extending from where it blends with comedy to where it merges
into tragedy, life assumes the same forms and moves toward the same confusions. The differences are of degree, not of kind.

at any given instant it will appear to have arrived at a fixed state
and definite form, but it is never at rest until its full cycle is completed; and its nature is defined by its completed pattern, not
by any single shape it assumes along the way. The fall of eternal
darkness and the arrival of absolute chaos do not occur until
the final lines of *The Dunciad*, but if we understand that these
are the shapes toward which life has been tending throughout
the poem, then we can see that the dunces have from the beginning
been bringing darkness and chaos in a host of smaller, less obvious
ways.

Frye's symbols are the shapes which dullness always assumes
in satire, but the essence of dullness is best understood not as
being cannibalism, torture, and dark towers, but as *moving* into
and through these and similar states. It is not a noun—cannibalism
—but a verb—eating other people. The advantage of putting the
matter this way is not only that is squares with our actual experience of literature, but that it also permits us to see dullness at
work in scenes and incidents where the chief symbols of satire do
not appear in their manifest, extreme forms. My argument is
that the world of satire should not be thought of as a number of
typical set scenes or symbolic entities but as characteristic actions
—such as darkening, disordering, preying—which in passing
assume the symbolic shapes Frye has isolated as the defining
forms of satire.

That literature should present not completed man but man in
action seeking form is really not surprising, since literature is
constructed from language; and language, considered as grammar,
logic, or rhetoric, takes static quantities—the single words—and
places them in the directional current of the sentence, the progression of the syllogism, or the thrust of the rhetorical figure,
where at least two qualities are always in movement in relation
to one another. In irony appearance is always shifting away from
reality or reality breaking up into contradictory parts; in bathos
the existent is falling away from the ideal; in chiasmus the two
qualities involved are exchanging positions; in metaphor one
quality is joining itself to another and maintaining the union

only with a good deal of tension. This "active" quality of rhetoric can be of use in locating the key actions or energies of satire and showing their workings on the verbal, presymbolic level of particular satires.

Except in certain rare cases, such as Elizabethan satire, where a harsh, elliptic phrasing and a stunted logic were mandatory, there is nothing very peculiar about the logic or grammar of satire. But there has always been a strange relationship between rhetoric and satire. One of its most persistent external characteristics is an attack on the false styles and elaborate rhetoric of other writers and other kinds of poetry. In fact, satire draws much of its nourishment from these false styles, delighting in parodying and inflating them until they burst. But these are for satire relatively delicate methods of attack, and satirists—who as a species trust very little to the intelligence of their audience—regularly deliver open attacks on false rhetoric. Aristophanes begins it in *The Clouds* with Strepsiades apprenticing his son to Socrates to be taught sophistic rhetoric and wrong logic—"to talk unjustly and prevail"—in order to avoid paying his debts. George Orwell is still at it when in *1984* he provides a grammar of Newspeak, a parody of the pseudoscientific sign language of modern politics and advertising which is robbing English of its rich complexity of truth and threatening to make it the instrument of human enslavement. In between, Petronius offers a hilarious picture of the orator Agamemnon and his fashionable finishing school of rhetoric in the early Roman empire; Juvenal thunders against the writers of innumerable epics who recited their elephantine poems in public theaters; Erasmus in his *Praise of Folly* and Rabelais in *Gargantua and Pantagruel* mock the pedantic language and logic of the scholastic philosophers and rhetoricians; Ben Jonson in his plays provides a catalogue of all the fashionable styles of his time—the lover's, the soldier's, the puritan's, the entrepreneur's, the politician's—and reveals each as mere cover for ignorance, roguery, and greed; Swift in his *Tale of a Tub* reproduces the garbled language and thought of the political

pamphleteer and "modern"; and Pope in *The Dunciad* anatomizes the various styles of dullness.

In contrast, the satirist always presents himself, directly or indirectly, as a plain speaker who uses none of the elaborate tricks of rhetoric. He trusts to his love for the simple truth and his clear sight to provide him with the plain words needed to express what the world really is. He will even exclude himself from the "number of those called true poets" because, as Horace put it, he merely "writes talk,"[3] and he will speak of his muse as "pedestrian," "stuttering," and "homely."

This ironic modesty fools no one, and it has long been clear that satire is the most consistently and obviously rhetorical of all the major genres. Every reader is aware that the satirist cunningly manipulates feelings; deliberately scants, simplifies, and exaggerates reality; loads and slants language to give a particular bias to his material. Critics learned in rhetoric have been able to name and classify the rhetorical strategies and figures used by satirists, and in recent years they have regularly employed rhetoric to explain the art of satire.[4]

As it is ordinarily understood today and as it is usually presented in manuals ancient and modern, rhetoric is the art of persuading. It is language used to shape the attitudes of the audience and is

---

3. Horace, *Sermones,* 1.4.39ff.

4. The affinity of rhetoric and satire has frequently been explored. Juvenal's satires have, for example, long been treated by classicists as skillful developments in an intensely rhetorical style of certain themes which were set as exercises in the schools of first-century Rome. Nearly every major satirist since Juvenal has also been analyzed in rhetorical terms. See, for example, H. L. R. Edwards, *Skelton, The Life and Times of an Early Tudor Poet* (London, 1949), pp. 22–28; Alexander Sackton, *Rhetoric as a Dramatic Language in Ben Jonson* (New York, 1948); Maynard Mack, "The Muse of Satire," *Yale Review,* 41 (1951), 80–92; John Bullitt, *Jonathan Swift and the Anatomy of Satire* (Cambridge, Mass., 1953), esp. Ch. III, "The Rhetoric of Satire"; Martin Price, *Swift's Rhetorical Art* (New Haven, 1953). For general discussions of the relation of satire and rhetoric, see Ian Jack, *Augustan Satire* (Oxford, 1952); and David Worcester, *The Art of Satire* (Cambridge, Mass., 1940).

thus distinguished from poetry, which uses words to create a world or to mirror reality. Since rhetoric has ceased, in the popular mind at least, to be the art of speaking well and become the art of using contrived arguments for a bad cause—the art of linguistic deception—it has been possible to argue that simply because satire is so pronouncedly rhetorical, it is nothing more than propaganda, skillful lies told to further the authors' peculiar aims. But we have been working our way toward a more sympathetic under-standing of rhetoric, and there is some hope that, while avoiding the multiplication of meaningless distinctions and overly elaborate terminology of classical rhetoric, rhetorical theory and its analysis of the effects attainable in language will once again become useful critical tools. W. K. Wimsatt puts it this way:

> The terms of rhetoric, spurned by Croce and other moderns, did have a value for the ancients, even though they failed to connect all of rhetoric with meaning. To give the terms of rhetoric a value in modern criticism it would be necessary only to determine the expressiveness of the things in lan-guage to which the terms refer.[5]

If we can show then that there are a few dominant rhetorical figures in satire and can "determine the expressiveness of the things in language to which the terms refer," we should be able to locate the characteristic actions which shape the world of satire. We are searching for what may be called the "master tropes" of satire, with the understanding that a trope is not merely a persua-sive device but rather a way of showing some action in language.

---

5. *The Prose Style of Samuel Johnson* (New Haven, 1941), p. 11. Wimsatt goes on to point out that "this has been done for metaphor," and it has since been done for a number of other rhetorical figures. Harry Levin in *The Overreacher* (Cambridge, Mass., 1952), does it for hyperbole—which Putten-ham styled the "overreacher"—by showing that it is the master figure of Marlovian tragedy. Cedric Whitman in *Homer and the Heroic Tradition* (Cambridge, Mass., 1958) does it for the figure hysteron-proteron, which, he argues, provides the major image of life as it is conceived in *The Iliad* and

Fortunately, we have a rhetoric of satire which lists and analyzes the major figures used by satirists: *Peri Bathous: or Martinus Scriblerus His Treatise of the Art of Sinking in Poetry*. This piece, probably written largely by Pope, is an ironical, duncely version of Longinus' *Peri Hupsous* or *On the Sublime*. Where Longinus attempts to explain the art of rising to the heights of poetry, Pope, assuming the persona of a modern rhetorician, explains to the bad poets of his day the rules and art which will enable them easily to sink to the lowest levels of language, thereby winning fame and fortune by satisfying the vulgar tastes of the great mass of modern readers. The point of the joke is, of course, the implication that modern poets and their readers much prefer the bathetic to the sublime; and the cutting edge of the satire is further honed by drawing examples of the perfection of bathos largely from the works of popular poets of the late seventeenth and early eighteenth centuries. Thus, when he wishes to recommend and illustrate ways in which prolixity will aid in sinking in poetry, the "Rhetorician of the Profound" quotes as a masterful instance of this technique the lines from Blackmore's *Job,* where the poet "spreads out" the brief biblical line, "He wash'd his Feet in Butter" to

> With Teats distended with their milky Store,
> Such num'rous lowing Herds, before my Door,

---

becomes the organizational basis of the poem. N. W. Lund, *Chiasmus in the New Testament* (Chapel Hill, 1942) explores the meaning of this figure in its context in the New Testament. Kenneth Burke, whose works are filled with hints and brief discussions of the meaning of various tropes, argues that the oxymoron is the figure most useful to and favored by writers trying to express mystic experiences—*A Rhetoric of Motives* (New York, 1950), pp. 324–28.

The exploration of the meaning of metaphor, which has of course proceeded a great deal farther than work on any other figure, has already made clear one danger involved in this kind of criticism. Although certain tropes seem most naturally to catch in language one particular sense of life, each trope, like metaphor, is not fixed in its meaning but is filled with potential. It can be and has been exploited in very different ways in different poems and by different poetic sensibilities.

> Their painful Burden to unload did meet,
> That we with Butter might have wash'd our Feet.
>   (Ch. VIII)[6]

After a few pages of this kind of thing, it becomes quite clear that Pope's contemporaries have little need of further instruction in the art of sinking in poetry. They have already gone about as far as they can go. But with true Scriblerian zeal the Rhetorician doggedly moves on to schematize and turn to rule for the benefit of lesser writers those happy turns of bathos struck off from the genius of "those *Great Spirits,* who are born with a *Vivacité de pesanteur,* or . . . an *Alacrity of sinking."*[7]

Peri Bathous is not exclusively an attack on inferior poets, wretched styles, and pedantic rhetoric. Here, as in *The Dunciad,* bad writing is treated as but one, though crucial, symptom of a more general breakdown of taste and morality. It is but one expression of an essential vulgarity and primitive disorder of mind innate in man: "The Taste of the *Bathos* is implanted by Nature itself in the Soul of Man; 'till perverted by Custom or Example he is taught, or rather compell'd to relish the *Sublime."*[8] This original sin of vulgarity, uncorrected by education and society, not only shapes the bathetic style but also controls manners and moral codes: "Whoever is conversant in *modern Plays,* may make a most noble Collection of this [bathetic] kind, and at the same time, form a compleat Body of *Modern Ethicks and Morality."*[9] Vulgarity not only manifests itself in trivial poetry but creates trivial lives as well: "I doubt not but an active Catcher of Butterflies, a careful and fanciful Pattern-drawer, an industrious Collector of Shells, a laborious and tuneful Bagpiper, or a diligent Breeder of tame Rabbits, might severally excel in their respective parts of the *Bathos."*[10]

6. All citations of *Peri Bathous* are to *The Art of Sinking in Poetry,* ed. Edna Leake Steeves (New York, 1952).
    7. Ch. III, p. 14.
    8. Ch. II, p. 10.
    9. Ch. V, pp. 18–19.
    10. Ch. VI, p. 26.

THE RHETORIC OF SATIRE

The relationship between literary style and contemporary society and manners expressed in these lines is dramatized in the thoughts and style of the supposed writer of the piece. The Rhetorician regularly betrays ways of thinking which explain just why he and his readers prefer debased to elevated language. He is an incurable materialist who argues that the true end of writing poetry is "Profit or Gain," and, unable to distinguish between ideals and matter, he therefore sees nothing wrong with the images in which the spirit is reduced to a ludicrously material level. He delights, for example, in the comparison of God to a recruiting officer and a fuller, and, arguing for the bathos of the moderns over the sublimity of the ancients, his materialistic bent causes him to seek out and elaborate a mercantile figure such as this:

> When I consider (my dear Countrymen) the Extent, Fertility, and Populousness of our *Lowlands of Parnassus,* the flourishing State of our Trade, and the Plenty of our Manufacture; there are two Reflections which administer great Occasion of Surprize; the one, that all Dignities and Honours should be bestow'd upon the exceeding few meager Inhabitants of the Top of the Mountain; the other, that our own Nation should have arriv'd to that Pitch of Greatness [i.e. Bathos] it now possesses, without any regular *System of Laws.* (Ch. 1)

The Rhetorician's materialism comes out even more unpleasantly in certain literal statements such as his argument that "Poetry is a *natural* or *morbid Secretion from the Brain.*"[11]

Hand in hand with his materialism goes what we might call his "democratic principles of literature." He believes that the worth of the bathos and the triviality of the sublime are guaranteed by the fact that very few readers prefer the latter, while almost everyone enjoys the former: "The *Profund* strikes universally, and is adapted to every Capacity."[12] Then too, there is so much more bathetic writing than sublime that the former must be the better. This touching faith in numbers can only lead on to a delight in

11. Ch. III, p. 12.
12. Ch. II, p. 10.

language which is elaborate, stuffed, prolix; in descriptions and comparisons which are various and extended to infinity; and in poems which are long and filled with many different things to delight the simple taste.

The list of the Rhetorician's vulgarities and their manifestations in style could be considerably extended, but Pope's point is clear: a debased style is both an effect of and an index to debased ways of thinking. Underneath the figures recommended for sinking in poetry lie bathetic attitudes, primitive appetites, and childish, uninstructed ways of thinking. Therefore, the profound rhetoric offered in *Peri Bathous* provides at once both a list of the major faults of style and the vulgarities of nature which create them. We need not be concerned with most of the rules the Rhetorician offers —avoid common sense, cultivate prolixity, seek always the lowest thoughts—but his choice of major classes of the figures contributing most powerfully to the bathetic are of the greatest interest. "We shall content ourselves," says the Rhetorician,

> to range the Principal [figures] which most powerfully contribute to the *Bathos,* under three Classes.
> I. The Variegating, Confusing, or Reversing *Tropes* and *Figures.*
> II. The Magnifying, and
> III. The Diminishing. (Ch. X)

He then proceeds to take up each of these classes in turn and list their various subdivisions, providing suitable examples of each. Under Class I, Variegating Tropes and Figures, for example, he places catachresis, metonymy, synecdoche, aposiopesis, and the type of metaphor in which the highest and lowest things are compared—thunder becomes, *"The* Lords above *are* angry *and* talk big."

But in the midst of playing with rhetorical jargon and pedantry, Pope never allows us to forget that each major class of bathetic rhetoric is an expression of some fundamental human failing. The variegating, confusing, or reversing tropes and figures are the products of minds which have lost all sense of order and proportion. They have given themselves over to fancy and vanity,

and in their striving to show themselves unique and clever "say nothing in the usual way, but (if possible) in the direct contrary."[13] Such minds naturally express (and reveal) themselves corrupt forms of figures such as catachresis—"Mow the Beard" for "shave" —inept synecdoche—"Split-cause" for lawyer, and "draggle-tail" for woman—and indecorous metaphors—"The Spoil/Painful in massy Vomit shall recoil" to describe a miser forced to give up his treasure. Such minds naturally hesitate over what to say— aposiopesis—mix figures of speech recklessly and without regard for sense, seek out vulgar jargon, and construct antitheses which cancel out rather than balance.

The magnifying class of figures expresses not only a lack of common sense and a delight in the farfetched, but also man's incurable appetite for self-glorification. His lust for the impossible leads him on to all forms of extravagant, outsize forms of expression—periphrasis, macrology, and such hyperboles as

> He roar'd so loud, and look'd so wondrous grim,
> His very Shadow durst not follow him.

or such modest requests as

> Ye Gods! annihilate but Space and Time,
> And make two lovers happy.

The diminishing figures betray confusion of thought and a vulgar inability to distinguish the value of things. These ways of thinking inevitably turn parallelism to anticlimax:

> And thou *Dalhoussy* the great God of War,
> Lieutenant Colonel to the Earl of Mar.

emphasis into tautology:

> Divide—and part—the sever'd World—in two.

noble comparison into disabling ridicule:

> I cannot stifle this gigantic Woe,
> Nor on my raging Grief a Muzzle throw.

13. Ch. X, pp. 43–44.

If the inversions of taste and art which it catalogues are turned right side up again, *Peri Bathous* can be read as a serious neo-classical poetic. For example, the rule of avoiding common sense can be read in reverse as a rule always to follow common sense. Pope probably meant no more than this when he remarked that *"The Profound,* though written in so ludicrous a way, may be very well worth reading seriously as an Art of Rhetorick."[14] But the ironic subtitle, "The Art of Sinking in Poetry," suggests another sense in which the work is an art of rhetoric. Read in one way, taking the verbal "sinking" as intransitive, its sense is no more than "the art of writing badly, or making a fool of yourself and debasing the language." But read in another way, giving "sinking" a transitive force, "the art of sinking in poetry" becomes "the art of writing satire," a manual of the satirist's way of sinking dullards by deflating them and dropping them to their true level. The ambiguity of the title is realized in the substance of the work, which is at once a collection of ridiculous lapses of taste in thought and expression, a masterful ironic exposure of this idiocy, and a catalogue of the principal rhetorical strategies used by all satirists to show the actions of dullness. I am proposing that *Peri Bathous,* by accident or design, is a true "Art of Satire" which locates the definitive actions of dullness and their rhetorical equivalents. To see how this is so, it will be necessary to look briefly at the chief peculiarity of satiric rhetoric.

Since, ideally, rhetoric is the art of speaking and writing both sensibly and convincingly, the techniques recommended by better rhetoricians reflect the workings of a discriminating and orderly mind. Comparisons should illuminate, parts correctly define the whole, series build to a climax, causes properly contain their effects, language be adjusted to subject and audience, and compositions move logically from premises to conclusions. But the satirist does not deal with orderly minds or worlds. He pictures the inflated, the fragmented, the jumbled; he shows us men whose language is indecorous and whose pretensions to decency and

14. As reported by Joseph Spence in *Observations, Anecdotes,* and *Characters of Books and Men,* ed. Edmund Malone (London, 1820), p. 16.

honor are as much a sham as their speech; he creates worlds
where fools have tampered with the workings of nature and where
everything is falling apart. Because of this grotesque subject
matter the usual rhetorical strategies are not available to the
satirist. Quintilian remarks that "Style may . . . be corrupted in
precisely the same number of ways that it may be adorned,"[15]
and it is these corruptions which the satirist must use if he is to
render accurately in language the disorders of men and society.
Pope knows that the poet's language should not fall below the
"seemly" and that comparisons should not be drawn from below a
certain level. But as a satirist trying to catch precisely the vulgarity
and lack of originality in the so-called wits of his age, he will be
forced to such language and comparisons as this:

> Let Courtly Wits to Wits afford supply,
> As Hog to Hog in huts of *Westphaly;*
> If one, thro' Nature's Bounty or his Lord's,
> Has what the frugal, dirty soil affords,
> From him the next receives it, thick or thin,
> As pure a Mess almost as it came in;
> The blessed Benefit, not there confin'd,
> Drops to the third who nuzzles close behind;
> From tail to mouth, they feed, and they carouse;
> The last, full fairly gives it to the *House.*

(*Epilogue to the Satires,* "Dialogue II," lines 171–80)[16]

The two terms of a metaphor should never cancel one another
out, but in exposing a fool who has set up for a clever man,
Congreve must allow Witwoud such a stylish metaphor as

> Your horse, sir? your horse is an ass, sir!
> (*The Way of the World,* Act III)

15. *"Totidem autem generibus corrumpitur oratio quot ornatur."* Institutio
Oratorio, VIII,3,58.
16. Twickenham Edition of the Poems of Alexander Pope, *4, Imitations of
Horace,* ed. John Butt (London and New Haven, 1953).

Extravagant hyperbole and a series leading to an anticlimax may be faults of language, but they alone can convey the inflated pride and the ludicrous falling off of a Lord Steyne:

> Everybody knows the melancholy end of that nobleman, which befell at Naples two months after the French Revolution of 1830: when the Most Honourable George Gustavus, Marquis of Steyne, Earl of Gaunt and Gaunt Castle, in the Peerage of Ireland, Viscount Hellborough, Baron Pitchley and Grillsby, a Knight of the Most Noble Order of the Garter, of the Golden Fleece of Spain, of the Russian Order of St. Nicholas of the First Class, of the Turkish Order of the Crescent, First Lord of the Powder Closet and Groom of the Back Stairs, Colonel of the Gaunt or Regent's Own Regiment of Militia, a trustee of the British Museum, and Elder Brother of the Trinity House, a Governor of the White Friars, and D.C.L.—died, after a series of fits.
>
> (*Vanity Fair,* Ch. 64)

These are all brilliant pieces of satiric writing, and in each case the satirist has taken a figure which would be a stylistic fault if used unself-consciously and employed it to dramatize rhetorically some aspect of dullness. It is my contention that such is his regular practice, and that the three classes of figures Pope gives in *Peri Bathous* as the major faults of style locate for us the principal types of satiric rhetoric. And since these linguistic abuses reflect major flaws in thought, morality, and manners, *Peri Bathous* also provides us with an index of those kinds of activity which the satirist always shows busily at work fragmenting a culture, throwing up towers of fantasy and illusion, and perverting the workings of nature.

The world of satire is built up from these rhetorical figures and the moral failings they dramatize. But in considering satiric rhetoric, there is little profit in using the rhetorical jargon Pope ridicules in *Peri Bathous*—aposiopesis or pleonasm. Instead, it will be more useful to translate these terms to the "scenic" terms which they suggest. In doing so, we will be determining "the expressiveness of

the things in language to which the [rhetorical] terms refer,"
and we will then be able more easily to see the ways in which the
rhetorical figures expand into description of clothes, bodies, scenes,
and actions. The "variegating, confusing, or reversing tropes and
figures" are, for example, more usefully understood as the "mob
tendency." This primitive drive toward disorder is first expressed
by the various faults of style Pope includes in this class, but it
presses on to realize itself in such scenic elements as the wearing
of fantastic clothing, crowd and mob scenes, labyrinths and other
disordered buildings, huge, jumbled cities, and at last in primal
chaos and uncreation.

Each of Pope's three classes of disordered figures—the confusing, the magnifying, and the diminishing—could be plentifully
illustrated from *The Dunciad,* the masterwork of satire, or any
other great satire. But in order to expand our range and provide
the clearest possible examples, I have chosen to discuss each class
of disorder in terms of a satire where the particular tendency it
suggests is dominant. The three tendencies of dullness are not,
however, to be thought of as distinct and unrelated; though one
may be stressed in a particular satire, it always appears in conjunc-
tion with the others. Pope was well aware of this fact, and the
words of his Rhetorician sum the matter up very nicely: "The
Macrology and Pleonasm, are as generally coupled, as a lean
Rabbit with a fat one; nor is it a wonder, the Superfluity of Words
and Vacuity of Sense, being just the same thing.[17]

Each of the major tendencies or actions of disorder is in fact
either a necessary condition or consequence of the other two, and
I plan to take them up, not in the order Pope lists them, but
rather in a way which will show how one leads inevitably to the
other and suggest the kind of world they ultimately create in
combination.

17. *Peri Bathous,* Ch. XI, p. 58.

3. The Magnifying Tendency: Gay's *Trivia;*
or The Art of Walking the Streets of London

> Above all, preserve a laudable *Prolixity;* presenting the Whole
> and every Side at once of the Image to view. For Choice and
> Distinction are not only a Curb to the Spirit, and limit the
> Descriptive Faculty, but also lessen the book.
>
> (*Peri Bathous,* Ch. VIII)

The greatest satirists have always taken for their subject not mere
petty stupidity but the more "heroic" and self-satisfied forms of
vice and dullness, which, blind to reality, create grand inflated
images of themselves and pompously attempt to reconstruct the
world. A dunce sets himself up for a great wit, a self-seeker for
a man of piety, and an ugly woman as a great beauty. The first
step in these grand transformations is always achieved by language,
for in the world of satire, as Voltaire remarked, *"La pudeur s'est
enfuite des coeurs, et s'est refugiée sur les lèvres."*[1] The sonority
of epic, the thunderous tones of Old Testament prophecy, the
vocabularies of science and philosophy, the terms of wit and learning, the styles of refinement and morality are all appropriated—
and mangled—by dullness attempting to enlarge itself.

Dullness never limits its reach for grandeur to language alone
but always goes on to try to create vast images of itself in extravagant clothing, elaborate manners, oversize gestures, huge accum-
ulations of goods and titles, and vast, pretentious buildings. As
fatuousness and insolence swell, these modest violations of nature
expand into ever larger and grander schemes. We find the master
dunces of satire busily constructing perpetual motion machines,
industriously mixing chemicals to create the philosophers' stone,

1. *Lettre de M. Eraton à M. Clocpitre Aûmonier de S.A.S.M. de landgrave,*
1759. Quoted by Byron, *Don Juan,* "Preface to Cantos VI, VII, and VIII."

stirring up the elixir which will confer eternal life on its possessor, creating utopian societies which by scientific regulation banish all pain and hardship from life. Marching under the banner of progress, dullness is always incurably optimistic about its ability to rework nature into a brave new world and to make itself over in the image of its own desire.

Trimalchio is only a mean and greedy ex-slave who has found his way to riches in the early Roman Empire by the exercise of the lowest cunning and by the lack of any standards or decency. But the frescoes on his walls tell a different story:

> First came a panel showing a slave market with everything clearly captioned. There stood Trimalchio as a young man, his hair long and curly in slave fashion; in his hand he held a staff and he was entering Rome for the first time under the sponsorship of Minerva. In the next panel he appeared as an apprentice accountant, then as a paymaster—each step in his career portrayed in great detail and everything scrupulously labeled. At the end of the portico you came to the climax of the series: a picture of Mercury grasping Trimalchio by the chin and hoisting him up to the lofty eminence of the official's tribunal. Beside the dais stood the goddess Fortuna with a great cornucopia and the three Fates, busily spinning out Trimalchio's life in threads of gold.
>
> (*The Satyricon of Petronius,* Ch. V)[2]

Such inflation of the self as this and the magnifying tendency which it expresses lie at the basis of some of the most standard techniques of satire: high burlesque, mock epic, mock utopia, and the "great man" theme, all of which render in the largest terms the ludicrous pretensions to greatness and nobility of men completely lacking these virtues.

Pope calls attention to the fact that the magnifying tendency is also manifested by a fondness for amplification, sheer multiplication of words and indiscriminate amassment of vast numbers of

2. Trans. William Arrowsmith (Ann Arbor, 1959).

sounds. The amplifying tendency appears in language in elaborate periphrasis, macrology, pleonasm—in short, the prolix style. In scenic terms it takes the form of the profusion of things and objects which dullness so regularly delights in. If a crafty ex-slave can magnify his worth by showing himself as the favorite of the gods and wearing a toga with the senatorial purple stripe, he can at the same time further amplify his image by surrounding himself with innumerable expensive objects and giving incredibly varied dinners, in which this is only one course:

> Spaced around a circular tray were the twelve signs of the zodiac, and over each sign the chef had put the most appropriate food. Thus, over the sign of Aries were chickpeas, over Taurus a slice of beef, a pair of testicles and kidneys over Gemini, a wreath of flowers over Cancer, over Leo an African fig, virgin sowbelly on Virgo, over Libra a pair of scales with a tartlet in one pan and a cheesecake in the other, over Scorpio a crawfish, a lobster on Capricorn, on Aquarius a goose, and two mullets over the sign of the Fishes. The centerpiece was a clod of turf with the grass still green on top and the whole thing surmounted by a fat honeycomb.

But this is considered "wretched fare" by Trimalchio, and he calls in four slaves who whisk the top off this concoction:

> Underneath, in still another tray, lay fat capons and sow-bellies and a hare tricked out with wings to look like a little Pegasus. At the corners of the tray stood four little gravy boats, all shaped like the satyr Marsyas, with phalluses for spouts and a spicy hot gravy dripping down over several large fish swimming about in the lagoon of the tray.
>
> (*The Satyricon,* Ch. V)

The magnifying and amplifying powers of dullness are active in most satires, where they account for the many various kinds of pomposity and the vulgar profusion of objects so characteristic of the satiric scene. Petronius' *Satyricon,* Jonson's *Volpone* and *The Alchemist,* Samuel Butler's *Hudibras,* Fielding's *Jonathan*

Wild, and Huxley's *Brave New World,* to name a few instances, all feature the magnifying tendency of dullness, showing worlds in which men for various reasons and in various ways seek to elevate themselves to ridiculous heights. I intend, however, to pass over these more obvious and familiar illustrations of the magnifying tendency and to discuss instead a much neglected and in many ways puzzling work that handles the magnifying tendency in a most subtle and intriguing manner.

Since John Gay's *Trivia; Or the Art of Walking the Streets of London*[3] is not very well known, it will be useful to begin with a description of it. The poem is spoken by "The Walker," a man who knows his way about London and undertakes to give us advice on how to walk safely and cleanly through the dangerous and dirty town. He sets forth his program in the first five lines:

> Through winter streets to steer your course aright,
> How to walk clean by day, and safe by night,
> How jostling crouds, with prudence to decline,
> When to assert the wall, and when resign,
> I sing.

After an invocation to the goddess Trivia—Diana, the deity of the crossways or public places, *tri via*—the Walker describes the kind of gear, coats, shoes, and canes to be preferred for walking the streets of London and offers advice on forecasting the weather in order to be prepared with the proper clothing. He supports his advice with vivid examples of success and disaster drawn from his past experiences on the streets, and he diversifies his speech with such *obiter dicta* as a patriotic discussion of the superiority of English streets to Italian or French and a little myth about how pattens (shoes with raised soles for walking in wet weather) were invented by Vulcan when he became enamored of a mortal maiden, the "blue-ey'd Patty," who was sickening from walking the wintry ways.

3. *The Poetical Works of John Gay,* ed. G. C. Faber (London, 1926), pp. 57–87.

In Book II the Walker takes us out for an actual tour of the London streets by day. Our journey begins early in the morning when the milkmaids are on their rounds in donkey-drawn carts and rows of drummers stand beating their instruments outside a church where a wedding is taking place. Then the world wakens and business begins:

> Shops open, coaches roll, carts shake the ground,
> And all the streets with passing cries resound.
>
> (II, 23–24)

We pick our way through the crowd, trying to save our clothing by avoiding contact with the bloody butcher, the perfumer, the dusty baker, the chimney sweep, and the dustman. When we encounter the helpless, we give them the wall, but the bully who tries to thrust us into the street is defied and goes off muttering curses. At St. Giles Cripplegate a countryman is wandering lost in the maze of streets, and the Walker points him out and compares him with Theseus lost in the Labyrinth. Crossing sweepers spatter the unwary passerby with dirt, porters lower huge hogsheads from carts, and brewers carry barrels of beer into tavern cellars. A bootblack's cry is heard, and the Walker stops to tell a long myth about the origin of bootblacks. Cloacina, goddess of sewers, smitten with a "scavenger," a street-cleaner or garbage man, becomes pregnant, but unwilling to accept disgrace, she drops the child "beneath a bulk" in London. The helpless orphan, starving, is pitied by the gods who teach him the useful trade of cleaning shoes. The different gods each contribute, as in the arming of the epic hero, some piece of equipment: the brush, the foot-rest, the oil, the blacking.

Greatly instructed by this story, we move on to the stocks, where some poor wretch is being pelted with garbage, but we pass on quickly lest our clothes be stained. Loaded carts, thundering wagons, straining horses being savagely beaten mark the passage into Watling Street, from whence we continue on to Cheapside, to Fleet Ditch, and then down Thames Street with its ripe odors of fish, meat, tallow, and cheese. Here we leave the old City and go on to Pall Mall with its wide, safe walks and the bright cos-

tumes of fashionable promenaders. But this attractive scene bord-
ers on narrow alleys down which the broker with his large beaver
hat walks on his way to foreclose a mortgage, where an old lecher
taps on the door of the "fair recluse," and where the "lavish rake"
sneaks about to avoid his tailor's dun. Emerging into the open
again, we watch the juggler and the shell-game man at their trades,
see a wit urinating on a sentry box, hear the dangerous crack of
the coachman's whip, avoid the urchin's snowball, and follow a
young seamstress to her work in the Exchange. In Covent Garden
a crowd of football players rushes headlong at us, but the ball
sails over our heads to a glazier above repairing a window. He
bats it away, but into another pane. The Walker pauses to tell
of the time when the Thames was frozen over and a carnival
town grew up on the ice. All was festive until one day an apple-
seller fell through the ice, and her severed head went sliding
away still crying "pip-pip-pip." This diverting tale, which seems
to have as moral the dangers of any kind of nonproductive frolic,
is ended when a bear and a bull are led up the street beneath the
mops being shaken out by maids above. We are surrounded by
beggars crying out for alms; half-pence are judiciously bestowed.

The Walker now meets a lawyer friend at the Temple and
walks with him through the Strand, looking down toward the
river and lamenting that only Burlington House remains of all
the stately buildings and centers of culture which once lined
the shore. The greatness of the past and the vulgarity of the
present having been glanced at, we move on to examine the various
city markets and to browse in the used-book stalls, where morals
can be picked up from "Plutarch's tatter'd page." We next come
on an overturned coach and a splintered sedan chair, and our
guide, after congratulating himself on having chosen such a safe
means of getting about as walking, delivers a tirade on the wicked-
ness of *riding:*

> What walker shall his mean ambition fix
> On the false lustre of a coach and six?
> Let the vain virgin, lur'd by glaring show,

Sigh for the liv'ries of th' embroider'd beau.
    See yon bright chariot on its braces swing,
With *Flanders* mares, and on an arched spring;
That wretch, to gain an equipage and place,
Betray'd his sister to a lewd embrace.

                    .   .   .

Here the brib'd lawyer, sunk in velvet, sleeps;
The starving orphan, as he passes, weeps;
There flames a fool, begirt with tinsell'd slaves,
Who wastes the wealth of a whole race of knaves.
That other, with a clustring train behind,
Owes his new honours to a sordid mind.
This next in court-fidelity excells,
The publick rifles, and his country sells.
May the proud chariot never be my fate,
If purchas'd at so mean, so dear a rate;
O rather give me sweet content on foot,
Wrapt in my virtue, and a good *Surtout!* (II, 569–90)

In Book III the Walker takes us on a tour of the streets by night.
As darkness falls, the shutters of the shops are lowered, workmen
walk home carrying planks and ladders, and people swarm the
streets. We are immediately in trouble where Fleet Street meets
the Strand. No posts protect the sidewalk from the busy street,
and strings of combs for sale dangle in the face and blind the
walkers. A traffic jam occurs and swells rapidly into a riot.

Team follows team, crouds heap'd on crouds appear,
And wait impatient, 'till the road grow clear.
Now all the pavement sounds with trampling feet,
And the mixt hurry barricades the street.
Entangled here, the waggon's lengthen'd team
Cracks the tough harness; here a pond'rous beam
Lies over-turn'd athwart; for slaughter fed
Here lowing bullocks raise their horned head.
Now oaths grow loud, with coaches coaches jar,

And the smart blow provokes the sturdy war;
From the high box they whirl the thong around,
And with the twining lash their shins resound:
Their rage ferments, more dang'rous wounds they try,
And the blood gushes down their painful eye.
And now on foot the frowning warriors light,
And with their pond'rous fists renew the fight;
Blow answers blow, their cheeks are smear'd with blood,
'Till down they fall, and grappling roll in mud. (III, 27–44)

Pickpockets, sword stealers, and boys carried high in baskets to reach out and snatch wigs are attracted by the tumult and work their trades in the throng. A petty thief is detected, the cry of "Stop thief" raised, and a hue and cry pursues the boy through the streets until he is caught and nearly drowned under a pump. Turning to look at a handsome "damsel," another walker is drenched with dirty water from a fish stall; forgetting himself for a moment, he is beaten down in a turnstile; crossing a dark street, he falls over a porter's load, is splattered with mud from a barrow's wheels, falls down dark cellar steps, and overturns a huckster's stall. More skilled, our Walker leads us around such dangers and avoids the dark alleys and open spaces of Lincoln's Inn Fields, where the beggar waits to use his crutch as a club on his surprised victim.

As night deepens, the dangers intensify. A rude chairman moving, contrary to law, along the dark sidewalk tries to thrust us into the street. He fails, but a brutal footman leading a train carrying torches before a lady of fashion on a midnight visit forces us from the wall. Thundering coaches nearly crush us with their wheels. The whores from Drury Lane and Catherine Street appear in their silks and paint to leer familiarly, twitch the sleeve, or pat the cheek with their fans. To show us the danger of these creatures, the Walker provides a "dreadful example" of a young countryman from *"Devon's* plain" who was robbed by a harlot of the money he had received for the sale of his cattle, and infected to boot. As the story finishes, the sound of breaking windows is

heard. One of the roaming street gangs, the Nickers, have begun their quaint practice of throwing half-pence at windows. Another gang, the Mohocks, roll a matron down Snow Hill in a barrel. Night and evil increase: the warning lights placed in front of open ditches and sewers flicker out, and a coach crashes with cracking axle and struggling horses into the void. Finally the cry of "Fire" is heard, the blaze roars up, firemen rush to pull the burning buildings down, but the fire still spreads. As a last measure, gunpowder is brought, a train is laid, and a block of houses is blown up to create a fire line.

Looking back on the dangers and toils he has passed, the Walker addresses us in the following fashion:

> Consider, reader, what fatigues I've known,
> The toils, the perils of the wintry town;
> What riots seen, what bustling crouds I bor'd,
> How oft' I cross'd where carts and coaches roar'd.
>
> (III, 393–96)

But he feels that his labors will be well repaid if his poem shows others the way to walk the streets in safety, and he rests happy in the thought that when other such distinguished poets as Ward and Gildon—they were actually hacks—are forgotten, his work will still be "high-rais'd on *Fleet-street* posts, consign'd to fame." In a last epic comparison he compares his journey through London to bold travels through *"Asia's* desert soil, the barb'rous *Arabs* haunt," and "Dark *Greenland's* mountains of eternal frost."

There is, I believe, no question that the Walker intends this, as well as his other epic comparisons, quite seriously. He believes that he has shown the streets of London to be as barren and as savage as the Asian desert or the mountains of Greenland, and the inhabitants of the town to be barbarians. Certainly he has shown us the grime, the brutality, the confusion, and the pain which are characteristic of the satiric world; and we have seen labyrinths, jungles, Towers of Babel, holocausts, and animals where we had supposed there was a great city and civilized men.

The Walker has even pinpointed for us the source of the trouble as he sees it: The Riders. This term sums up, for him, all the vanity, venality, laziness and attempts to rise above man's natural condition, which stand in opposition to the humble walking along life's path in simple, stout clothing.

Yet all this will somehow not do. As much as it resembles the Rome of Juvenal's Third Satire—some passages are direct imitations—the London of *Trivia* is not the corrupt city of the early Caesars. The great, confused, polyglot metropolis—The Cities of the Plain—frequently appears in satire as the symbolic form assumed by dullness' magnifying and disordering tendencies— Samuel Johnson's *London,* Blake's *London,* or James Thomson's *The City of Dreadful Night.* But Gay's London, though it certainly has its dark spots, is in a good many places most attractive: the carnival city on the ice, the bustling game of football in the streets, the fish market,

> The golden-belly'd carp, the broad-finn'd maid,
> Red-speckled trouts, the salmon's silver joul,
> The joynted lobster, and unscaly soale,
> And luscious scallops . . . . (II, 414–17)

These spots where life leaps through the Walker's sober disapproval suggest a complex richness and vitality everywhere present in the city but dampened down and distorted by the Walker. The poem is, remember, spoken entirely by the Walker, and enough has been quoted, I hope, to suggest his peculiar strained tone. But Gay is sufficiently explicit in his irony at times to force us to look critically at the Walker and to become aware of him as, not a neutral telling voice, but a warped mirror giving its own peculiar distortions to the scene it reflects.

"Wrapt in my virtue, and a good *Surtout*" is the Walker's happy description of himself, and it sums up very nicely his basic reduction of life. For him virtue and a stout greatcoat, morality and serviceability, are identical. And he is "wrapt" in both of these, enclosed, insulated, in a smug sense of his own righteousness

and practical wisdom in choosing a stout garment which protects
him by keeping all the world outside. This basic reduction of life
to self and sound economic practices dictates his announced purpose in the poem, which is no more than "How to walk clean by
day, and safe by night." When in the course of his tour of London
he offers any other reason for being abroad, that reason is always
businesslike. He does not go out, and cannot conceive of others
going out, just to visit a friend, seek amusement, or see the sights.
The approved step is never "loitering," but always quick, busy,
hasty, on business bent. In his walking there is nothing that delights him quite so much as "the voice of industry" in rich trades-
men or poor bootblacks. When he tells us of a young countryman
who was robbed by whores and sent home to his new bride with
a foul disease, he adds as a climax that the unhappy young man
was saddled with large doctors' bills. The Walker's choice of
shoes, coat, walking stick, and other clothing is based entirely
on serviceability. Light colors and fancy dress which dirty easily
or do not keep out the weather manifest foolishness, vanity, and
sin. These fopperies, like coaches with arched springs, or rich
foods—blood sausages, frogs' legs, ragousts—are favored by the
Riders of the world and lead, the Walker insists, to ill health.
Meanwhile, the Walker, moving on the legs God gave him for
locomotion, can congratulate himself on growing constantly more
robust, more wise, and less subject to accident.

The Walker is as narrow in politics and religion as he is in
economics and morals, and here Gay's irony is a good deal broader
than is usual in either this poem or his other writings. The Walker
is a true-born British man who despises foreign food, prefers
English cloth and styles, and delights that he does not walk the
streets of France,

> Where slav'ry treads the street in wooden shoes; (I, 86)

or through the town of Rome,

> Where frequent murders wake the night with groans,
> And blood in purple torrents dies the stones. (I, 95–96)

Later, in terms which suggest a Protestantism as stout as his shoes
and cloak, he pauses to compare the happy reign of law in England
with the anarchy of other lands:

> Happy *Augusta!* law-defended town!
> Here no dark lanthorns shade the villain's frown;
> No *Spanish* jealousies thy lanes infest,
> Nor *Roman* vengeance stabs th' unwary breast;
> Here tyranny ne'er lifts her purple hand,
> But liberty and justice guard the land;
> No bravos here profess the bloody trade,
> Nor is the church the murd'rer's refuge made.
>
> (III, 145–52)

No sooner is this boast out of his mouth than the Walker encounters a chairman walking on the sidewalk where the law
forbids him to be; and in a few more lines he is describing all the
frauds and "petty rapines of the night," and the wild activities
of the Nickers and the Mohocks, which the law was helpless to
stop.

We have noted that reduction and magnification go together in
satire, and so it is no surprise to discover that after reducing life
to extremely narrow dimensions, the Walker goes on to express
an enormous sense of his own importance, all half-hidden under
a surface of creeping humility. This is, perhaps, most apparent
in his announcement of his action:

> How to walk clean by day, and safe by night,
> How jostling crouds, with prudence to decline,
> When to assert the wall, and when resign,
> I sing.   (I, 2–5)

What a reduction and magnification are here at once when we
think of the other subjects announced in this epic formula: the
wrath of Achilles, the transferal of Troy to Latium, "Man's first
disobedience and the fruit / Of that forbidden tree." The exag-
geration of what is after all rather trivial is central to the tone

of the poem, and the Walker is quick to use epic terms and devices for unsuitable subjects. If a carriage is wrecked in a ditch, the Walker reminds us of the destruction by storm of the Eddystone and all the ships that were afterwards broken on the coast. Bootblacks are raised to "the sable race"; brawls in the street to epic combats, "with coaches coaches jar"; decisions about which side of the street to take to choices between Scylla and Charybdis; and a quarrel about who will take the wall to a Theban incident:

> O think on *Oedipus'* detested state,
> And by his woes be warn'd to shun his fate.
>   (III, 215–16)

The dislocation of values and the subsequent magnification of the trivial suggested directly by the Walker's fondness for the epic style is extended further in a number of subtle and unusual ways. Concerned for his own safety and cleanliness alone, isolated in his virtue and his surtout, the Walker sees menace everywhere he turns. He finds malevolence in the paving stone which tilts under his foot, in the crack of the coachman's whip, in the rain which pours from the gutters, and even in the maid shaking out the mop. These ordinary events become dangers as real to him as the street gangs and the fire, and he invests them with a significance out of all proportion to what they deserve. And so it is with the rich, bustling, at times overly active city as a whole, which he translates into a place of cunning traps and ever-present dangers to the person. In the end he defeats his own argument, for he treats everything he sees with such solemnity and such caution that after a time even the more startling sins of the city come to seem not so important after all.

Though the Walker is a remarkably cold man, he magnifies out of all proportion certain situations requiring an emotional response. Sentimentality replaces genuine concern for other living things. He is extremely fond of the word "little," never misses a chance to refer to the orphan's tear and the widow's groan, cannot bear to see animals mistreated, and speaks constantly of "virgins." His sentimentality operates, however, only so long as the victim is industrious in some honest trade, but when a thief

is caught and placed in the stocks, the Walker can address him with these comforting words:

Ill-fated boy!
Why did not honest work thy youth employ? (III, 71–72)

Both sentiment and morality find their natural reduction and magnification in a pronounced sententious streak. The Walker cannot see an elaborate funeral (of a "fair virgin nipt in beauty's bloom") without stopping to moralize:

How short is life! how frail is human trust!
Is all this pomp for laying dust to dust? (III, 235–36)

Young girls playing a game of shuttlecock lead him on to this,

These sports warm harmless; why then will ye prove,
Deluded maids, the dang'rous flame of love? (II, 341–42)

Sentimentality, maxims, stern patriotism and a fear of foreign lands, strict concern for business and practicality, and an overriding concern for cleanliness and safety, these are the constituents of the Walker. Taken together, they add up to a type familiar to us, and not unknown in any age, but one who must have seemed odd to a cultivated gentleman of the early eighteenth century, who was apt still to regard himself as an inheritor of Western culture rather than an Englishman, who knew of a scheme of values in which epic and tragic ideals did not mingle with business practices and squabbles between wagoners, whose morality was realistic enough to exclude the sentimental, and who could accept the world in all its mysterious variety and odd vitality without seeing it as a constant threat to his safety and cleanliness.

No doubt Gay uses his Walker to good effect to satirize some of the crudeness and beastliness of Augustan London, but the main thrust of the satire is, I am arguing, directed at the attitudes embodied in the Walker. It is his materialism which reduces all he describes to things, to a consideration of business efficiency. It is his solemnity and literal-mindedness which allow him to magnify simple matters of daily life with epic devices, making mechanics into gods and every street occurrence into an Odyssean

trial. It is, finally, his limited moral view and his insulation which turns a complex city with all its human interactions into *trivia*.

In order to make my point, I am, of course, treating the Walker far more seriously than Gay does, for his irony is mild and Horatian. He laughs at the fool he has created, but he does not lash him savagely with the heavy whip used by Swift and Pope against the same forms of dullness. But the final point Gay makes about his Walker is serious enough. This strange man has set out only to walk the town cleanly and safely, and this he succeeds in doing. In achieving his purpose, he makes the town a meaningless jumble, and his journey has in the end the same meaninglessness. He walks but he goes nowhere. His path back and forth through London is mere wandering. At one moment he is on Lower Thames Street, and then he is at Pall Mall; he moves from watching a horse struggle up Ludgate Hill to the market in Covent Garden to the Temple. This aimless movement about the town would be far more apparent to a contemporary of Gay's than it is to us, but enough of it can be puzzled out from old maps to recover the point that the Walker is always busily hastening on his way, but that he has no way. He begins in Book I walking the streets of London, and by the end of the poem he is still walking the streets, clean and safe. His values have magnified the movements of the busy city into a source of endless dangers and have made his own industrious steps into mere wandering.[4]

4. It has long been recognized that *Trivia* is in some ways a mock form of Vergil's *Georgics,* a "town Georgic." Changes in season and weather, for example, which are marked in Vergil by occurrences in nature are marked in Gay by such town changes as the shift to brightly colored, light clothing and coachmen dozing in the sun. There has been, however, no close exploration of the relationship between the two poems, and the accepted view has been that partly expressed by Gay's latest critic (Sven Armens, *John Gay Social Critic* [New York, 1954], Ch. III), who argues that the *Georgics* serves as a model of the proper life and stands in contrast to the ways of the wicked town—as *The Aeneid,* say, stands in contrast to the actions of the fools in *The Dunciad.* Such, I think, is not the case. Rather, the echoes of Vergil serve to bring into play our sense of the various but unified and interacting world of nature and man realized in *The Georgics,* and to transfer these feelings to the urban life. But the Walker does not, of course, feel this pulse of life because he lacks the sensibility Vergil brought to bear on his subject.

4. The Diminishing Tendency: *The Mechanical Operation of the Spirit*

Since bathos is literally "the diminishing," nearly all the advice the Rhetorician gives in *Peri Bathous* bears on this subject. He recommends such general strategies for sinking as dwelling "upon the dregs of nature," vulgarizing material taken from the great poets, and cultivating the prurient by drawing metaphors "from two most fruitful Sources or Springs, the very *Bathos* of the human Body, that is to say . . . and . . . *Hiatus magnus lachrymabilis.*"[1] More specifically, the Rhetorician offers for the consideration of the bathetic poet such rhetorical devices as comparisons of the noble with the gross, tautology, and anticlimax. Satire makes heavy use of these figures, and the diminishing tendency of dullness which they manifest at the verbal level always expands into larger terms of composition. Swift, for example, uses an elaborate series of anticlimaxes to capture the human tendency to reduce all things to a selfish consideration of "private ends." Several of the Dean's friends, while playing cards, have received the news of his death:

> "The Dean is dead, (*and what is Trumps?*)
> "Then Lord have Mercy on his Soul.
> "(Ladies I'll venture for the *Vole.*)
> "Six Deans they say must bear the Pall.
> "(I wish I knew what *King* to call.)[2]
> > ("Verses on the Death of Doctor Swift,"
> > lines 228–32)

Pope, wishing to show the diminution of literature resulting from the writing of slander and scurrilous pamphlets, extends the kind

1. Ch. XII, p. 67.
2. *The Poems of Jonathan Swift,* ed. Harold Williams (London, 1958), 2, pp. 551–72.

of sinking in conversation found in Swift's lines into scene and physical action. His Dunces, the mightiest pamphleteers in the land, come to the edge of Fleet Ditch where they stop for a mud-diving, slandering, contest, the object being to see who can plunge the deepest into the sewage and remain the longest on the mud at the bottom:

> In naked majesty Oldmixon stands,
> And Milo-like surveys his arms and hands;
> Then sighing, thus, "And am I now threescore?
> "Ah why, ye Gods! should two and two make four?"
> He said, and clim'd a stranded lighter's height,
> Shot to the black abyss, and plung'd down-right.
> The Senior's judgment all the crowd admire,
> Who but to sink the deeper, rose the higher.
>   (The Dunciad, II, 283–90)[3]

This descent from the high air to the mud and garbage traces in concrete terms the path which dullness takes in satire: it rises high (magnifies) only to plunge deeper. All instances of the bathetic involve the reduction of some high ideal, some spiritual quality, some ineffable, to the level of the grossly substantial, the material, the solid thing. This materialistic drive toward the diminution of idea to thing is most obvious in the stock satiric character who substitutes some objective thing for a subjective reality: a pious expression, a cowl, folded hands, and frequent references to the Deity for true religion; paint, elegant clothing, and genteel ways of speaking for beauty and cultivation; pedantic phrases, long words, heavy books, and a grave manner for wisdom. Jonson's *Volpone* is made up of a great number of such substitutions which ultimately resolve into two master reductions: heavy, drossy gold for life and virtue; and acting for honesty, love, concern for others. Even when some brand of dullness is attacked

---

3. I owe this point to Aubrey Williams, *Pope's Dunciad*, pages 54–55, where he discusses the possibility of "whether mock-epic poetry may not be defined as a very self-conscious exploitation of the qualities of bathos by an arrangement of the high alongside the low."

for its departure from common sense and its soarings into the realm of the abstract, there is usually some reduction to the material involved. Ferdinando Flosky (Coleridge) in Peacock's *Nightmare Abbey* may be a transcendental metaphysician who has never a practical thought, but in the end all of his vague ramblings are shown to be no more than big words, impressive noises. He never leaves the earth at all.

These are the local effects of the diminishing action of dullness, and as they accumulate they create larger, more general patterns: the reduction of man to meat in *A Modest Proposal,* to chemicals and statistics in *Brave New World,* and to political objects in *1984.* The accepted name for this action, when it is considered as a rhetorical strategy, is "low burlesque," which always involves the reduction of something high and noble to something low and mean. Out of low burlesque come some of satire's most common patterns, such as the beast fable (*Mother Hubberd's Tale, Animal Farm,* Gay's *Fables*) or the representation of men as children or tiny creatures (*Lord of the Flies* and Book I of *Gulliver's Travels*).

Having risen high, dullness always plunges to the depths of life, carrying all that was meaningful and valuable to the lowest levels of being. This reduction of life to its grossest constituents has taken many forms, but the two most persistent directions it has followed are the diminishing of the vital to the mechanical and the spiritual to the vulgarly material. The attempts of satirists to dramatize the latter direction have generated those distasteful vulgarities which spot satire so much more frequently than any other genre. Many readers are frankly appalled by such scenes as the meeting in Juvenal's Ninth Satire with the male whore who complains in the most explicit terms of the treatment he has had from a rich man who has now abandoned him; the Yahoos in the trees defecating on the passersby below in *Gulliver's Travels;* the urinating contest in *The Dunciad;* or the cannibalism in the open boat in *Don Juan,* where one lucky fellow is excused from being the victim because he has a venereal disease. The usual explanation offered for these scenes is the poets' obsession

with filth, and case histories have been manufactured to support these views. Swift's frequent references to ordure are, for example, regularly diagnosed as expressions of coprophilia. Most satirists are not fortunate enough to draw such a distinguished name for their mental conditions and have to be satisfied with being styled "dirty-minded."

It does, I believe, require a certain kind of man to write satire, and among the qualifications is no doubt a certain fascination with what is usually thought vulgar, indecent, and downright filthy. But whereas the ordinary "dirty mind" is limited to scribbling on toilet walls, the satirist of genius can and does make use of his curious fascination with the vulgar to express not just his disgust with the world but to dramatize the grossness to which dullness reduces life.

George Orwell is a case in point, and documents exist which make it much easier than it is with Swift to discuss the relationship of his peculiar character to his satires. In the years since his death in 1950, Orwell's character has been the subject of a great deal of controversy. For some writers, such as V. S. Pritchett, Orwell was the "conscience of his generation," while others, such as Rayner Heppenstall, who once shared lodgings with Orwell, have stressed his instability, his moral naiveté, and his inability to deal with complex ethical and social questions. Anthony West has gone on to argue that Orwell's miserable childhood built into him certain fears and patterns of terror, which he projected onto the world in his satires.[4] According to West's theory, works like *Animal Farm* and *1984* are more dramatizations of Orwell's personal fears than artistic extensions and intensifications of real dangers at work in our world. From the evidence offered it is impossible, I believe, to deny that Orwell's childhood was trau-

---

4. The argument over Orwell's character and its relation to his writing is summed up by D. J. Dooley, "The Limitations of George Orwell," *Univ. of Toronto Quarterly*, 28 (1958–59), 291–300. See also Anthony West, "George Orwell" in *Principles and Persuasions* (New York, 1957), pp. 164–76, and Rayner Heppenstall, "The Shooting-Stick," *Twentieth Century*, 157 (1955), 367–73.

matic, that he lacked sophistication in his approach to moral
problems, and that he wrote his fears into his books. But far from
disabling his satire, his terrors functioned to sensitize him to
very real problems of our time and to give him the terms in which
to present these problems.

Among Orwell's peculiarities was one that particularly concerns us here; he was extraordinarily sensitive from early childhood to the grossness in life and unusually pained by the heavy,
stinking material world in which he found himself trapped:

> It is not easy for me to think of my schooldays without
> seeming to breathe in a whiff of something cold and evil-
> smelling—a sort of compound of sweaty stockings, dirty
> towels, faecal smells blowing along corridors, forks with old
> food between the prongs, neck-of-mutton stew, and the
> banging doors of the lavatories and the echoing chamber-
> pots in the dormitories.
>
> ("Such, Such Were the Joys . . .")[5]

Even when older and more accustomed to the odors of life,
Orwell still felt that "one seems always to be walking the tightrope
over a cesspool." Doubtless such extreme sensitivity is abnormal,
but could any abnormality have been more useful for the satirist
of modern materialism, of a world which seemed "to breathe
forth a smell of the more vulgar, un-grown-up kinds of luxury,
a smell of brilliantine and creme de menthe and soft-centred
chocolates . . . this oozing, bulging wealth of the English upper
and upper-middle classes"? Orwell is here specifically describing
the pre-1914 world, but the peculiar distaste for the material
built up in this period enabled him to smell and record with
power the grossness of a reductive materialism which substituted
hard cash, possessions, and physical power for honor, taste, and
justice in a fashionable boys' school, in the jungles of Imperial
Burma, in the industrial and commercial wastelands of the great
cities of the West, in the power states of modern dictators, and,

5. In *George Orwell, A Collection of Essays* (New York, 1954), pp. 9–55.

finally, in socialist utopias. It enabled him also to nose out and write with rare vividness of the grime and filth on which this materialism ultimately and revealingly rests in such places as a Burmese jail, the kitchen of a fashionable French hotel, a London flop house, and the houses of the English industrial poor.

The second of the major directions taken by the diminishing tendency of dullness is the reduction of the vital to the mechanical, and Henri Bergson in *De Rire* has identified the various devices which have been used in literature to convey life become thing-like, machinelike. Bergson perceives that some form of what we now call the conditioned response is at the base of mechanical motions of life. In language, the mechanical response, which results from a rigid habit of thought, appears as the constant repetition of the same word or phrase no matter how varied the circumstances, the use of jargon to explain whatever occurs, and such ridiculous lapses of meaning as malapropisms or the confusion of the literal and the figurative. In action, the mechanical takes such forms as wearing stiff, ornate clothing which makes free movement difficult, doing the same thing over and over (Jack-in-the-box), being manipulated by another individual or some force outside the person (Dancing-Jack or puppet), and being caught in chain reactions and moved in the way that one domino is by others when they are lined up and knocked over (Snowball). Bergson is, of course, interested in mechanical movement only in comedy, but his analysis is useful for satire, since the two genres share this understanding of human idiocy but develop it in different directions.

Swift, more than any other writer in our tradition, was aware of the vulgarity of life as it is ordinarily lived and of the tendency of men to mechanize thought and action. His dullards are always offering schemes, plans, mechanical systems, modest proposals, and arguments which express eighteenth-century optimism about man's ability scientifically to perfect himself and his world. Two of the distinctive marks of Swift's style are the use of images drawn from machinery and the mock-solemn arrangement of argument into stiff, pseudological patterns. No work shows this

tendency more clearly than the short *Discourse Concerning the Mechanical Operation of the Spirit,* published in 1704 along with *A Tale of a Tub,*[6] and no work shows better the perennial tendency of dullness to reduce ideas to things and the vital to the mechanical. ✓

The Mechanical Operation of the Spirit is written in the form of a letter intended for publication, a mode rather fashionable about the beginning of the eighteenth century, which was particularly favored by scientific investigators of the kind associated with the Royal Society and Gresham College (the type parodied as the Virtuosi in Book IV of *The Dunciad*) who wrote to one another about their experiments and discoveries. The author of this letter is a Greshamite writing to a friend "at his Chambers in the Academy of the *Beaux Esprits* in *New-Holland*" to explain his investigations and theories on the subject of Enthusiasm or Fanaticism. He notes that every art and science has its "Fanatick Branch," such as the search for the Philosopher's Stone or the attempts at Squaring the Circle, and he acknowledges that this common trait of mankind has created numerous political revolutions and caused frequent disorders in religion. It is religious enthusiasm which is his particular subject, and he narrows his field of inquiry even further by limiting himself to a study of only those varieties of religious experience which are induced by art or some mechanical method. He then proceeds to probe and explain these enthusiasms in a hostile manner.

The immediate object of the satire is, then, those self-induced enthusiasms or ecstatic visions which lead an individual to believe that he is in direct communication with some transcendental power which authorizes him to speak and act out some kind of wild truth. More specifically, the object of attack is the "Assembly of Modern Saints," the various reformed sects and dissenters—Presbyterians, Quakers, Anabaptists—who emphasized the necessity of a personal vision of God for salvation, and who, acting on these visions, had been destroying tradition and disrupting civil life in the Kingdom for well over a century.

6. All citations are to *A Tale of a Tub, With Other Early Works,* 1696–1707, ed. Herbert Davis (Oxford, 1957), pp. 171-90.

The attack on Dissent is sharpened and the range of reference extended by constructing in the letter a history of fanaticism which reaches back to the orgiastic rites of Osiris, Dionysus, and Bacchus and comes forward through the heretics of the early Christian period, the Mohammedans, and up to such great sixteenth-century reformers as Martin Luther. This lineage convicts Dissent of being but a modern form of heresy and paganism at the same time that it suggests that these more ancient forms of Dissent are no more than varieties of self-induced, mechanically contrived enthusiasms.

The main attack on Dissent is managed by describing a number of the more pronounced eccentricities of reformed preachers and congregations and then treating these as the causes of their visions. Cutting the hair short, squeezing the face, and wearing a black cap produces the favored spherical or Round-Head appearance. Hats are never removed—a reference to both the obdurate pride of the Dissenters before civil and ecclesiastical authorities and their custom of wearing hats in meeting. This practice, the letter writer assures us, prevents the internal spirit from escaping through the head via perspiration, which is "a great Spender of Mechanick Light." Reason is overcome and the spirit released in meeting by rocking back and forth, keeping up a gentle "hum," rolling the eyes backward in the sockets, and proceeding in this manner:

> The Eyes being disposed according to Art, at first, you can see nothing, but after a short pause, a small glimmering Light begins to appear, and dance before you. Then, by frequently moving your Body up and down, you perceive the Vapors to ascend very fast, till you are perfectly dosed and flustred like one who drinks too much in a Morning. Mean while, the Preacher is also at work; He begins a loud Hum, which pierces you quite thro'; This is immediately returned by the Audience, and you find your self prompted to imitate them, by a meer spontaneous Impulse, without knowing what you do. The *Interstitia* are duly filled up by the

Preacher, to prevent too long a Pause, under which the *Spirit* would soon faint and grow languid.

The dissenting Preachers are most adept at achieving enthusiastic states in themselves and their auditors by such means. They cultivate dark, unkempt appearances to manifest the presence of the inner light—"As Lanthorns, which the more Light they bear in their Bodies, cast out so much the more Soot, and Smoak, and fuliginous Matter to adhere to the sides." They pour out the spirit in the hawking, spitting, and belching, which are the "Flowers, and Figures, and Ornaments" of their unconventional, rough pulpit rhetoric. In their language "*Cant* and *Droning* supply the Place of *Sense* and *Reason,* in the Language of Men: Because, in Spiritual Harangues, the Disposition of the Words according to the Art of Grammar, hath not the least Use, but the Skill and Influence wholly lye in the Choice and Cadence of the Syllables." Their sermons are "plentifully fraught with Theological Polysyllables, and mysterious Texts from holy Writ, applied and digested by those Methods, and Mechanical Operations already related."

The point of all this is of course not only to ridicule the crudity and outlandishness of the Dissenters' ways but to suggest, as was often done, that they substitute physical appearances for true religion. Somber clothing, the wearing of hats, spouting biblical quotes, the disdain for conventional manners, and the rejection of simple, grammatical ways of speaking are all shown to be mere outward signs used to manifest piety where there is none. These conventional satiric reductions of ideal to thing involve not only the reduction of religion to clothing and sounds but the absolute debasement of a number of other ideals, such as reason, learning, clarity, and style.

But the edge of the satire cuts even deeper than these charges of pretense and vulgarization. It was common to refer to the Dissenters as religious hypocrites, and Swift treats them in this way on one level; but on another level he takes them perfectly

seriously. They may unconsciously substitute the appearances of religion for religion, but their actual aim is to reach the enthusiastic state, "A lifting up of the Soul or its Faculties above Matter." Here and in his other writings Swift makes it clear that as a Christian he believes in the possibility of genuine divine inspiration, but as a rational man and something of a cynic he believes that the Age of Miracles is past and that the possibilities of direct communication with God are fairly limited. Man's knowledge of truth and God's ways are far more likely to be found in the traditions—religious, literary, and social—which embody the discoveries about ultimate matters made in the rare encounters with the Divine in the past. The Dissenters, however, believe that every man has it in him to be a prophet and lift up his soul above matter. They attempt to force the issue by the mechanical means already described, believing that the spirit can be found "entirely from within." Truth, God, and all divine powers are thus located for them within the self, where they can be aroused and released by any kind of artificial excitement or by any dark urge to self-aggrandizement. Ultimately, the writer of the letter isolates the sexual drive as the final cause of the search for enthusiastic states. He offers a number of examples to prove that heresy everywhere has centered on women and free love, and he then goes on to describe a number of extremely unpleasant incidents which prove that,

> the Seed or Principle, which has ever put Men upon *Visions* in Things *Invisible,* is of a Corporeal Nature: For the profounder Chymists inform us, that the Strongest Spirits may be extracted from *Human Flesh.* . . . thus much is certain, that however Spiritual Intrigues begin, they generally conclude like all others; they may branch upwards toward Heaven, but the Root is in the Earth. Too intense a Contemplation is not the Business of Flesh and Blood; it must by the necessary Course of Things, in a little Time, let go its Hold, and fall into *Matter.*

As a realist Swift had no illusions about the fact that man is

largely matter and that he lives in a world of matter, but he also believed that there were some ways of transcending this condition to a modest degree. Certainly there was no reason for falling lower than nature requires; but this is exactly what the Dissenters and Enthusiasts of all kinds do: seeking to soar higher than is possible —"to lift up the soul or its faculties above matter"—they manage to fall far lower than is needful, to fall in fact to that level which Pope describes as "the very *Bathos* of the human body, that is to say . . . and . . . ." Specifically, it is the Dissenters' search for sexual and other bodily pleasures which in *The Mechanical Operation of the Spirit* reduces all ideas to gross matter and the vital to the mechanical. And as always in satire, the reduction is masked as its opposite, an exaltation.

The range of Swift's satire is, however, somewhat wider than an attack on Dissent and the more obvious kinds of fanaticism. The writer of the letter is one of the new breed of Royal Society investigators, the forerunners of the modern scientist in some respects. Widely read in arcane documents, scrupulous in his references, and completely objective in his approach, the writer has only contempt for the wretched, superstitious, emotional enthusiasts who are his subject. Secure in his sense of being an emancipated thinker free from ancient confusions of thought, he resolves "immediately, to weed this Error out of Mankind, by making it clear, that this Mystery, of venting spiritual Gifts is nothing but a *Trade,* acquired by as much Instruction, and mastered by equal Practice and Application as others are." He proceeds to his task with all the vigor and confidence carried in the tone of this passage; but, irony of ironies, he succeeds in revealing that he too has the same type of materializing, mechanical mind which he exposes in the other enthusiasts. This becomes clear in a number of ways.

First, his choice of the epistolary form is not dictated by any such abstract ideal as the suitability of form and content but by the very practical discovery, made after walking among the booksellers' stalls for several days, that no form of writing "holds so general a Vogue, as that of *A Letter to a Friend.*" Though he

speaks of the urgency of writing on the subject of Enthusiasm, there is still a dark hint that this subject and form may have been chosen after discovering that it was fashionable to write letters on such learned subjects as "long schemes in Philosophy" and "Advice to Parliaments." The irony expands, in a manner usual in Swift, when our writer, completely innocent of the epistolary tradition, takes this form of writing for an actual letter and wonders why letters should be written to such unlikely persons as "a Neighbour at next-Door" or "a perfect Stranger." Resolved not to be caught in such foolishness, our writer addresses himself to a reader over the seas in New Holland!

Whatever the immediate advantages of the epistolary form, it is soon discarded:

> And now, Sir, having dispatch'd what I had to say of Forms, or of Business, let me intreat, you will suffer me to proceed upon my Subject; and to pardon me, if I make no farther Use of the Epistolary Stile, till I come to conclude.

The writer now launches into an allegory of the most mechanical, contrived sort in which one thing, apparently, stands arbitrarily for another. But in one of the grotesque little jokes played on the writer to show his incredible literal-mindedness and the depths of ignorance lying below the show of vast learning, Swift causes him to reverse the terms of allegory. The writer begins with an obscure parable about Mahomet riding to heaven on his ass and remarking that many Christians since that time had chosen the same conveyance. Next he tells us that to avoid giving offense he will leave off "discoursing so closely to the Letter" and proceed by the way of allegory. He then gives the literal equivalents for the allegorical terms: for *ass* we are to understand "Gifted or enlightened Teacher" and for *Rider* "Fanatick Auditory." He has gone out of allegory when he said he was going in; or has he? Perhaps *ass* (with all its connotations) *is* the thing being talked about in the *Discourse* and "Gifted or enlightened Teacher" is only a figure for the animalism and the sexual urges which are ultimately shown to be the basis of enthusiasm and fanaticism.

At any rate, it is quite clear that the writer bungles the distinction between figure and reality and in doing so he demonstrates once more his inability to work on the level of concept and idea.

The method of composition and the style of the writer are as mechanical as his choice and management of form. He is a careful keeper of a commonplace book, and his collection of references to *ass* and his way of using these references reveal his method of composition: whenever he encounters some reference to "this our Fellow-Creature, I do never fail to set it down, by way of Common-place; and when I have occasion to write upon Human Reason, Politicks, Eloquence, or Knowledge; I lay my *Memorandums* before me, and insert them with a wonderful Facility of Application." He does work this mechanic way in the *Discourse,* for references to riding and to the ass occur frequently and gratuitously. The logical organization of the piece is of the one-two-three variety, and while confusion is always the ultimate product, problems are always laid out in a schematic fashion suggesting the manuals of rhetoric or the modern student's outline: heading A, subheading I, parts a, b, c, etc.

Just as the writer takes all elements of inspiration, living idea, and spirit out of writing, reducing it to various forms of mechanics, so he diminishes every subject he touches to a thing. This tendency appears continuously in his choice of metaphors. Most metaphors involve a concrete and an abstract term, but here the concrete falls to an unseemly level and is extended in this direction until it achieves a massive solidity. A few examples will convey this quality: if enthusiasm has "found a root in the fields of Empire and of knowledge, it has fixt deeper, and spread yet farther upon Holy Ground"; every effort must be used "to divert, bind up, stupify, fluster, and amuse the Senses, or else to justle them out of their Stations"; "the Spirit is apt to feed on the Flesh, like hungry Wines upon raw Beef"; the spirit and the flesh engage in "a perpetual game at Leap-Frog . . . and sometimes, the Flesh is uppermost, and sometimes the Spirit."

Perhaps even more startlingly reductive are the numerous instances of the confusion of the literal and the figurative in

which the figure is taken for an actual thing. The spirit, for example, is often compared to a light, but for our writer it becomes an actual "Mechanick Light" which can be conveyed out of the body or spent by perspiration. An idea becomes a substance in the head which can be *contained* no longer and must be purged for the sake of health. Enthusiasm becomes a literal *grain* placed in every person. The person becomes a *composition*.

The direction of all this is quite clear. Our writer is some variety of objective scientist, what we would now probably term a logical positivist. He can conceive of nothing which is not substantive and present to the senses, he can think of no action which is not a mechanical operation. Whatever he touches he reduces to this level. The brain, for example, "is only a Crowd of little Animals, but with Teeth and Claws extremely sharp, and therefore, cling together in the Contexture we behold, like the Picture of *Hobbes's Leviathan,* or like Bees in perpendicular swarm upon a Tree." Action results from these little animals biting upon the nerves, and sickness results from their reactions to eating and climatic conditions. Intense heat gives the animals vigor to bite, and "if the morsure be Hexagonal, it produces Poetry; the Circular gives Eloquence; If the Bite hath been Conical, the Person, whose Nerve is so affected, shall be disposed to write upon the Politicks; and so of the rest."

This kind of scientific materialism eventuates in self, making its particular consciousness and senses the measure of all things. Its final monument achieved by the concerted efforts of both fundamentalists and scientists to reduce all ideas to matter, is the discovery that good and evil, God and Devil, are only the inventions of man:

> After Men have lifted up the Throne of their Divinity to the *Cœlum Empyræum,* adorned him with all such Qualities and Accomplishments, as themselves seem most to value and possess: After they have sunk their *Principle of Evil* to the lowest Center, bound him with Chains, loaded him with Curses, furnish'd him with viler Dispositions than any *Rake-*

hell of the Town . . . I laugh aloud, to see these Reasoners,
. . . engaged in wise Dispute, about certain Walks and Pur-
lieus, whether they are in the Verge of God or the Devil.

The view which depresses all of life to material terms is finally
stated proudly and openly; "I think, it is in *Life* as in *Tragedy,*
where, it is held, a Conviction of great Defect, both in Order and
Invention, to interpose the Assistance of preternatural Power,
without an absolute and last Necessity."

We have long ago come to accept in physiology, pyschology,
sociology, comparative religion, and many other fields the materialism which Swift exaggerates and ridicules in *The Discourse.*
But this does not, I believe, invalidate Swift's major point that
there are human experiences to which a materialistic view cannot
be extended without ludicrous results—the Enthusiasts' reduction
of all religion to sex and the writer's reduction of philosophy and
art to collecting and mechanics. In a historical sense Swift's accomplishment in *The Discourse* is equally impressive, for he is
among the first to point out the close relationship between extreme
forms of Protestantism—represented by the Enthusiasts—and
scientific materialism—represented by the writer. But while English Dissent and the New Science are the specific objects of the
satire, the reduction of life to things and mechanics for which
Swift's targets are condemned is one of the perpetual actions of
dullness in the satire of all times.[7]

7. James L. Clifford, "Swift's Mechanical Operation of the Spirit" in *Pope
and His Contemporaries,* eds. James L. Clifford and Louis A. Landa (Oxford,
1949), pp. 144ff., has suggested an intimate connection between *A Tale of a
Tub* and *The Mechanical Operation.* His suggestion has been expanded and,
I believe, demonstrated by Ronald Paulson, *Theme and Structure in Swift's
"Tale of a Tub"* (New Haven, 1960), esp. pp. 188–235. Though the operations of the mechanical and the reduction of life to the material are equally
present in *Tale of a Tub,* it is sufficient to deal only with *The Mechanical
Operation,* for my purpose of demonstrating the tendency of dullness to
reduce all that it touches.

5.   The Mob Tendency: *The Day of the Locust*

> [The Profund Poet should] consider himself as a *Grotesque*
> Painter, whose Works would be spoil'd by an Imitation of Na-
> ture, or Uniformity of Design. He is to mingle Bits of the most
> various, or discordant kinds, Landscape, History, Portraits, Ani-
> mals, and connect them with a great deal of *Flourishing*, by
> *Heads* or *Tails*, as it shall please his Imagination, and contribute
> to his principal End, which is to glare by strong Oppositions of
> Colours, and surprize by Contrariety of Images . . . . His Design
> ought to be like a Labyrinth, out of which no body can get you
> clear but himself. (*Peri Bathous*, Ch. V)

The central character of Nathanael West's *The Day of the Locust*[1]
is a young painter, Tod Hackett, who has been brought to Hollywood to design costumes for one of the studios, and his problems
as a painter of Hollywood parallel exactly the problems of West
and other writers as satirists, who are driven to more and more
bizarre styles to catch the disordering tendencies of dullness. When
Tod leaves the Yale School of Fine Arts, his masters are the realists
Winslow Homer and Thomas Ryder; he paints such solid, orderly,
familiar subjects as "a fat red barn, old stone wall or sturdy
Nantucket fisherman." But once in Hollywood he abandons realism and turns, "despite his race, training and heritage" to the
caricaturists Goya and Daumier in search of an adequate style to
portray the fantastic world of the Golden West. As he sees more
of Hollywood, the fantastic turns to the nightmarish, and Tod
begins

> to think not only of Goya and Daumier but also of certain
> Italian artists of the seventeenth and eighteenth centuries,

1. In *The Complete Works of Nathanael West* (New York, 1957), pp.
257–421.

of Salvator Rosa, Francesco Guardi and Monsu Desiderio, the
painters of Decay and Mystery. Looking downhill now, he
could see compositions that might have actually been arranged from the Calabrian work of Rosa. There were par-
tially demolished buildings and broken monuments, half-
hidden by great, tortured trees, whose exposed roots writhed
dramatically in the arid ground, and by shrubs that carried,
not flowers or berries, but armories of spikes, hooks and
swords.

For Guardi and Desiderio there were bridges which
bridged nothing, sculpture in trees, palaces that seemed of
marble until a whole stone portico began to flap in the light
breeze. (Ch. 18)

After a tour of such churches as the "Tabernacle of the Third
Coming" where the "Crusade against Salt" is preached, Tod is
forced to reject Goya and Daumier altogether because they treat
their subjects with too much pity and without enough respect for
their "awful anarchic power." Tod turns at last to Alessandro
Magnasco and thinks how well he "would dramatize the contrast
between . . . drained-out, feeble bodies and . . . wild, disordered
minds."

Tod's master painting, "The Burning of Los Angeles," is a huge
satiric canvas in which he uses the techniques of the painters of
Decay and Mystery and creates those grotesque images which Pope
sees as characteristic of the bathetic style:

Across the top, parallel with the frame, he had drawn the
burning city, a great bonfire of architectural styles, ranging
from Egyptian to Cape Cod colonial. Through the center,
winding from left to right, was a long hill street and down
it, spilling into the middle foreground, came the mob carrying baseball bats and torches. For the faces of its members,
he was using the innumerable sketches he had made of the
people who come to California to die; the cultists of all sorts,
economic as well as religious, the wave, airplane, funeral
and preview watchers—all those poor devils who can only

be stirred by the promise of miracles and then only to violence. A super "Dr. Know-All Pierce-All" had made the necessary promise and they were marching behind his banner in a great united front of screwballs and screwboxes to purify the land. No longer bored, they sang and danced joyously in the red light of the flames.

In the lower foreground, men and women fled wildly before the vanguard of the crusading mob. Among them were Faye, Harry, Homer, Claude and himself. Faye ran proudly, throwing her knees high. Harry stumbled along behind her, holding on to his beloved derby hat with both hands. Homer seemed to be falling out of the canvas, his face half-asleep, his big hands clawing the air in anguished pantomime. Claude turned his head as he ran to thumb his nose at his pursuers. Tod himself picked up a small stone to throw before continuing his flight . . . . the tongues of fire . . . licked even more avidly at a corinthian column that held up the palmleaf roof of a nutburger stand. (Ch. 27)

Both Pope's advice to the Profund Poet and "The Burning of Los Angeles" serve as expanded glosses on the root meaning of the word "satire." The Latin root, the adjective *satura,* originally seems to have meant "filled or charged with a variety of things"— a hodgepodge, a farrago. In the course of time this adjective came to be used to form a noun which designated the type of poetry written by Lucilius, Horace, Persius, and Juvenal. Its meaning was then gradually extended to cover any piece of writing "which contains a sharp kind of irony or ridicule or even denunciation."[2] Though largely forgotten, the root meaning of "satire" remains functional, for the world of satire is always a fantastic jumble of men and objects. Whatever particular form dullness may take in a given satire, it moves always toward the creation of messes, discordancies, mobs, on all levels and in all areas of life. Pope

2. Elliott, *The Power of Satire,* p. 101. Elliott, pp. 100–12, provides an excellent summary of the origin of the word *satire* and the gradual growth of its meaning.

in *Peri Bathous* shows vulgarity creating disorder in poetry and language, and in *The Dunciad* he shows Dulness manufacturing confusion in grammar, literature, thought, the theater, education, religion, politics, and the human personality. Dulness' genius for disorder assumes the visible shape of the routs, straggling processions, and ever-growing mobs which her sons form throughout the poem, until at last, in Book IV, they achieve the ultimate mythic shape of the mob, Chaos and Uncreation, the primal mess from which the Cosmos was once constructed by the Creating Word.

As a moralist Nathanael West would seem to be about as far from Pope as it is possible to get. The neoclassical values of tradition, culture, common sense, and Nature are so diminished for West that he could once write, wryly but accurately, that "there is nothing to root for in my work and what is even worse, no rooters."[3] But the particular form of dullness which is the disintegrating force in *The Day of the Locust* still seeks out and expresses itself in those jumbles and mobs which it finds so "naturally" in *The Dunciad,* or which new wealth and lack of taste create in Petronius' *Satyricon,* or which pedantry, ignorance, and the burning desire for fame discover so regularly in that greatest image of confusion, Swift's *Tale of a Tub.* A poet like Pope will often dramatize the mob tendency of dullness in a single line, using, or purposely misusing, some rhetorical device such as zeugma or antithesis: "Or lose her heart, or necklace, at a ball"— "Puffs, Powders, Patches, Bibles, Billet-doux." In a novelist like West the crowding effect is not so obviously rhetorical or so concentrated; it is built up in blocks of semirealistic description of scenes, characters, and actions. But the effect is still to show dullness' disorganization of all the fundamental patterns of sense.

The dynamics of *The Day of the Locust* are focused in Tod's painting, "The Burning of Los Angeles." In the background is the mob which exerts a downward and outward pressure on the

---

3. Unpublished letter written in 1939 to George Milburn, quoted by Richard B. Gehman in his introduction to *The Day of the Locust* (New York, 1957), p. xx.

people below and on the picture as a whole. The mob is made up of "the people who come to California to die." These are the retired farmers from the midwest, the "senior citizens" tired of ice and snow, the housewives and clerks and small merchants dissatisfied with their dull, dreary lives in some small town, who come to California for sunshine, orange juice, and excitement. But these people are already sophisticates in violence.

> Every day of their lives they read the newspapers and went to the movies. Both fed them on lynchings, murder, sex crimes, explosions, wrecks, love nests, fires, miracles, revolutions, war. (Ch. 27)

Only disappointment can follow, and they quickly discover that you can get enough orange juice and sunshine, that one wave in the ocean looks much like another, and that airplanes almost never crash and consume their passengers in a "holocaust of flame." As simpler entertainments fail, these people, dressed in their dark mail-order suits, begin to loiter on street corners staring with hard, bold gazes at the brighter passersby. Themselves empty of talent; lacking beauty, vitality, and intelligence; and completely without compassion, the people who come to California to die search more and more wildly for the life that is not in themselves. They attend funerals waiting for the collapse of a mourner or some other show of strong emotion, they follow movie stars hoping that their personalities will magically be changed by proximity to beauty and dynamism, they take up fad diets which promise health and vigor if they avoid meat and cooked vegetables, they learn "Brain-Breathing, The Secret of the Aztecs" in a search for contact with mysterious powers which will bring them to life. But nothing works, for "Nothing can ever be violent enough to make taut their slack minds and bodies. They have been cheated and betrayed. They have slaved and saved for nothing." As this realization comes home to them, their expressions change to "vicious, acrid boredom" that trembles on the "edge of violence," and their fury at being cheated becomes "an awful, anarchic power" that can "destroy civilization."

Before the destroying mob in "The Burning of Los Angeles" runs a group of fugitives made up of the principal characters of the novel. These men and women are imperfect, but each has some one virtue which the mob lacks. Faye Greener is completely emptyheaded, but she has a breathtaking beauty, "structural like a tree's, not a quality of her mind or heart"; her father Harry Greener is a clever vaudeville actor, a master of the art of staying alive in a world fraught with dangers; Claude Estee is a writer and a talented wit; Tod Hackett a painter; and Homer Simpson a simple man capable of and needing love and kindness. But they are not complete people. It seems as if some god with a wry sense of humor had decided to give them only one virtue apiece while withholding the auxiliary virtues needed to make the gift meaningful.

The relationship of these people to the mob in the background is not simple. They are in one way, as the picture suggests, the victims of the mob, pursued and destroyed because they are different and talented. In another sense they are the purveyors of excitement to the mob, the representatives of all those people in the "entertainment industries" who make a living manufacturing the fake "amour and glamor" needed by the tired barber in Purdue who has spent his day cutting hair. But these people with their single talents, while contemptuous of the mob which follows them, "run before" in another sense, for they too are people who have come to California to die. They too seek vicarious pleasure or strange experiences to compensate for lives which, despite their gifts, are still inadequate. Because they have money or are cleverer and more attractive, their escapes into fantasy are more expensive and glossed over with a show of indifference and sophistication. But they are still escapes. Claude Estee puts a dead horse made of inflated rubber at the bottom of his swimming pool, and he and his friends visit a fancy bawdy house to see pornographic films with such titles as "Le Prédicament de Marie, ou La Bonne Distraite." He lives in an exact reproduction of an old southern mansion where he stands on the porch trying to look like a Civil War colonel and calling "Here, you black rascal! A mint julep,"

to a Chinese servant who comes up with a scotch and soda. Faye Greener's beauty is so overwhelming that she can be described only as a Botticelli Venus, "smiling a subtle half smile uncontaminated by thought . . . just born, everything moist and fresh, volatile and perfumed." Yet because her beauty is joined with no other virtue, she cannot find her life in the world and seeks it instead in daydreams built on Hollywood plots. In her dream world she becomes a rich-young-girl cruising on her father's yacht in the South Seas. Engaged to a Russian count, she falls in love with a young sailor, and they alone are saved in the inevitable shipwreck. They swim to a desert island where she is attacked by a huge snake while bathing, etc., etc.

The major portion of *The Day of the Locust* is made up of a panorama in which each of these talented people "dies" in some fashion. Harry Greener literally dies of a bad heart, exhausted and feeling cheated because he never became the great actor he thought he was. Homer Simpson's dreams of love sour into hate. He ends by killing a most unpleasant small boy and is in turn torn apart by an excitement-seeking mob. Claude and Faye survive physically, but their abilities, thwarted, lead only to sterility and emptiness. Tod Hackett ends as a wailing madman after being caught in the maelstrom of the mob.

This is West's image of Hollywood, but, as Richard Gehman says, "West used Hollywood as a microcosm . . . because . . . everything that is wrong with life in the United States is to be found there in rare purity, and because the unreality of the business of making pictures seemed a most proper setting for his 'half-world'."[4] The same point is made in *The Day of the Locust* where the people who come to California to die are described as the "cream of America's madmen" which is skimmed from a milk "just as rich as violence." West is not condemning all of American life but isolating and exposing in grotesque forms a peculiar danger or brand of dullness within it. This is, specifically, the peculiar emptiness of many people and lives, and the search for compensation in vicarious excitement and glamor. This appetite

4. Gehman, p. xviii.

is always fed and sharpened by sensational newspapers, lurid writing, impossibly romantic movies, enthusiastic religions, health fads, and quackery of all kinds which trade on dullness, fear, and hatred. These substitutes for life, West shows, are necessarily illusions, and because they are such, they—like Jonson's alchemy or the contemporary half-world created by television and Madison Avenue—cannot but fail in the end to satisfy the impossible desires they have fed and fanned. When the inevitable drop to reality comes and it is discovered that sunshine, orange juice, and waves are not really very exciting, the cheated fools will turn to mobs and destroy civilizations to revenge themselves and "get a little fun out of life."

West offers no specific cure for these empty lives. In fact, like many satirists, he deliberately leaves any positive, reforming element out of his work in order to intensify the shrillness of the siren announcing disaster.

> If I put into *The Day of the Locust* any of the sincere, honest people who work . . . [in Hollywood] and are making such a great, progressive fight, those chapters couldn't be written satirically and the whole fabric of the peculiar half-world which I attempted to create would be badly torn by them . . . I believe there is a place for the fellow who yells fire and indicates where some of the smoke is coming from without actually dragging the hose to the spot.[5]

I doubt if West really had any cure, except the dynamite blast of satire, for the deep-seated ills which he isolates, but he did diagnose the disease and predict its course with remarkable accuracy. Because he believed in no traditional value systems, he could only denote the disease in pragmatic and symbolic terms. He could not say, for example, that men were wrong to try to escape from unsatisfactory lives because each man is created by God as a part of a great plan; nor could he argue that every man has his allotted work in society which, properly done, will be richly rewarding and

5. Letter to Jack Conroy, quoted by Gehman, pp. ix- x.

serve the best interests of the society and the individual. But he could show again and again that while the phony may momentarily satisfy some desire for the impossible, that it can only disappoint more painfully, and dangerously, in the end. Eggs bathed in a rich cream-colored light in the supermarket can only turn out to be plain eggs when you get them home, and romantic dreams of passion and adventure lived in the darkness of the Bijou can only make more unsatisfactory the ordinary lives which inevitably begin again at the sidewalk.

The particular horror of West's satiric world is that in their search for romance the people who have come to California to die, and those who pander to their appetites, create such a grotesquely phony and pitifully illusionary world. Whatever they put their hand to is unreal, and unreality begins to build on unreality—furniture "painted to look like unpainted pine," or movie indians cracking jokes in fake German accents, "Vas you dere Sharley?" As the fake encrusts itself on the fake, obeying no law except the need for the novel, the result can only be fantastic disorder, combinations of things unrelated, great jumbles, and the division of those things which properly belong together. The search for glamor creates the strange dress of the Angelenos:

> Their sweaters, knickers, slacks, blue flannel jackets with brass buttons were fancy dress. The fat lady in the yachting cap was going shopping, not boating; the man in the Norfolk jacket and Tyrolean hat was returning, not from a mountain, but an insurance office; and the girl in slacks and sneaks with a bandanna around her head had just left a switchboard, not a tennis court. (Ch. 1)

A dwarf in a high green Tyrolean hat, black shirt, and yellow tie may be an amusing, harmless kind of disorder, but the disintegration of architecture and a city into a dream world sounds a more serious note:

> Only dynamite would be of any use against the Mexican ranch houses, Samoan huts, Mediterranean villas, Egyptian

and Japanese temples, Swiss chalets, Tudor cottages, and every possible combination of these styles that lined the slopes of the canyon.

When he noticed that they were all of plaster, lath and paper, he was charitable and blamed their shape on the materials used. Steel, stone and brick curb a builder's fancy a little, forcing him to distribute his stresses and weights and to keep his corners plumb, but plaster and paper know no law, not even that of gravity.

On the corner of La Huerta Road was a miniature Rhine castle with tarpaper turrets pierced for archers. Next to it was a little highly colored shack with domes and minarets out of the *Arabian Nights*. (Ch. 1)

The dreams that know no law, not even such impersonal laws as gravity and complementary colors, also ignore the simple laws of chronology and distance. The movies which feed this hunger for romance make cheap pretenses and a jumbled heap—"a Sargasso of the imagination"—out of the long history of human efforts to achieve a civilization. Tod Hackett wanders through the "dream dump" of a studio lot, moving from a giant *papier mâché* sphinx across a manmade desert to the front of the Last Chance Saloon, from where he can see a conical grass hut in a jungle compound, a charging Arab on a white stallion, a truck loaded with snow and sled dogs, a Paris street, a Romanesque courtyard, and a group of people in riding costume eating cardboard food on a fiber lawn in front of a cellophane waterfall. Crossing a bridge, he comes to a "Greek temple dedicated to Eros. The god himself lay face downward in a pile of old newspapers and bottles." Tod moves on through a

tangle of briars, old flats and iron junk, skirting the skeleton of a Zeppelin, a bamboo stockade, an adobe fort, the wooden horse of Troy, a flight of baroque palace stairs that started in a bed of weeds and ended against the branches of an oak, part of the Fourteenth Street elevated station, a Dutch windmill, the bones of a dinosaur, the upper half of the

Merrimac, a corner of a Mayan temple, until he finally
reached the road. (Ch. 18)

After this we can only ask, "What road?"

Not only does the search for dreams mangle history, making it
impossible to believe in it or see in it such simple patterns even
as enduring human courage or ingenuity; it fragments and jumbles
the human character as well. *The Day of the Locust* is populated
with strange inhuman mixtures and the broken wholes of men.
A small child brought to Hollywood to win fame and fortune
combines a childish innocence with phony adult manners, learned
from the movies, such as bowing low and clicking his heels together when introduced. He moves his small body in a suggestive
manner while dancing and singing sexy songs, which he does not
understand. Men yearn to be women and croon lullabies to imagi-
nary babies they pretend are real, and then they pretend to be men
again. An incredibly beautiful young woman speaks always in the
most vulgar tones and voices the most trivial of clichés. A
"dried-up little man with the rubbed features and stooped
shoulders of a postal clerk" pretends that he is a southern colonel
and at the same time dresses in ivory shirts, black ties, red-checked
trousers, and enormous rust-colored shoes.

This division of human nature becomes most apparent in
Homer Simpson, the quiet hotel clerk who has wandered to
Hollywood looking for health and for the love of which he is
capable but can never find. He is described as large and muscular
yet not looking strong or fertile. "He was like one of Picasso's
great sterile athletes, who brood hopelessly on pink sand, staring
at veined marble waves." He sleeps whenever he can, seeking in
unconsciousness the peace he cannot find in the world. The disintegration of self which he has suffered is clearest in the disjunc-
tive, awkward movements of his body, and particularly in his
hands, which have become separated from the rest of his being:

> He got out of bed in sections, like a poorly made automaton,
> and carried his hands into the bathroom. He turned on the
> cold water. When the basin was full, he plunged his hands

in up to the wrists. They lay quietly on the bottom like a
pair of strange aquatic animals. When they were thoroughly
chilled and began to crawl about, he lifted them out and
hid them in a towel. (Ch. 8)

Beaten by a world where he cannot find or take what he needs,
he retreats in on himself and coils back into the position of
Uterine Flight. Then, in the final scene of the book, this kindly
but ineffective man, frenzied by finding nothing but hatred and
violence in people where he hoped for love and gentleness, turns
into a savage murderer who stamps to death the small boy who
throws a stone at him. Homer's simple dream of love and peace
is more acceptable than the dreams of most of the people who
come to California to die, but West's point would seem to be
that Homer's is still a dream which, because it is not realistic and
is therefore hopeless, leads to the same fragmentation and violence
that grows from the more grotesque dreams of fame, passion,
and adventure. The retreat into sleep to find peace is finally as
fatal a dream as the visit to the movies to find love.

In *The Day of the Locust,* as in most satires, there is no consistent story and, therefore, by the usual standards, no plot. The
narration does come back frequently to the life of a few major
characters, and we are most often led on our tour of Hollywood
by Tod Hackett. But the total effect is of phantasmagoria now
thrusting forward a vaudeville act filled with brawny acrobats
tossing a helpless clown about; then a shift to the charge
of an army of extras up a plaster Mont St. Jean at Waterloo for
the glory of Grotenstein Productions. We stop to watch a lizard
emerge from a tin can and trap flies, pass on to a funeral, a scene
on Hollywood Boulevard, and move in to look at the furnishings
of a house. We attend the showing of a blue film in which all
the members of a household attempt to seduce the maid, who is
attempting to seduce the young daughter, and then move on to
the Church of Christ Physical "where holiness was attained
through the constant use of chestweights and spring grips." As
disjunct as these scenes may seem to be, each shows the dream

seekers searching for satisfaction and achieving only the flimsiest illusion, which in turn creates what is at first an amusing and then a terrifying disorder. This recurring movement from dream through illusion to disorder is the basic action of the novel. As these madmen search more and more feverishly for what is missing in their lives they turn all they touch to a mob. Clothing, furniture, architecture, history, the human personality are jumbled into monstrous collages, and under the pressure of the need for excitement and dreams every relationship, every ritual occasion, every social meeting turns to bedlam, babel, riot. A funeral becomes a sideshow as an Eskimo family, the Four Gingos, grunts in time to a record of Bach's chorale, "Come Redeemer, Our Savior," and the sensation-seekers pour in from the street to look at the corpse. A church service turns to a scene in a madhouse as a man "from one of the colonies in the desert near Soboba Hot Springs where he had been conning over his soul on a diet of raw fruit and nuts" explodes in anger against the wicked world:

> The message he had brought to the city was one that an illiterate anchorite might have given decadent Rome. It was a crazy jumble of dietary rules, economics, and Biblical threats. He claimed to have seen the Tiger of Wrath stalking the walls of the citadel and the Jackal of Lust skulking in the shrubbery, and he connected these omens with "thirty dollars every Thursday" and meat eating. (Ch. 19)

The search for amusement creates cock-fights in which one bird cuts another to pieces and then eats its eyes. A typical "party" ends with a dwarf, frantic with lust for the cold Venus, Faye Greener, being kicked in the stomach when he tries to break in between two dancers.

> The dwarf struggled to his feet and stood with his head lowered like a tiny ram. . . . He charged between Earle's legs and dug upward with both hands. Earle screamed with pain . . . then groaned and started to sink to the floor, tearing Faye's silk pajamas on his way down.

Miguel grabbed . . . [the dwarf] by the throat. . . . Lifting
the little man free, Miguel shifted his grip to his ankles and
dashed him against the wall, like a man killing a rabbit
against a tree. He swung the dwarf back to slam him again.
(Ch. 23)

The pressure toward disorder evident in each of these scenes
is embodied in the episodic form of the novel, and it takes its
final form in the great mob scene with which the book ends.
Here, as in the scene of chaos and uncreation with which *The
Dunciad* closes, all forms of dullness are gathered together to express their ultimate nature and to achieve the final shapelessness
toward which they have been constantly moving. The crowd begins
to gather to see the moving-picture stars arrive at a premiere at
Khan's Persian Palace—"Mr. Khan a Pleasure Dome Decreed." As
the people who came to California to die come up to the crowd they
look "diffident, almost furtive," but once they enter it all their in-
hibitions are released and they become arrogant and pugnacious.
The inevitable panders are present to stir the mixture more violently and amuse the folks at home who couldn't make it this year.
Colored lights flash madly about, and a radio announcer stands
above the crowd asking, in a high, hysterical voice broadcast
over a national network and amplified for the benefit of those
present, "can the police hold them? Can they? It doesn't look so,
folks." The mob grows every moment, shoving, bulging, pushing,
breaking out of any lines authority attempts to impose on it.
Within, it mills about, stumbling and swirling and releasing the
most primitive powers, hatred, lust, dislike for anyone different,
and the desire to break and kill to avenge a life of emptiness.

Only a spark is needed to touch the mob off and release its full
destructive power, and this comes when Homer Simpson, who
has wandered into the crowd in a state of shock resulting from the
loss of his own dream, kills the small boy who is tormenting him.
One form of riot releases another: the rumor sweeps through the
crowd that a pervert has attacked a child, and it explodes, surging
and churning over all barriers. Homer is torn apart, Tod's leg

is broken, an old man attacks a young girl pinned helpless by other bodies, men and women are crushed and trampled down. Here is "The Burning of Los Angeles," the great Vortex of Dulness sucking all down into nothingness, the final expression of the mob tendency.

Broken by the mob's awesome power, the satirist Tod Hackett goes mad. Taken to a police car, he begins to imitate the siren as loudly as he can. In the end the only style which the satirist can turn to is the wail sounding all the fires, bombings, accidents, and violences of a world which has tried to cure emptiness with illusion.[6]

6. The progress in *The Day of the Locust* of the painter-satirist from realist, to painter of grotesques, to the loud wail of disaster is but one instance of the classic pattern which most satirists picture themselves as following. They usually begin as young idealists of some variety, who usually write love poetry or pastorals, but because the world is so gross and corrupt they are forced, if they wish to write truthfully, to abandon their pleasant verses and gentle ways for the writing of harsh, crabbed satire. Pope, for example, presents himself in this manner in the *Epistle to Dr. Arbuthnot* and in the *Epilogue to the Satires.* In the Renaissance the satirist was conventionally pictured as a disappointed scholar; see my *The Cankered Muse* (New Haven, 1959), pp. 17–18, 148.

6. Irony

To this point we have treated the major actions of dullness as if they were simple, uncomplicated movements. The dunces always begin by constructing outsize, heroic images of themselves and building colossal monuments to their self-importance. At the same time, and in order to achieve this end, they drive all spirit down to matter and reduce the vital to mere mechanics. As this work goes forward, the ideas which provide the organizational forms for the material world are inevitably destroyed, and the world ceases to be arranged in meaningful patterns and becomes instead an endless number of disjunct objects, a series of mobs. But it has become obvious that these actions of dullness are all self-defeating, not because we judge them by some outside standard of what constitutes the good and valid life but rather because they always achieve the exact opposite of what is intended. The more the dunces speak to show their learning, the more they reveal their ignorance; the more frantically they pursue sensationalism and pleasure, the farther they move from the possibility of any real satisfaction; the more gigantic the monuments they construct to show their taste and importance, the more clear they make their meanness and vulgarity. Dullness unerringly seeks out the very actions and statements which define it truly as the opposite of what it would show itself to be. This pattern of movement is, of course, known as irony, the rising *and* falling figure, and in turning to a consideration of it we are moving closer to the full plot of satire.

The claim has been made that all irony is satire. While this is obviously not so, it is true that nearly all satire makes use of irony—ranging from the broadness of sarcasm to the extreme understatement of litotes—to such a degree that it is now very

nearly impossible to think of satire without thinking of irony. The satirist never seems to attack directly but always pretends not to be doing what in fact he is doing. He praises what he loathes, speaks with enthusiasm of utopias which he proves to be wastelands, creates pleasant little tales about the beasts and never seems to notice that his animals are reductions of human beings, solemnly dresses his contemporaries in epic robes far too large for them, and confidently puts Achille's spear in hands which cannot hold it. Many of the structural devices consistently used in satire are large-scale ironic techniques: mock encomium, mock epic, mock utopia, the beast fable, the adventures of the simpleton, and the wise fool.

Irony is capable of immense variation in the hands of poets,[1] but for working purposes there is no need to define it more precisely than the generally accepted meaning: a situation, spoken or dramatized, is ironic when what seems to be and what is are in some way opposed. In modern critical usage the term has been expanded to refer to situations in which the two components of an ironic situation are not what seems and what is, but rather two different and seemingly contradictory aspects of reality, both equally true. Irony then blends into ambiguity, tension, paradox, and ambivalence. This expansion of the term grows out of the facts of literature, for in tragedy and certain kinds of poetry, particularly the Metaphysical, the movement is from pure irony into paradox, from a situation in which one term of a pair of opposites seems true and the other false, to a situation where both are true. Oedipus at the end of his play is at once the greatest of men and the most miserable, Othello becomes both judge and criminal. In satire, however, the two poles of irony are ordinarily kept separate.

But why should satirists be so fond of irony? Most answers to

1. Norman Knox, *The Word Irony and Its Context, 1500–1700* (Durham, N.C., 1961), provides a catalogue of the various meanings of the word "irony" and in doing so demonstrates that there are numberless ways to achieve irony. But irony always involves two things in opposition, and the major differences in the kinds of irony turn around the way in which the writer makes it clear that the opposite of the obvious or literal is true. Overstatement and understatement appear to be the two principal methods.

this question have not moved beyond the undeniable remark of
the consistently ironic Horace that "ridicule more often cuts deeper
into important matters than does seriousness."[2] But this leaves
the real questions unanswered: Why is irony, which is what
changes the serious to the ridiculous in satire, witty and amusing?
What gives it its cutting edge? Another explanation frequently
offered by the satirists themselves—and supported by Freud—is
that it is necessary to deal with vice in an indirect, ironic manner
because a direct attack would invite physical reprisals from dangerous enemies. This argument is itself often ironic, for it convicts
the satirist's enemies of being vicious brutes before he begins to
expose them. But while Ben Jonson may have "beat Marston and
took his pistol from him" for representing him on the stage in an
unfavorable way, and while Dryden may have been roughed up
by Rochester's thugs in the Rose Alley Ambuscade, satirists on the
whole have fared little worse at the hands of their enemies than
other types of poets. Besides, irony never really fools anyone, and
it removes the sting from a deadly insult only if the victim is a
witty man. A third, less common, explanation of the marriage of
satire and irony is that this way of writing permits its user at once
to state the ways of dullness and to provide the norm against
which folly can be known and judged. This is one of the prime
functions of irony in satire and a junction point of the morality
and wit which Dryden made the two chief components of this
kind of poetry. We shall see in some detail how irony works to
state the norm and its violation in our examination of *The Dunciad, Volpone,* and the novels of Evelyn Waugh.

But the most immediate function of satiric irony is disclosed by
one of the satirist's regular defenses against the standard charge
that he attacks the unfortunate and helpless out of pure savagery.
Pope puts it this way:

> Deformity becomes the object of ridicule when a man sets up
> for being handsome: and so must Dulness when he sets up
> for a Wit. They are not ridicul'd because Ridicule in itself

see Wycherley

2. *Sermones,* 1.10.14–15.

is or ought to be a pleasure; but because it is just, to undeceive or vindicate the honest and unpretending part of mankind from imposition . . . Accordingly we find that in all ages, all vain pretenders, were they ever so poor or ever so dull, have been constantly the topicks of the most candid Satyrists, from the Codrus of Juvenal to the Damon of Boileau.

> (*The Dunciad,*
> "A Letter to the Publisher,"
> Twickenham Edition, p. 17,
> lines 11–22)

In other words, satire does not deal with the naturally dull and deformed, but with the pretense of these and other weaknesses to be what they are not. Plain villainy would seem to lie equally beyond the range of satire, which would concern itself only with the brute who seems to be the benefactor. Such pretenses need not be conscious, however; the fool who really believes that he is wise is as proper a subject of satire as the double-dealer. The pretense of virtue and lip service to morality are as necessary to satire as the dullness they express, and it is part of the satiric creed that the nature of man is such that you seldom find the failing without the pretense: *Plus les mœurs sont dépravés, plus les expressions deviennent mesurées; on croit regagner en langage ce qu'on a perdu en vertu.*[3] Irony is the perfect rhetorical device for catching the pretense which reveals itself as sham, since its two terms permit the poet to create both the pretense and the truth at once. He no longer need tell us, as the sermonist or reformer does, that men are not what they seem to be; he dramatizes the gap men drive between what they seem to be and what they are; he creates, like other poets, the very thing he exposes.

To make clear just how satiric irony operates, let us look at several examples. We can begin with an instance of scenic irony which makes clear the perspective inherent in all rhetorical and

---

3. Voltaire, *Lettre de M. Eraton à M. Clocpitre Aûmonier,* 1759. Quoted by Byron in *Don Juan,* "Preface to Cantos VI, VII, and VIII."

dramatic forms of irony. The speaker is describing his life as a
dishwasher in a very expensive and very fashionable French hotel:

> It was amusing to look round the filthy little scullery and
> think that only a double door was between us and the dining-
> room. There sat the customers in all their splendour—spot-
> less table-cloths, bowls of flowers, mirrors and gilt cornices
> and painted cherubim; and here, just a few feet away, we in
> our disgusting filth. For it really was disgusting filth. There
> was no time to sweep the floor till evening, and we slithered
> about in a compound of soapy water, lettuce-leaves, torn
> paper and trampled food. A dozen waiters with their coats
> off, showing their sweaty armpits, sat at the table mixing
> salads and sticking their thumbs into the cream pots. The
> room had a dirty, mixed smell of food and sweat. Everywhere
> in the cupboards, behind the piles of crockery, were squalid
> stores of food that the waiters had stolen. There were only
> two sinks, and no washing basin, and it was nothing unusual
> for a waiter to wash his face in the water in which clean
> crockery was rinsing. But the customers saw nothing of this.
> There were a coco-nut mat and a mirror outside the dining-
> room door, and the waiters used to preen themselves up and
> go in looking the picture of cleanliness.
>
> It is an instructive sight to see a waiter going into a hotel
> dining-room. As he passes the door a sudden change comes
> over him. The set of his shoulders alters; all the dirt and
> hurry and irritation have dropped off in an instant. He glides
> over the carpet, with a solemn priest-like air. I remember
> our assistant *maître d'hôtel,* a fiery Italian, pausing at the
> dining-room door to address an apprentice who had broken
> a bottle of wine. Shaking his fist above his head he yelled
> (luckily the door was more or less soundproof): *"Tu me fais*
> ————. Do you call yourself a waiter, you young bastard?
> You a waiter! You're not fit to scrub floors in the brothel
> your mother came from. Maquereau!" . . .
>
> Then he entered the dining-room and sailed across it dish

in hand, graceful as a swan. Ten seconds later he was bowing reverently to a customer. And you could not help thinking, as you saw him bow and smile, with the benign smile of the trained waiter, that the customer was put to shame by having such an aristocrat to serve him.[4]

Here the irony catches not a single individual but a society in its full pretense. On one side of the door it is assumed that men are civilized, mannerly, and prosperous, and that life is rich and orderly; on the other side we see the greasy reality on which this pretense rests, dirt, brutality, thievery, hunger, exhaustion. The door is "luckily" soundproof, so that the wealthy customers have no idea of the other face of their world, and the slaveys in the kitchen are either too dull to see the ironic gap or are forced by need to help maintain the pretense. But the satirist, though in this case he remains physically at the dirty sink, thinks himself into a position precisely at the soundproof door so that he can see and hear on both sides at once. He need not tell us that the world we think we live in is a sham, a play, and he need not denounce—though Orwell always goes on to do so—the blindness and selfishness that create a dream world and take it for real. His scenic irony has made all these points by creating an extended image in which seems and is are at dangerous variance.

The point at the soundproof door is the position the satiric ironist always occupies, though he may not always create the two components of the ironic situation and offer them side by side for inspection. Another type of satirist achieves his ironic effects by first describing whatever he despises and then peeling away the layers of pretense—manners, cosmetics, speech, clothes, faces— which cover the reality. Lucilius, who was, Horace tells us, the first man to compose formal verse satire, "stripped away the skin wherein everyone struts, flaunting his good looks in his neighbors' eyes while inwardly foul."[5] Juvenal is a master of this technique.

4. George Orwell, *Down and Out in Paris and London* (London, 1933), Ch. 12.

5. *Sermones*, II.1.62–5. In the more savage or Juvenalian type of satire this crude ironic function of stripping is symbolized in the tools the satirist

He offers a panorama of Imperial Rome, showing everywhere the masks of gravity, virtue, and patriotism with which the Romans cover themselves, and then in language so brutal that it seems literally to batter down all pretense, he shows us the terrible truth. His wealthy matron wears beautiful green gems around her neck, pearls hang from her ears, her face is covered with cosmetics, her body is drenched in perfume, and she bathes daily in asses' milk. But,

> Through the last layer of the mudpack, from the first
>   wash to a poultice,
> What lies under all this—a human face, or an ulcer?[6]

Such techniques as this are so direct and crude that most of us would perhaps deny them the name of irony. And perhaps we would also feel that the related device of contrasting-revealing scenes, a scene at a London party followed by a scene in the jungles of the Amazon, would not qualify as irony. But the same appearance-reality conflict which is at the heart of irony is at work in these methods, though they leave something to be desired. They separate two things, appearance and reality, which are in fact one, for the seeming and being which the ironist shows us are not distinct in time and place but simultaneous. Swift, I believe, claims for his own the introduction and refinement of the perfect ironic

---

metaphorically uses on dullness: the scalpel, the emetic, the whip for tearing away the skin and driving the madman back to sanity, instruments of torture such as the rack and the strappado for extorting the truth, flood and fire for annihilating the pretenses covering truth. These are connected with metaphors used for the satirist's sight and language, cutting, probing, cruel, piercing, keen, acid, etc. Mary Claire Randolph, "The Medical Concept in English Renaissance Satiric Theory," *SP, 38* (1941), pp. 135–57, connects such imagery with the magical curative functions which primitive satire was believed to have. This may be so, but its survival in more sophisticated literary satire is surely the result of its continued usefulness in manifesting the ironic function of the satirist, his stripping pretense away to show reality.

6. Satire VI, lines 460–72. The translation is Rolfe Humphries', *The Satires of Juvenal* (Bloomington, Indiana, 1958).

technique in which appearance and reality are collapsed into a single statement or image:

> Arbuthnot is no more my Friend,
> Who dares to Irony pretend;
> Which I was born to introduce,
> Refin'd it first, and shew'd its Use.
>
> ("Verses on the Death of Dr. Swift,"
> lines 55–58)

We may question whether Swift really introduced this kind of irony, but that he refined it and used it for maximum satiric effect, there is no question. The gap between appearance and reality is almost completely closed in the scene in which a group of fashionable ladies playing cards receive the news of Dean Swift's death:

> My female Friends, whose tender Hearts
> Have better learn'd to act their Parts,
> Receive the News in *doleful Dumps,*
> "The Dean is dead, (*and what is Trumps?*)
> "Then Lord have Mercy on his Soul.
> "(Ladies I'll venture for the *Vole.*)
> "Six Deans they say must bear the Pall.
> "(I wish I knew what *King* to call.)
> "Madam, your Husband will attend
> "The Funeral of so good a Friend.
> "No Madam, 'tis a shocking Sight,
> "And he's engag'd To-morrow Night!
> "My Lady Club wou'd take it ill,
> "If he shou'd fail her at *Quadrill.*
> "He lov'd the Dean. (*I lead a Heart.*)
> "But dearest Friends, they say, must part.
> "His Time was come, he ran his Race;
> "We hope he's in a better Place.
>
> (lines 225–42)

The ladies express pious sentiments and then return very quickly to what really interests them, the card game, so that they seem

to assume a mask and then take it down. But as the scene progresses, the masks themselves come to reveal the reality. The speed
of the four-beat line, the regularity of the rhythm, the patness of
the rhymes, the conventional quality of the phrasing, and the
subtle equation of people and cards, life and game—"He lov'd the
Dean. (*I lead a Heart.*),'' "My Lady Club," the rhyming of soul and
vole—all combine to create people who play at life as they play
at cards, or act their parts. The pretense itself contains the ex-
posure of the ghastly truth of human nature which lies at the
basis of the poem:

> In all Distresses of our Friends
> We first consult our private Ends.
> (lines 7–8)

If any slight distance still exists between seems and is in the card-
playing scene, it is closed altogether in such a speech as this in
A Modest Proposal: "It is true a Child, *just dropt from its Dam,*
may be supported by her Milk, for a Solar Year with little other
Nourishment; at most not above the Value of two Shillings; which
the Mother may certainly get, or the Value in Scraps, by her lawful Occupation of *Begging.*" The judicious phrasing, the reason-
ableness, the careful calculation, the scientific objectivity of this
speech create the character of the Modest Proposer, a learned
gentleman interested in the welfare of his nation, whose unaware-
ness that he is talking about *people* leads inevitably to the proposi-
tion, made in the most reasonable manner, that both the food-
shortage and the overpopulation of Ireland can be solved at once
by selling the young children of the poor for food. Pose and
reality are combined perfectly here to create a smug, emotionless,
completely self-centered and dangerous dunce, who can solemnly
assure us, and believe, that he has "not the least personal interest
in endeavouring to promote this necessary Work," for he has no
children by which he can "propose to get a single Penny; the
youngest being nine Years old, and . . . [his] wife past Child-
bearing." This is what Swift is attacking: not just the cruelty of
the social planner and the savage economic practices of the En-

glish landlords in Ireland, but the cruelty, and savagery, and heartlessness which can offer themselves as clear-thinking philanthropy, disinterested patriotism, and sound economic practice.

Irony is the perfect device for rendering such self-deceit and hypocrisy, and the consistent use of irony in satire suggests that the tendency of dullness to create masks for itself is one of satire's principal subjects. Irony might, in fact, be called the master trope of satire which sums up all the other major figures used to construct the satiric world. I have, for the sake of discussion, separated out the major actions of dullness and the various rhetorical and scenic devices which render them. But in actual practice, though one tendency or another may dominate because it suits perfectly the particular brand of dullness being attacked—as the diminishing tendency suits an overconfident materialism—all of these tendencies are present simultaneously. Whenever ideas are reduced to things and life to mechanics in the satiric world, there always follows a magnification of the unworthy and a multiplication of the number of things. The result of this is inevitably the jumble. Taken together, these tendencies indicate a loss of some sensible belief about the nature of reality, and they lead on to a world in which the real is buried under messes of the unreal. But dullness always persists in believing that its conglomerations and pretensions are very real indeed, and it is just such a situation which irony catches and holds up for inspection.

By now it is clear, I hope, that in discussing the actions of dullness we have really been discussing the plot of satire in terms of its smaller constituent parts. The tropes and objective shapes— the multiplicity of things, the oversize images of self, the crowds —which make up the language, the persons, the furnishings, the landscapes, and the architecture of the satiric world are themselves but the momentary forms taken or shaped by dullness on its way to the full realization of its nature in the total plot. To put it another way, the solid objects and characters which make up the satiric world are but the testaments of dullness' acts, its passing creations, or, considered ironically, its "uncreations." When we look at the rhetoric or the scenery of satire, we are looking at

the smallest manifestations of the actions of dullness, which taken in the aggregate constitute the plot of satire. We must now turn to a consideration of several full plots, trying to see how the materializing, magnifying, jumbling, and dividing actions of satire work themselves out in larger terms, and how the irony of the single incident grows into and shapes the plot as a whole.

III

THE PLOT OF SATIRE

The failure of criticism to define the word "plot" with any precision has had serious results for satire. It is generally held, though
seldom explicitly stated, that there is really only one kind of plot,
the Aristotelian progression made up of a series of events initiated
by some "human frailty" and having "a beginning, a middle, and
an end," which is of sufficient length "to admit a change of
fortune . . . brought about by a succession, necessary or probable,
of well-connected incidents," leading to reversal and discovery.
Such a description leaves a number of crucial questions unanswered: "What constitutes an *event* or an *incident?*" "In what
sense can a scene in a literary work be considered the *necessary*
or *probable* successor to the scenes before it?" "Must the *discovery*
be made by the chief character, or is it sufficient for the audience
to perceive the change in situation?" But the general drift of this
definition is clear enough, and from the fourth century B.C. to
the present critics have assumed that a plot should be a tightly
constructed chain of cause and effect moving inevitably toward
a revelation. It has also been assumed, as a corollary, that the
characters who initiate and drive the plot along should be consistent and not display any unrealistic changes in their natures.

A plot of this type manifests the rock-hard world of necessity
and the isolated individual caught in an inescapable train of
causation, and it is therefore a reasonably good description of the
tragic plot—which is all, it would seem, that Aristotle intended.
Such a description of plot will also fit to a lesser degree the arrangement of events and the movements of life in the epic or heroic
poem. But it will not describe the situation in comedy and satire.
Comedy, for example, has always a strong tendency toward the
episodic or even chaotic plot; and on those rare occasions when

the plot is allowed to develop "realistically," it will likely be resolved by some outrageous *deus ex machina:* the happy chance of a birthmark, the return of a rich uncle, a messenger from the king arresting the villain. Its themes, though charming, always lack high seriousness and deal with such "trivialities" as love and marriage and the possession of wealth and property. The young hero never gets the lady alone, he always gets her father's gold too. And in achieving these rich prizes the comic hero regularly displays the most alarming lack of moral scrupulousness, or, even worse for his dignity, he may reveal himself to be the completely inept child of good luck. Character changes with startling suddenness: villains become generous benefactors in a flash, love changes to hate and hate to love.

The perfect confrontation of tragic plot and comic life is *Tristram Shandy.* Poor Tristram, trying desperately to write the history of his life and opinions, wants his chronicle to fit the patterns of tragedy. He wants it to have a beginning, a middle, and an end, but no matter how he tries, every event is inseparable from an endless series of trivialities going before and through it. His story has no neccessary conclusion, no neat ending: the longer he writes, the more he falls behind his life. He wants his life to have dignity, and yet it is always entangled with such ludicrous minutiae as his mother asking Walter Shandy to wind the clock or the rivet in Doctor Slop's new forceps. He wants to be the contriver of his own fate like the tragic hero, but he is always in the hands of a careless fortune which in the guise of Corporal Trim removes the sashweights from the window, in the form of Susanna cannot pronounce Trismegistus, or in the form of death removes Bobby so suddenly from the scene and makes Tristram the heir to Shandy Hall. This is the comic vision and the forms required for its expression are by necessity different from those which express the tragic vision. To measure *Tristram Shandy,* or any comedy, by the standard of the tragic plot is to miss what is there, and to ask it to do things for which it was not designed.

Satire has been even more misunderstood than comedy, for the application of the Aristotelian plot formula to it can only result,

and often has in fact, in the decision that the genre is deficient in plot or altogether plotless. It is possible to visualize *Antigone* or *Othello* as linear progressions, but to call to mind *The Acharnians,* Horace's *Sermones, The Satyricon, In Praise of Folly, Tale of a Tub, The Dunciad,* or *Don Juan* is to evoke an image of a mob of characters whirling about in a great variety of scenes, and a succession of seemingly loosely related events with little apparent development.

Formal verse satire, such as the collected satires of Juvenal or Pope's "Imitations of Horace," usually offers the most disconnected panorama of scenes and characters.[1] Its plot is roughly that of a newsreel: the satirist stands before some scene, usually a bustling city street, and comments, to the world at large or to a specific *adversarius,* on the foolishness and depravity of those who pass before him or those whom he remembers. He never lingers long over any one character or event, but swivels his gaze rapidly from dunce to dunce and scene to scene. He will stop from time to time to deliver a brief sermon and then suddenly pass on to attack something else. In the best instances of this type of satire, the satirist restricts himself in each satire to the discussion of one general subject, such as the characters of women—Juvenal's Sixth Satire—or the dangers of writing satire—Pope's imitation of Horace's First Satire of the Second Book. But in the next satire a new series of characters and scenes is introduced to illustrate some other aspect of the general corruption of society, the main theme holding the collection of satires together. At the conclusion of however many satires the author may choose to include in his collection, there is little sense of any movement from one point to another. The dunces and the vicious go merrily on their way, lying, swindling, drinking, eating, and boring one another; the satirist stands in the foreground shouting or wryly mocking, de-

---

1. The mixture of scenes, events, and rhetorical devices characteristic of this type of satire is well described by Mary Claire Randolph, "The Structural Design of Formal Verse Satire," *PQ,* 21 (1942), 368–84. She notes also the relationship of this mixture to the original meaning of the word *satura,* an adjective meaning "stuffed or filled with many different things."

pending on his nature, and using every device of rhetoric to throw into relief the corruption of his world. His voice is never stilled, and dullness is never converted to wisdom. Formal verse satire thus appears to be organized in a rhetorical rather than a dramatic fashion; its incidents are used to illustrate and drive home a thesis rather than to create a plot in which one event leads on to another and the whole imitates an essential movement of life.[2]

In satires which have a fable of sorts, there is still only an appearance of what is usually taken as plot. Gay's nameless walker in *Trivia* marches through the city streets carefully noting their condition, gravely remarking on the state of the weather and the best areas in which to walk in certain seasons, reflecting solemnly on the dangers, meticulously examining and describing cheeses, fish, and other merchandise. In the end he is still walking on, apparently without any purpose to his journey or any end in sight. He has simply walked the streets of London, and done it in a very precise and careful fashion. Even in satires which appear to have something more like a "normal" plot, there is usually something "wrong." In *Candide* a young simpleton and his even simpler tutor pass through a series of adventures which take them all over the Western world, beginning in Germany and ending on a Turkish

2. The question of whether rhetoric itself cannot have a plot has been raised in connection with Juvenal's satires by William S. Anderson in a series of articles which show that some of the individual satires "depend upon a self-contradiction or . . . paradox." Satire III, for example, the famous description of Rome, which was the model for Samuel Johnson's "London," is spoken by a stout, honest old Roman, Umbricius, who is leaving the city because he can no longer earn a living or endure the indignities forced upon him. Umbricius "takes the Rome of traditional associations—its majesty, justice, wealth, beauty, and honesty—and exposes its self-contradiction . . . the lack of opportunity, the aliens, the fires, the thieves, etc., all of which signify the loss of the traditional Roman qualities and cumulate in a totally negative picture of an uninhabitable city." By the time Umbricius has finished describing the degradation of Rome, he has proved that Rome is no longer *Rome*. And since he is the last of the Romans, his leaving is not a departure from Rome but a departure of *Rome* from a heap of stones and a mob of people on some hills along the Tiber. "Studies in Book I of Juvenal," *Yale Classical Studies*, 15 (1957), pp. 33–90. See also "Juvenal 6: A Problem of Structure," *Classical Philology*, 51 (1956), pp. 73–94.

farm. They know a little more about life in the end than they did at the beginning, but they continue to discuss such insoluble problems as the origin of evil, the nature of the soul, and the pre-established harmony of the world. Pangloss is still talking about "the best of all possible worlds," the German Baron is still arguing that no commoner like Candide may marry his sister Cunegonde, and every week the great ones of the world—effendis, pashas, and cadis—go by on their way to exile, while other great ones—cadis, pashas, and effendis—return to power. The world goes round and round, and dullness never dies. Even the adventures which form the substance of the book constitute no real progression. Each episode drives home the point that men are cruel and senseless, life filled with unexpected disasters, and nature wantonly destructive. But one episode does not grow inevitably out of another, and most of them could be relocated without loss of meaning. Life is, Voltaire shows, a wandering, chancy affair which teaches the same lesson over and over.

If we go one step further and look at a satire which seems to be very tightly plotted in a conventional sense, William Golding's *Lord of the Flies,* we still find something "wrong," or at least very peculiar. The novel tells the story of a group of boys evacuated from England during a great war of the future. They are wrecked on a tropical island, a new Eden, but innate human fears and hatreds immediately begin to work in them, and they proceed to make an absolute hell of their island. Step by step the author traces a movement from their first attempts to order their lives in the manner taught them at home and in their public schools to the eruption of primitive fears and struggles for power. They change the beneficent nature of their island into a source of dark terrors responding to their own fears, they disintegrate into warring groups, and by the end of the novel the destructive powers in the boys have annihilated all that is reasonable and sensible in themselves and their small world. Like barbarians, the gang of hunters chases down the last boy with any decency or moral intelligence. He runs before them through the jungle and staggers at last out onto the beach to find a British naval officer, trim and

clean in his white uniform and polished brass buttons. Saved! But though the officer is shocked by the boys' condition and horrified by the barbarism, he fails to see that the heavy guns, powerful engines, and splendid discipline of the cruiser anchored off the island are merely more effective instruments of the old-brain forces which on the island have found expression in fists, teeth, sharpened sticks, and heavy rocks. Savagery has run out onto the beach to meet savagery in another, more deceptive, more powerful, form. Bestiality, having discovered itself in the individual and the isolated group, turns outward to find itself again in society and history.

It is clear that satire never offers that direct, linear progression which is ordinarily taken as plot. Instead, we get collections of loosely related scenes and busyness which curls back on itself— darkness never really moves on to daylight but only to intensified darkness. Disjunctiveness and the absence of change are then the chief "faults" of the satiric plot. But can we then say that satire is plotless because it takes these particular shapes? I think not. What has happened is that one type of plot, the tragic variety, has gradually come to be accepted as the only kind of plot. A species has been taken for a genus because the necessary questions have not been asked about the nature of "events" and the meaning of the words "probable" and "necessary" when applied to a succession of actions in a literary work.

My own position is that any work of literature in which there is action, in which there is a shift of position or scene, in which there is any kind of physical or psychic movement, has a plot. This is to say, of course, that all literature has plot, and that the term should be applied to any arrangement and connection of events which a writer constructs to image his sense of the way the world goes. The term "plot" should not carry with it any prescription for a particular kind of agency, linkage of events, or type of action; it should only point toward that aspect of a literary work which involves movement and the relationship of parts occurring at different points of time. In other words, we must take our plots where and how we find them rather then expecting

that they will give shape to some particular view of the dynamics of life.

It is usual to consider only the largest elements of construction, the main events of the fable or story, as the components of plot. But if a plot is, as Aristotle says, "The imitation of an action,"[3] and if Coleridge is correct in pointing out that unity of action is "in itself the great end, not only of the drama, but of the epic, lyric, even to the candle-flame of an epigram—not only of poetry, but of poesy in general, as the proper generic term inclusive of all the fine arts, as its species," then it follows that *all* acts (speaking included) and all movements in a literary work are a part of the plot. The smallest gesture and motion as well as the largest event will manifest the action which the poet is imitating. The crooking of a finger, the splashing of the rain on a windowpane, and the way in which a metaphor is assembled are as much expressions of the basic action as the murder of a king or the sack of a town. It should therefore be possible to locate the basic action of a work in its smaller expressions and then follow these on to their larger manifestations in the events of the story. We have already isolated the basic actions of satire and seen the way in which these manifest themselves in language, character, and scenery. And we have discovered that as aimless and various as the activities of dullness

3. Just what Aristotle means in *The Poetics* by the term "action" is a vexing question. Most simply it is, of course, the root idea or subject to which the play—or, by extension, the dramatic poem—gives expression or "imitates" and which is distinguished from plot by making the plot the primary mode of imitation. But by using the word "action" rather than some other term, such as "theme," Aristotle is insisting that the play imitates some active, moving, dynamic force in life, not a static "quality." Francis Fergusson in *The Idea of a Theater* (Princeton, 1949) and several subsequent articles has argued that the term "action" is best translated as "motive." But present usage has motive referring primarily to psychic motive, mental drives, and this is the way Fergusson applies the term. I agree that the action or motive of a work can be located in character and can be expressed by a character's movements and language, but it is also, I believe, a more general force at work in all aspects of a dramatic work. Thus, we can expect to find that the particular action or "nature" of life—that pressure toward a particular fulfillment which is the soul of any active thing—which the writer wishes to imitate can be

may appear, the dunces are perfectly consistent in their actions
of magnifying their own importance, reducing the vital to the
mechanical and material, producing chaos, and driving a wedge
between appearance and reality.

Considering the disordering nature of these actions, it should
not be at all surprising that the ultimate result should be dis-
orderly, that the "plot" of satire should appear disjunct. Dullness
drives toward a dismemberment of form, and this drive is manifested—consistently—on all levels of the plot. But we have also
noted a complex, ironic quality in the movements of dullness: it
strives in spite of nature to create Progress yet always produces its
opposite. The rise becomes a fall, the advance a circular wandering,
the brave new world a living hell; the search for the philosophers'
stone eats up the wealth it was intended to produce; the dunce
who sets up for a wit only succeeds in making his weaknesses apparent. In satire we are shown that it is the very nature of dullness
to defeat itself, even when it *appears* to succeed, believes it has
succeeded; but dullness remains extremely dangerous because in
its inevitable movement toward self-defeat it will casually, often
unintentionally, destroy the society and culture which the sense
and courage of the past have patiently and arduously constructed.

The titanic and random efforts of dullness are always self-
defeating because they defy what is and what is possible for man;
this is the general "action" which every satirist sees in the particular idiocies of his time, and it is this action which his plot
imitates. Swift describes perfectly this tendency of dullness and

---

seen moving in his re-creation of such natural events as a storm at sea or
the swing of a clock's pendulum, in the operation of such institutions as a
court of law, or in the shape of a battle as well as in the activities of the
characters. Wherever there is movement—in the pounding of the sea on the
land or in the gradual decay of a body—the action has traced its passage
in matter. The motive of a character is often directly opposed to the action
of the world in which he finds himself, and then the character may be forced
to conform to the action of the world (naturalism), or he may force the
world to conform to his action (romance), or the action, and the plot which
imitates it, will be the complex result of the interaction of man and world.

provides two of the major schemes employed in satiric plots to reflect this self-defeating movement:

> And, whereas the mind of Man, when he gives the Spur and Bridle to his Thoughts, doth never stop, but naturally sallies out into both extreams of High and Low, of Good and Evil; His first Flight of Fancy, commonly transports Him to Ideas of what is most Perfect, finished, and exalted; till having soared out of his own Reach and Sight, not well perceiving how near the Frontiers of Height and Depth, border upon each other; With the same Course and Wing, he falls down plum into the lowest Bottom of Things; like one who travels the *East* into the *West;* or like a strait Line drawn by its own Length into a Circle.
>
> (*A Tale of a Tub,* Section VIII)

The large plot movements of satire described by Swift are, of course, built by a multitude of smaller movements, already described as magnifying, reducing, and jumbling. Each of these smaller actions manifests, when seen ironically, the same self-defeating pattern which Swift traces in large-scale terms. Magnifying the self is a rising, and since the attempts at self-glorification always end by revealing the dunce for what he is, it becomes a falling. Each of the attempts to create a world corresponding to man's maddest dreams is undertaken with enormous energy and purpose (the straight line) but ends by curling back on itself to create something less than it started with. In the following chapters we will examine these large-scale plots which Swift describes. *Volpone* is a perfect instance of the rise which becomes a fall, and the satiric novels of Evelyn Waugh are arranged in the straight-line circular pattern. At the same time we can see how these patterns, and the action they imitate, give shape to the actual contemporary practices, social conditions, and attitudes toward life which are the substance of the satires and the immediate specific objects of the satirists' attacks. The specific forms of dullness change from age to age and satirist to satirist, but the action of dullness and the plots which imitate it remain the same.

But the patterns Swift describes are only two examples of the general movement of satire, and before turning to Jonson and Waugh, I want to look at another satire, Pope's *Dunciad,* which uses a variant scheme, what can be called the "everything-nothing" pattern. *The Dunciad* serves as a good place to begin for another particular reason: while it is the greatest of English satires, it has been consistently charged with lacking a plot.

Dullness—that quality of mind and being which is the subject of *The Dunciad*—is not only inertness, the ponderous movement, and the vacant stare; it is busyness, briskness, and pertness as well. Pope's Dunces swirl and swarm about the City of London, engaging in fantastic parodies of epic games, urinating contests, mud-diving, and noise-making. They race about pursuing butterflies, collecting coins, growing flowers. They beat students savagely, make long speeches, and write endless numbers of bad poems and dreary political pamphlets. Their styles, become substantial, a "mob of metaphors," "motley images" and "similes unlike," break out of the printed page to join the Dunces in their "mazy dance" about the town. The mad machinery of the new Italian opera spills out into the streets to swell the hurly-burly to monstrous dimensions:

> All sudden, Gorgons hiss, and Dragons glare,
> And ten-horn'd fiends and Giants rush to war.
> Hell rises, Heav'n descends, and dance on Earth:
> Gods, imps, and monsters, music, rage, and mirth,
> A fire, a jigg, a battle, and a ball,
> 'Till one wide conflagration swallows all.
>
> (III, 235–40)[1]

1. My references throughout this chapter are to *The Dunciad* (B), the 1743 version of the poem in four books with Cibber rather than Theobald as King of the Dunces. Even the few critics who argue stoutly for the integrity of the poem hesitate to say that Book IV, first published in 1742 as *The New Dunciad*, fits very smoothly into the poem as a whole. I have no wish to argue that Pope *planned* any elaborate connection between the first three books and the last one, but the evidence offered in the following pages does, I believe, suggest that *The Dunciad in Four Books* of 1743 is, however it came about, much more of a unity than has previously been thought.

The poem is filled with all the activity of a monkey-cage, but all this various busyness has a felt common quality. To find this quality is to come at the root action of the poem and the spring of its plot.

There exists at the heart of at least the very greatest literature an action, or a verbal quality, anterior to any particular word and unlocalized in any single shape or substance. This essential active quality in a satire will be related to, and a variant of, the actions we have seen to be the essential movements of satire as a genre, but at the same time it will have a specific quality of its own. In this uniqueness resides the distinctiveness of the particular satire. No one verb ever quite captures this ground movement, but we are closest to it in the particular verbals of the poem and in the simple movements of things and people. Without attempting for the moment to define the basic movement which underlies *The Dunciad,* I will offer a selection of the kind of verbs which occur most frequently and then pass on to some of the simple movements which elaborate the basic verbal quality.

Dullness in the many forms and shapes it assumes, pours, spreads, sluices, creeps, drawls on, stretches, spawns, crawls, meanders, ekes out, flounders on, slips, rolls, extends, waddles, involves, gushes, swells, loiters, decays, slides, wafts, lumbers, blots, o'erflows, trickles. Such words and their variants are omnipresent in *The Dunciad,* and the quality of movement they manifest achieves more extended form in such lines as the following:

The goddess Dulness looks into the chaos of her poets' minds,

> Where nameless Somethings in their causes sleep,
> 'Till genial Jacob, or a warm Third day,
> Call forth each mass, a Poem, or a Play:
> How hints, like spawn, scarce quick in embryo lie,
> How new-born nonsense first is taught to cry,
> Maggots half-form'd in rhyme exactly meet,
> And learn to crawl upon poetic feet.

Here one poor word an hundred clenches makes,
And ductile dulness new meanders takes.

(I, 56–64)

The King of Dunces views his own past productions,

Nonsense precipitate, like running Lead,
That slip'd thro' Cracks and Zig-zags of the Head.

(I, 123–24)

Dullness is to the heads of fools

like byass to the bowl,
Which, as more pond'rous, made its aim more true,
Obliquely wadling to the mark in view.

(I, 170–72)

The dunces play

where Fleet-ditch with disemboguing streams
Rolls the large tribute of dead dogs to Thames,
The King of dykes! than whom no sluice of mud
With deeper sable blots the silver flood.

(II, 271–74)

Sleep spreads over those assembled to listen to Henley's orations
and Blackmore's endless epics like ripples from a stone dropped
in the water:

What Dulness dropt among her sons imprest
Like motion from one circle to the rest;
So from the mid-most the nutation spreads
Round and more round, o'er all the sea of heads.

(II, 407–10)

"Like a rolling stone," Cibber's

giddy dulness still shall lumber on,
Safe in its heaviness, shall never stray,
But lick up ev'ry blockhead in the way.

(III, 294–96)

Dulness advises her scribbling followers to

> spread, my sons, your glory thin or thick,
> On passive paper, or on solid brick.
>
> (IV, 129–30)

In certain scenes in *The Dunciad* this swelling, onward pressure
of Dulness becomes larger and louder. For example, at the end
of Book I, after Cibber is proclaimed the King of Dunces by his
goddess, the news spreads outward through the City and voices of
praise resound from every corner:

> Then swells the Chapel-royal throat:
> "God save king Cibber!" mounts in ev'ry note.
> Familiar White's, "God save king Colley!" cries;
> "God save king Colley!" Drury-lane replies:
> To Needham's quick the voice triumphal rode,
> But pious Needham dropt the name of God;
> Back to the Devil the last echoes roll,
> And "Coll!" each Butcher roars at Hockley-hole.
>
> (lines 319–26)

In Book II the duncers amble in a roundabout way through the
City, and when they reach its limits, the noisiest fools broadcast
their nonsense in loud voices to every area in Westminster. At
the end of their epic games the assembled multitude of duncery
tries desperately to stay awake while "Henley's periods" and
"Blackmore's numbers" are read aloud, but sleep spreads irresist-
ibly through them, until they lie stupefied. In Book III Settle
shows the King of Dunces the barbarian flood expanding out
of the north and east over civilization, carrying dullness and
darkness to China, Greece, Rome, and Egypt. In Book IV duncery
takes the form of a great rout of idiots who come forward to
announce themselves the true subjects of Dulness. As their numbers darken the land, the Muses are destroyed and art after art
and light after light is extinguished, until all is blackness.

Looking at these verbs and scenes, we can begin to understand
the basic action of dullness. It has a complex, not a simple, move-

ment. On first appearance it is heavy, formless, and directionless, a vague slipping, oozing movement like a sliding sea of mud going in any and all directions. This shapeless pressure catches exactly the formlessness and meaninglessness of dullness. But though the spread is without guiding purpose and therefore moves in a random fashion, it is still relentless and never-ceasing, "obliquely wadling to the mark in view." It flows on and on, covering all that it encounters, and in the end it has spread over everything; all that is rational and useful is buried beneath it.

The primal "action" of dullness observable at the level of the single verb, the limited movement, and in the individual scene is exactly duplicated in the over-all arrangement of incidents and scenes in *The Dunciad*. There are four major incidents corresponding to the four books. Book I is located in the center of the City of London in a setting into which Pope compresses Bedlam, Grub-street, the booksellers' shops, and Guildhall. This is the native home of dullness. The action opens with a fantastic scene in which the goddess Dulness looks happily on while the scribblers of the realm—"who hunger, and who thirst for scribbling sake"—work frantically over their mad writings and their grotesque styles. The scene passes to Bays (Colley Cibber) chief of the scribblers and king of the dunces to be, who "swearing and supperless" sits in his room lacking sufficient dullness to plunder another author or combine old idiocy into a new play. In despair he builds an altar of his works and lights it as a sacrifice to the goddess, but she swoops down, extinguishes the fire, and crowns Cibber king of dunces. A Dionysiac attendant train is formed, chaos breaks loose in the streets, and "God save King Colley" resounds from the Chapel Royal to Hockley Hole.

Book II opens on a new scene: the King is now seated where Drury Lane meets the Strand, and around him assemble all the many kinds of literary dullness. In honor of their new chief, they engage in various parodies of epic games, and then after the noise-making contest which broadcasts the sounds of idiocy and nonsense over all Westminster, they move back by Fleet Street and Bridewell to Fleetditch and the mud-diving contest. From

here the royal procession passes on to Ludgate and back to Guildhall, where, trying to keep awake to listen to a reading of Blackmore's poems and Henley's oratory, all of Duncedom at last falls asleep, to dream of a glorious future. Book III contains this vision. In his sleep Cibber descends to the underworld where —in a parody of the meeting of Aeneas and Anchises—the spirit of Elkanah Settle, the old city poet, greets him and shows the past glorious accomplishments of dullness, its lineage stretching back to the beginning of time, its ancient heroes and martyrs, its triumphal invasion of past civilizations—China, Greece, Egypt, Rome—and the fathering of vast numbers of dunces in England to restore "this favorite isle" to the kingdom of Dulness once again. In the Argument to Book III Cibber, his sacred mission understood, is granted a prophecy of the future: "how first the nation shall be overrun with *Farces, Operas,* and *Shows;* how the throne of Dulness shall be advanced over the *Theatres,* and set up even at *Court;* then how her Sons shall preside in the seats of *Arts* and *Sciences:* giving a glimpse or Pisgah sight of the future Fulness of her Glory, the accomplishment whereof is the subject of the fourth and last book."

This accomplishment of "the future Fulness of . . . Glory" takes the form of a parody of the Day of Judgment, with Dulness rather than God on the throne, and, rather than Christ, "Soft on her lap her Laureate son reclines." In the earlier scenes it was possible to perceive through the fantastic landscape the outlines of the City of London, but now we have passed to an apocalyptic, nightmare world where the familiar landmarks have disappeared. The throne seems to sit in the midst of a vast, flat plain, and around it stands a group of murderers and torturers who bind, gag, and strangle the Muses and the Sciences. Beyond this inner circle gathers a vast rout of dunces, the heroes of dullness, and as they move inward toward the throne they gather to them "a vast involuntary throng." Out of this mob, to address the goddess, step the champions, each announcing the destruction of sense in some particular area of life—in education, government, scholarship, science, philosophy, religion, and morals. Then, after it has

become clear that intelligence, order, and morality are everywhere
dead, darkness begins to move over the face of the land, "*Art*
after *Art* goes out" and at last the world reverts to chaos and
night:

> Lo! thy dread Empire, Chaos! is restor'd;
> Light dies before thy uncreating word:
> Thy hand, great Anarch! lets the curtain fall;
> And Universal Darkness buries All.
>
> (IV, 653–56)

There is no point in looking in this sequence of events for the
relentless movement of an Oedipus tracking down the killer of
Laius, or a Lear moving step by inevitable step toward the heath
and the sight of the dead Cordelia. The sons of Dulness do not
set out to restore night and chaos, to bring about the apocalyptic
scene with which *The Dunciad* concludes. They are only out to
win fame, to make money, to gain a political office, to indulge
themselves and have a good time. And so they write books and
plays, curry favor with the great, collect butterflies and coins
publish smut and slander, and argue over minute and meaningless
scholarly points. Each following his own shortsighted aim and
exercising his simpleminded love for being busy in the great world,
they rush forth into the public scene to create the confusion and
chaos which Pope renders again and again as mobs and various
kinds of din and confusion:

> An endless band
> Pours forth, and leaves unpeopled half the land.
> A motley mixture! in long wigs, in bags,
> In silks, in crapes, in Garters, and in rags,
> From drawing rooms, from colleges, from garrets,
> On horse, on foot, in hacks, and gilded chariots.
>
> (II, 19–24)

> Now thousand tongues are heard in one loud din:
> The Monkey-mimics rush discordant in;
> 'Twas chatt'ring, grinning, mouthing, jabb'ring all,

And Noise and Norton, Brangling and Breval,
Dennis and Dissonance, and captious Art,
And Snip-snap short, and Interruption smart,
And Demonstration thin, and Theses thick,
And Major, Minor, and Conclusion quick.

(II, 235–42)

Here is no purposeful activity, but only random movement and a fantastic mingle-mangle caused by each man following his own "intelligence" and seeking his own good. And so they move, one mob giving place to another, no one dunce particularly willing the sequence of events which leads from Grubstreet to universal darkness, but yet it happens. The very lack of any tight cause-and-effect linkage between the four major scenes of the book is a crucial part of the definition of the "action" of dullness, which always moves, as we have seen, in a rambling, waddling way. In a world in which Dulness is the guiding force, things always will seem to "just happen," and therefore the incidents which form the plot on its most obvious level must be shaped and related in a manner which will express this kind of movement.

We have seen, however, in our examination of the verbs and the simpler movements which form the undercurrent of the plot, that while dullness may move in a haphazard, purposeless way, that it nonetheless continues to spread out until it has enveloped all. And while there is no definite single-line thrust discernible in the major incidents of the poem, we find there too a slow but steady seepage of dullness from its native residence in the center of the City and the garrets of the Grubstreet hacks out into the polite world of Westminster and then into history itself until finally it spreads over all England and all creation. This slow progress is also apparent in the gradual change in the nature of the scene. At the opening of *The Dunciad* dullness has transformed London into a fantasy world, distorted but still rather gay and amusing, like the spectacular Italian opera with its magical scenic effects of which the dunces are so fond. But as the oozing of dullness continues, the scene becomes more grotesque and more

frightening, until at last in Book IV the transforming power of dullness reduces all the great world to a flat wasteland and universal darkness. The passage, we might say, is from a burlesque and parody world to a surrealistic horror.

The fantastic shapes which the dunces and the world assume in *The Dunciad* are, of course, to be taken quite seriously, for they express the monstrous metamorphoses of which dullness is capable. But amid the fantasy, peering out at us, we can still discern very clearly—as in a burlesque drawing—the faces of actual people—Cibber, Bentley, Blackmore—and familiar realistic activities and practices. Pope's actual subject in *The Dunciad* is the very real progress through a society of certain ways of thinking and acting. Since it is the nature of dullness to act in a random manner, this progress is not schematic. That is, Pope does not show dullness operating first at the lower levels of society and then working its way up step by step through the various social hierarchies, as a medieval satirist like Skelton does. But we are aware as *The Dunciad* progresses that dullness continues to invade more and more crucial professions and social institutions. In Book I its operations are confined to bad poets of the past, to literary hacks, to dull writers in general, and to the vulgarity of the city merchants. Each succeeding book, with its lists of new names and its references to additional occupations, creates a gradually widening circle of dullness, and in the last book the corrupted professions and institutions of the realm which parade before the throne—of Dulness and the Hanoverian King—include all ranks and all crucial functions of society.

Aubrey Williams in *Pope's Dunciad*[2] has recently shown in a conclusive fashion that while the poem may lack the kind of plot in which all episodes are bound neatly together in a single-line

---

2. (London, 1955). This book has completely reoriented the study of *The Dunciad*, showing order, pattern, and scheme where critics once found only a jumble. My own argument about the basic plot of the poem rests solidly on Williams' work, and I am generally indebted to him here and elsewhere for his clear discussions of the nature of certain problems connected with satire.

progression, it does in fact have an "action," a continuing movement from one place and condition to another. This action, which
we have been discussing in general terms, appears in proper epic
fashion at the beginning of the poem: to bring "the Smithfield
Muses to the ear of Kings."[3] This suggests the gradual corruption
of taste and the translation of vulgarity from the City to the Court,
from the center of commerce to the polite world. But the serious
meaning of dullness is expanded and the relentlessness of its en-
croachment on wit intensified, Williams shows, by the introduction
of several "progresses" or related plots, which appear not in a
schematic but in a random fashion—random because it is not the
nature of dullness to move with the directness and known purpose
of the powers in some of the parallels. There are frequent bathetic
parallels to *The Aeneid* and its action, "the Removal of the empire
of *Troy* to *Latium*." There is a grotesque parody in Book II of the
Lord Mayor's Progress, a civic procession in which a newly
elected mayor journeyed from the center of the City to Westminster. In Book III there is an inversion of the *translatio studii*
in which Cibber in the underworld is shown not the traditional
progress of light and learning from east to west, but the step-by-
step engulfment of one great civilization after another by the
forces of darkness and dullness. Frequent use of Miltonic language
and references to the Satanic quest for new dominions to replace
those lost suggest the demonic urge of dullness to enslave men
and return the world to its original chaos. Finally, an anti- or uncreation myth running through *The Dunciad* inverts the creative

3. It should be noted that whenever we state the action of a work in
the terms provided by the work itself, as here, we are still dealing in metaphor.
If, for example, we say as Francis Fergusson does in *The Idea of a Theater*
(Princeton, 1949) that the action of *Oedipus Rex* is "the quest for Laius'
slayer" or that the action of *Hamlet* is "to find and destroy the hidden
'imposthume' which is poisoning the life of Claudius' Denmark," we are
locating the central issue of the plot, or perhaps restating the plot in a
condensed form, but we are still talking about the plot which the poet made
to imitate an action. The action itself lies beyond the plot as a perceived
quality of certain kinds of life, and since paraphrase is not only a critical
heresy but seemingly an impossibility, it may well be impossible to talk
about the action except in the terms of the plot.

acts described in Christian myth. Dullness and duncery proceed
to the destruction of light and the world, not with the same directness, but with the same invincible, inevitable power with which
the Creating Word moves onward in Christian history from *fiat
lux* to the Last Judgment. These various actions running through
the events of the poem serve as metaphors which work, either
directly or ironically, to identify and define the true nature of the
various specific instances of dullness which are the substance of
the poem. But they also mark the steady progress of the empire
of Dulness as the dunces carry the Smithfield Muses to the ear of
Kings, as darkness, chaos and sleep spread over all creation.

The Dunciad has, contrary to received opinion, a most pronounced plot, a characteristic movement, which originates in the
verbs and the simple activities of the characters and takes full
expression in the arrangement of the incidents of the story. This
movement is further strengthened by the use of several subplots
realized by metaphor and parallels. But Pope has managed his
plot in such a way that the bringing of "the Smithfield Muses to
the ear of Kings" is but one half of a more complex movement
or plot, for this expansion of dullness is at once a contraction.
At the very moment that dullness becomes everything, everything
becomes nothing, for dullness is finally nothingness, vacuity, matter without form or idea. This expansion which is a contraction
can be seen in a passage in Book IV where as the number of dunces
swells to a larger and larger mob, the great shapeless mass draws
in on Dulness and becomes smaller and smaller:

> The gath'ring number, as it moves along,
> Involves a vast involuntary throng,
> Who gently drawn, and struggling less and less,
> Roll in her Vortex, and her pow'r confess.
>
> (lines 81–84)

The vortex which Pope uses here renders in geometrical terms the
"plot" of the poem. The turbulent outer lip swirls round and
round, growing ever larger and engulfing more and more. It sucks
water and rubbish into a tumbling confusion and whirls them

downward through narrowing circles, which end at last in the pin-
point of nothingness.

This general expanding-contracting pattern is exemplified and
translated to social, moral, and personal terms in the activities and
speeches of the various spokesmen of dullness who parade before
their goddess in the last book. Each one represents the triumph
of dullness in some crucial area of life, and each boasts the destruction of reason and the contraction of man and mind in some
way. The brutal teacher, forming minds with whip and precept,
comes first to announce an educational theory which disposes of
all questions and doubts:

> When Reason doubtful, like the Samian letter,
> Points . . . two ways, the *narrower* is the better.[4]
>
> (lines 151–52)

Philosophy, history, and classical literature are dismissed. The
curriculum is reduced to the sterile study of words alone. The
ancient and fruitful union of ethics, logic, and rhetoric—the good
man, the clear thinker, and the good speaker—is dissolved, and
in place of the traditional ideal of the educated man trained to
reason clearly and express his thoughts in suitable language, the
schools produce an empty-headed, noisy kind of dunce charged
with rhetorical examples, rules, tropes, and figures learned by rote:

> We ply the Memory, we load the brain,
> *Bind* rebel Wit, and *double chain on chain,*
> *Confine* the thought, to exercise the breath;
> And keep them *in the pale of Words* till death.
>
> (lines 157–60)

An educational system as confining as this can only reduce its
students to fractional men who value smallness to the point where
they can believe "a perfect Epigram to be as difficult a performance
as an Epic Poem."[5]

4. I have in this and the following passages italicized the words which
carry the narrowing, constricting action.
5. This statement is attributed to Dr. South by Pope in his note to IV, 174.

The political form taken by dullness is despotism and tyranny, and the dull goddess longs for the return of "Arbitrary Sway" and a pedant king like James I. Only one principle is necessary for the foundation of the kingdom of dullness, "The Right Divine of Kings to govern wrong." The implication here and elsewhere in *The Dunciad* is, of course, that tyranny and arbitrary rule have once again conquered England in the persons of the Hanover kings and the corrupt ministry of Walpole and the Whig politicians. Here again the spread of dullness is a contraction, for despotism is shown to be a reduction of the traditional personal liberties of Englishmen.

The duncely variety of scholarship and literary study is represented by Pope's old enemy, Richard Bentley, "that awful Aristarch." He and his fellows have taken literature as their province, and, looked at in one way, their careful study of texts can be viewed as a valid extension of the scientific spirit to literary problems. But in Pope's view these critics only succeed in reducing something once great to something infinitely small. In their hands great poetry turns to prose, and that traditionally moral activity, the reading and explanation of great literature, disintegrates into quibbles over grammar and pronunciation, the study of minute textual problems, examination of erudite sources and parallels, speculations on particular readings, and the endless examination of minutiae. Bentley and his followers commit every possible sin against the tradition of humane letters, and in each case the sin is a reduction of literature to its smallest components:

> The critic Eye, that *microscope* of Wit,
> Sees hairs and pores, examines *bit by bit:*
> How parts relate to parts, or they to whole,
> The body's harmony, the beaming soul,
> Are things which Kuster, Burman, Wasse shall see,
> When Man's whole frame is obvious to a *Flea.*
>
> (lines 233–38)

And since in the world of *The Dunciad* expansion and contraction

always go together, the less and less the critics see, the more and more they read and write. "For thee [Dulness]," says the critic,

> we dim the eyes, and stuff the head
> With all such reading as was never read:
> For thee explain a thing till all men doubt it,
> And write about it, Goddess, and about it.
>
> (lines 249–52)

The triumph of Dulness in education, politics, and letters is repeated in the training of the young gentlemen of fashion, the future governors of the realm. Having been well educated in duncery at home, the young man undertakes the grand tour, visiting all countries and seeing the ways of all men. But the result of all this "broadening" travel is that he returns "with nothing but a Solo in his head." Having visited all the countries of Europe and seen all the sights—though he and his tutor principally sought out vice and fashionable ignorance—the young man can remember nothing but an air from a popular opera. He is narrowed even further by his loss of his moral sense. In his exploration of various depravities he has found his moral "freedom" and returns to England with a French whore. Dulness, that always generous goddess, greets him fondly and *frees* him "from sense of shame."

Pope and *The Dunciad* have often been criticized for the large number of antiquaries and virtuosi who next appear before Dulness. Such trivial offenders against sense, it has been argued, have no place in a catalogue of the great and dangerous forms of ignorance. After all, when you are dealing with world-shaking duncery why stop to berate coin and butterfly collectors? The answer to this charge is, of course, that the triviality of these occupations is precisely what is needed at this point. Pope is showing a world in which as dullness spreads, human intelligence contracts into ever smaller and smaller areas; what could be better for this purpose than to show the well-to-do and potentially intelligent exclusively occupied with collecting coins, classifying butterflies and mosses, cultivating exotic breeds of hothouse flowers, and arranging sea shells? These typical Royal Society activities represent the scientific approach to the natural world, and Pope's charge

against science, both the professional and amateur varieties, is the same as that leveled against the duncely kind of scholarship: it reduces something very large and filled with meaning to something small and meaningless.

> O! would the Sons of Men once think their Eyes
> And Reason giv'n them but to study *Flies!*
> See Nature in some *partial narrow shape,*
> And let the Author of the Whole escape:
> Learn but to trifle; or, who most observe,
> To wonder at their Maker, not to serve.
>
> (lines 453–58)

These are only the more outstanding ways in which world and man grow ever smaller in Book IV. In general, what we have here is a world in which the grand scheme of a divinely ordered universe is contracted to a mechanical operation, in which religion falls off to elaborate cookery, and in which all forms of virtue, intelligence, and art are scaled down to their corresponding, or antithetical, forms of dullness. The cause of all the many specific reductions is an ultimate and general reduction of all things to self:

> Make God Man's Image, Man the final Cause,
> Find Virtue local, all Relation scorn,
> See all in *Self,* and but for self be born:
> Of nought so certain as our *Reason* still,
> Of nought so doubtful as of *Soul* and *Will.*
>
> (lines 478–82)

By making self-interest the moral touchstone, by trusting to what he alone can see and understand, by turning away from the literary productions and social values bequeathed by the past—in short, by pride—man reduces all the world to his own puny size. Reduction of all to self lies underneath all the particular forms and activities of dullness which make up the body of *The Dunciad,* Blackmore's long, dull epic poem, the writing of political pamphlets for hire, the mad excesses of opera, the greedy willingness of publishers to print slander and obscenity, the sycophantic birth-

day odes addressed to the King by Colley Cibber, and the obliteration of literary and moral standards. The result is a new and
narrower kind of man, the true subject of Dulness:

> First *slave* to Words, then *vassal* to a Name,
> Then dupe to *Party;* child and man the same;
> *Bounded* by Nature, *narrow'd* still by Art,
> A trifling head, and a *contracted* heart.
>
>   (lines 501–04)

✓   The spread of dullness is a contraction of life. This would seem
to be the central irony of *The Dunciad* and the formula on which
the plot is constructed.[6] Throughout the poem we are aware of
the shapeless but ceaseless onward movement of Dulness and her
sons over the face of the world, and yet as dullness spreads out and
out, it narrows down and down, until at the end of the poem it is
both everything and nothing at once. This everything–nothing
pattern is central to *The Dunciad,* and it is supported by a number
of other ironic movements which also make the point that while
dullness is frighteningly real, it is also an empty illusion, a something which is somehow a nothing. The dunces are unbelievably
solid, heads of bone and foreheads of brass, and yet they are misty,
vague, unsubstantial. The light which they bring to the world in
various forms turns out always to be darkness, and the knowledge
they offer turns out to be ignorance. They rise high in poetry,
oratory, and other heroic activities only to plunge deeper down
into the bathetic. Their levity becomes gravity, their wakefulness
a sleep; their briskness ends in lethargy, and their triumphs in the
defeat of all humanitas.

6. Swift would seem to be working with a variation of this expansion-
contraction formula in *Gulliver's Travels.* In Book I Gulliver is very large
and gross in comparison to the Lilliputians, while in Book II he is very small
in contrast to the Brobdingnagians. In Book III man is shown as very ingenious
in various scientific activities, while in Book IV he is shown as an obscene
animal, the Yahoo. As a result of these shifting perspectives, man is seen
as both great and small, a creature of intellect and of appetite. See Samuel
Holt Monk, "The Pride of Lemuel Gulliver," *Sewanee Review, 63* (1955),
pp. 48–71, for a full discussion of the satiric scheme of *Gulliver's Travels*
and its relation to the thought of the time.

Ben Jonson was the great comic and satiric writer of the English Renaissance, and his consistent subject was the incredibly exaggerated optimism of the period. What we take to be the source of Renaissance grandeur, Jonson regards with a critical eye. The merchant adventurers, the daring explorers, the bold economic spirits, the white-hot zealots of the reformed religion, the inquiring scientists, the great captains, and the ingenious poets, all those figures who people our image of the Renaissance and invest it with magnificence, in his plays become mad dreamers and self-deluded hypocrites acting in ridiculous defiance of an unchanging and limited Nature. Their gaudy clothes, their flamboyant gestures, their bold dreams, and, above all, their profusion of vivid words become mere shams, pretenses thrown up to cover lack of substance. In short, Jonson attacked the new dream of man that he was free to make himself and his world over in the image of his desires, rather than working slowly and patiently with a stubborn Nature.

Volpone is the most cutting exposure of the emptiness of this dream and Jonson's most profound exploration of its psychological sources and its effect on man and society. In the persons of the Venetian merchant prince Volpone and his parasite, Mosca, confederated to cheat the world by holding out to the greedy the bait of a nonexistent inheritance, Jonson incorporated and intensified the immense dreams of riches, power, and pleasure which animated the Renaissance mind. The nature of the dream is dramatized fully in the first twenty-seven lines of the play where Volpone rises from his bed, greets the day perfunctorily, turns with joy to his gold, which is heaped in chests in a "shrine" near his bed, and begins to celebrate its virtues. He elevates—as the host is raised in the mass—a round gold coin, and the shining, yellow piece of

metal, the "son of Sol," in that instant replaces the sun which has
for ages past brought life to the "teeming earth" and which on the
first day of creation was "struck out of chaos," driving the primal
darkness to the lowest place in all creation, the center of the earth.
Gold is the new center of the *Volpone* universe, the unmoved
mover,[1] the still point, around which all existence now circles and
from which it must draw its life. Having completed his new
cosmology, Volpone hastens on to construct his new religion, his
new history, his new society, and his new man. As high priest of
the new cult, Volpone kisses "with adoration" the "relics of sacred
treasure" and bursts into rapturous praise of his "dear saint":

> Riches, the dumb god that giv'st all men tongues,
> That canst do nought, and yet mak'st men do all things.
>
> (lines 22–23)

Where the traditional view of history held that mankind had
degenerated from an innocent, simple way of life distinguished
by a lack of precious metals, Volpone as economic historian re-
defines human history by making it a movement controlled by
man's search for material prosperity beginning in an age of riches,
the "Golden Age":

> Well did wise poets by thy glorious name
> Title that age which they would have the best . . .
>
> (lines 14–15)

As sociologist he substitutes hard cash for the forces of blood,
piety, friendship, and love which have in the past bound men
together:

> Thou [gold] being the best of things, and far transcending
> All style of joy in children, parents, friends,

---

1. "Riches, the dumb god . . . /That canst do nought, and yet mak'st
men do all things" (I.1.22–23). The resemblance of this to Aristotle's Prime
Mover is noted by Edward Partridge, *The Broken Compass* (New York, 1958),
p. 74. All citations of *Volpone* are to my edition in The Yale Ben Jonson
(New Haven, 1962), the introduction to which is an expanded version of
this chapter.

Or any other waking dream on earth.
Thy looks when they to Venus did ascribe,
They should have giv'n her twenty thousand cupids,
Such are thy beauties and our loves!

(lines 16–21)

As philosopher-psychologist he quickly defines man as a seeker of
gold, who when he attains it achieves at one stroke all the goals
for which men in the past have struggled so confusedly and painfully:

Thou [gold] art virtue, fame,
Honor, and all things else. Who can get thee,
He shall be noble, valiant, honest, wise—

(lines 25–27)

Volpone, an apostle indeed blessed by his "dumb god" with the
gift of tongues, is announcing in the opening lines a new act of
creation; and as we watch the play we are watching this new gold-
centered world coming into being. The brave new world begins in
the house of Volpone, where life is given over to voluptuousness,
freedom, and cunning; and these values create a new type of household. Here there is no wife, child, parent, ally, or servant, only
grotesque relationships based on gold. Master and servant are
confederated to cheat the world, and one another if possible; dwarf,
eunuch, and hermaphrodite are said to be the unacknowledged
bastards of the householder, begotten only for pleasure and used
only for entertainment. To this house come "friends" mouthing
concern for the supposedly sick Volpone but in reality longing
only for his death and willing to hasten it with poison or suffoca-
tion, that they may inherit his fortune. For Volpone these friends
and fellow Venetians are no more than fools who can be coined
"into profit."

From this golden center the infection spreads outward, re-
creating the world beyond. In hope of fortune Corbaccio disinherits
his son, Corvino is willing to whore his wife, Lady Wouldbe offers
her virtue, and Voltore, who for a few pennies would "plead

against his Maker," dishonors his profession. Judges in a court of law change their attitude toward men when they learn that they are rich; with money learning becomes possible, for you need only, as Mosca says, "hood an ass with reverend purple . . . and he shall pass for a cathedral doctor"; gold becomes a "sacred medicine" and physicians practice only for their fees, flaying a man before they kill him. Not only are individuals, professions, and social institutions remade by the power of gold, but the yellow metal ultimately becomes the standard by which all things material and spiritual are measured. Celia's beauty can find no greater praise in Mosca's mouth than to be styled "Bright as your gold, and lovely as your gold"; and her concern for her virtue when she resists bedding with Volpone can be discredited by her husband's conclusive argument, "What, is my gold the worse for touching?" In the world of *Volpone* gold, like grace in a Christian world, appears finally to have no limits to its miraculous power:

> Why, your gold
> Is such another med'cine, it dries up
> All those offensive savors! It transforms
> The most deform'd, and restores 'em lovely . . .
> .   .   .   .
> It is the thing
> Makes all the world her grace, her youth, her beauty.
>   (V.2.98–105)

I have spoken of the *Volpone* world as crudely materialistic and gold-centered, but Volpone and Mosca, despite the fact that they are the resident deities of this world, seem to transcend mere miserliness. They adore gold with a passion usually reserved for religion or love, but they treat it not as something possessed for its own sake, the attitude of the miser, but rather as an instrument used to purchase other delights, or as a symbol of their genius. Early in the play Volpone tells us that he glories "More in the cunning purchase of . . . wealth, / Than in the glad possession" (I.1.31–32). And farther on he explains that the proper way for a

man to live is to "cocker up [his] genius and live free / To all
delights . . . fortune calls [him] to . . ." The word "genius" is not
used here in the restricted modern sense of "extraordinary ability,"
but in the Latin sense of "essential spirit" or "that fundamental
quality which makes a thing what it is," i.e. soul. For Volpone,
the essence of man is, then, the exercise of cunning in order to
gain wealth, and the proper life for a man is to nurture, "cocker
up,"[2] this essential power.

Most immediately this means that Mosca and Volpone put all
their minds and energies into bilking the fools and enjoying those
pleasures of the senses and the mind which fortune calls them to.
But the particular form their cunning takes is of central importance
in the play. They are above all else master actors; not the kind of
actors who learn their lines beforehand and move according to a
pre-established plot, but improvisers like the *commedia dell'arte*
players—referred to in the text in several places—who extempo-
rize their lines and action and make up their plot as they go along.
Volpone is an unusually impressive actor. He plays a sick and
dying man to perfection, coughing at the right moment, seeming
to recover slightly when necessary, moving his hands weakly or
lying perfectly immobile as the situation requires. When stirred
by lust for Celia, he typically solves the problem of how to see her
by assuming another disguise, of mountebank, which he plays so
well that the mountebank himself could not have been sure, as
Mosca tells him, that he was an impostor. After Bonario interrupts
his attempted rape of Celia, Volpone is called on to play his most
difficult part, an absolutely impotent and dying old man. Despite
the stringent requirements of the role—that he lie absolutely still
and *look* as if he were on the verge of death—he delivers a magnificent performance. Mosca, with all the professional perfectionism
of a Stanislavsky, accuses him of sweating while he lay there; but
it is nevertheless an excellent piece of work. And finally, in order
to torment even more the fortune hunters who already have been

---

2. Volpone's "cocker up my genius" is very close to Iago's declaration of
his fundamental purpose, "to plume up my will" (*Othello*, 1.3.392).

cheated of their money, Volpone puts on the costume of a sergeant of the court and plays an excellent clown, an ironic Dogberry.

But as excellent an actor as Volpone is, he is surpassed by Mosca, who can, he exults, "change a visor swifter than a thought." His great dramatic forte is flexibility. Where Volpone once having assumed a role continues to play it without much change, Mosca shifts roles from moment to moment. He can in swift succession be the humble servant of the legacy hunters, the crying friend of virtue who advises Bonario that his father is about to disinherit him, the smiling pander, the modest but stern inheritor of Volpone's fortune, the impressive and sober *magnifico*. There seems no end to his resources, and all that he plays he plays superbly. He is what he chooses to be. But even beyond the range of his acting, we must not forget that with such rare exceptions as the soliloquy at the beginning of Act III, he is playing two roles simultaneously: to Volpone he plays the subtle and obsequious servant; to the fools he plays whatever the occasion requires him to be; but underneath he remains the clever opportunist simply waiting for a chance to bilk his master.

Mosca has other theatrical talents as well. He is an excellent make-up man who carefully anoints Volpone's eyes to appear like those of a dying man; and he sees to it that they are kept sufficiently dulled. As costumer he arranges Volpone's fur robes on the "sick" man, and later finds the uniform of a sergeant for him. As producer he oversees the erection of the mountebank's platform stage in Act II. As a director he truly excels. In the first four acts of the play, Mosca arranges the scenes of all the little plays within the play. In the sick-room play of Acts I and III he prepares Volpone for his role, directs him when to enter the bed, coaches him on how to act, and then opens and closes the curtains of Volpone's bed-stage at the proper moments.

His masterwork is, however, the court-room play of Act IV. Here he takes a variety of actors of widely differing capabilities and interests—Volpone, Voltore, Corbaccio, Corvino, and Lady Wouldbe—and creates a smoothly working ensemble. First, he

passes among them, distributing their parts, i.e. making sure they know the lies they will tell. The lead is assigned to Voltore the lawyer, who is, as befits his profession, a considerable actor, able to speak

> To every cause, and things mere contraries,
> Till . . . hoarse again, yet all be law;
> That, with most quick agility, could turn,
> And re-turn; make knots, and undo them . . .
> (I.3.54–57)

After Voltore struts about and delivers his rather old-fashioned speech, accompanied by elaborate gestures, the witnesses are smoothly introduced to play their stock parts: Corbaccio, the kind old father cruelly treated by his son; Corvino, the gentle, forgiving husband taken advantage of by his lewd wife; Lady Wouldbe, an innocent, outraged wife. When Corbaccio or Corvino have doubts or hesitate, Mosca is there to prompt and reassure them. At just the right moment the apparently dying Volpone is carried into court. So well-designed and smoothrunning is Mosca's theatrical machinery that the innocents Bonario and Celia, despite their own efforts to state the truth, are drawn into Mosca's plot and forced to play the villains of the piece.

As *Volpone* proceeds, the acting theme is strengthened by the knaves' constant use of the language of the theater: plot, forced posture, epilogue, scene, feign, mask, zany, action, Pantalone; we begin to have the odd feeling that we are watching a play within a play or—as the levels of deception multiply—a play within a play within a play. At times the theatrical quality present in language and action is fully realized on stage, and we are presented openly with a theater within a theater. The grotesque interlude presented by Nano and Androgyno in Act I, Scene 2, and the performance of Volpone as mountebank on the platform stage erected on the real stage are clear-cut instances, like "The Murder of Gonzago" in *Hamlet,* of smaller performances within the larger.

But Volpone's huge bed with its movable curtains and acting space on which he plays out his sickness is also a small stage—an "inner stage"—and in Act V, Scene 2, Volpone and Mosca, using a traverse, construct a second theater in which Mosca plays out the comedy of driving each of the fortune hunters out of his humor, stripping him of his hopes and of his pretenses. Volpone and Mosca, and to a lesser degree Voltore and the other fools, think of man as *homo ludens* and his genius as *ludere,* to act, to play. Where for a fool like Voltore this means no more than pretending to be the honest advocate for the cause that pays the best, for a Volpone and a Mosca playing becomes the exercise of a godlike power. Playing the roles of dying men and humble parasite are for them only rehearsals for metamorphosis, complete transcendence of reality. Volpone's belief in the powers of acting appears most clearly in his sensuous and passionate temptation of Celia, one of the best-known speeches in Renaissance drama. His imagination runs riot as he pictures for her the incredible wealth they will enjoy and the sensual pleasures they will share, if only she will submit to him. All the world will be plundered to supply them with a moment's delight, a jewel, a rare dish, a luxurious bath; and then they will pass on to the greatest of pleasures, love:

> my dwarf shall dance,
> My eunuch sing, my fool make up the antic.
> Whilst we, in changèd shapes, act Ovid's tales,
> Thou like Europa now, and I like Jove,
> Then I like Mars, and thou like Erycine;
> So of the rest, till we have quite run through,
> And wearied all the fables of the gods.
> Then will I have thee in more modern forms,
> Attirèd like some sprightly dame of France,
> Brave Tuscan lady, or proud Spanish beauty . . .
>   (III.7.219–28)

His appetite for infinite variety and his fertile imagination hurry him onward to describe even more shapes which she will assume

to avoid satiety: Persian, Turk, courtesan, "quick negro," "cold Russian"; and he will "meet" her,

> in as many shapes;
> Where we may, so, transfuse our wand'ring souls
> Out at our lips, and score up sums of pleasures,
>   That the curious shall not know
>   How to tell them as they flow . . .

The action discernible in these lines is the action of human genius as Volpone understands it: to "flow" by means of acting, to change shapes from mere man to the immortal gods—Jove, Mars, Erycine—and thus enjoy endless pleasures and endless change.

Mosca is not so flamboyant as Volpone, but the achievements of his acting put Volpone to shame:

> Success hath made me wanton. I could skip
> Out of my skin, now, like a subtle snake,
> I am so limber.
>   (III.1.5–7)

But as he warms to the praise of his own acting, the ability to skip out of his skin becomes a minor accomplishment, for he feels that he:

> can rise
> And stoop, almost together, like an arrow;
> Shoot through the air as nimbly as a star;
> Turn short as doth a swallow; and be here,
> And there, and here, and yonder, all at once;
> Present to any humor, all occasion;
> And change a visor swifter than a thought . . .
>   (III.1.23–29)

Here is man altogether freed by his ability to act from the limitations reality imposes on ordinary men! Not only can he be anything he wishes, he can be several persons in several places at once!

Acting is for Volpone and Mosca a magical power, a short cut to fulfillment of boundless desire which avoids such unpleasant

realities as old age, decay, satiation, poverty. Acting opens up for
them a brave new world of the imagination where man can con-
tend with the gods themselves, as Volpone boasts to Celia:

> In varying figures I would have contended
> With the blue Proteus.
>
> (III.7.152–53)

If their adoration of gold suggests Volpone's and Mosca's materialism, their faith in acting marks them as believers in the theory
that man can make of himself whatever he wills to be, even a god.
They are thus the spokesmen for progress, the kind of progress
based on increase of material possessions and rugged individualism.
And in this they are one with such titans as Tamburlaine, Faustus,
Richard III, Edmund, Lady Macbeth, and Milton's Satan, who all
express—before coming to tragic awareness—the optimistic
Renaissance view:

> The mind is its own place, and in it self
> Can make a Heav'n of Hell, a Hell of Heav'n.
>
> (*Paradise Lost,* I, 254–55)

We cannot help being moved by the power of such a belief, and
a comic figure such as Volpone, as well as a defiant Satan thundering from the depths of hell, has a magnificence about him, a gusto
for experience and a turbulent vitality that is attractive. To understand, however, the full grandeur which this attitude toward man
and his possibilities is capable of reaching, we must look at a
passage in the *Oration on the Dignity of Man* written by Pico della
Mirandola in 1486, where transformation, i.e. acting, is argued
very seriously as the source of human greatness. Pico is describing
creation. God, he says,

> took man as a creature of indeterminate nature, and assigning
> him a place in the middle of the world, addressed him thus:
> "Neither a fixed abode, nor a form that is thine alone, nor
> any function peculiar to thyself have we given thee, Adam,
> to the end that according to thy longing and according to thy

judgement thou mayest have and possess what abode, what form, and what functions thou thyself shalt desire. The nature of all other beings is limited and constrained within the bounds of laws prescribed by Us. Thou, constrained by no limits, in accordance with thine own free will, in whose hand we have placed thee, shalt ordain for thyself the limits of thy nature. We have set thee at the world's center that thou mayest from thence more easily observe whatever is in the world. We have made thee neither of heaven nor of earth, neither mortal nor immortal, so that with freedom of choice and with honor, as though the maker and molder of thyself in whatever shape thou shalt prefer. Thou shalt have the power to degenerate into the lower forms of life, which are brutish. Thou shalt have the power, out of thy soul's judgement, to be reborn into the higher forms, which are divine . . ." Who would not admire this our chameleon? Or who could more greatly admire aught else what ever? It is man who Asclepius of Athens, arguing from his mutability of character and from his self-transforming nature, on just grounds says was symbolized by Proteus in the mysteries. Hence those metamorphoses renowned among the Hebrews and the Pythagoreans.[3]

The freedom of will which this passage celebrates so joyfully is, of course, orthodox Christian doctrine, but Pico gives man a great deal more freedom in choosing his own ends—"the maker and molder of thyself"—than had ever been allowed. And the Catholic Church condemned as heretical the theses which Pico proposed to argue in 1487 and for which the *Oration* was intended as a preface. This passage, though Pico would surely have objected, would have been acclaimed by Volpone and Mosca as an exact statement of their own beliefs in man's limitlessness; but Ben Jonson held more traditional views than either Pico or the characters in *Volpone*.

The substitution of gold for all virtues and acting for reality

3. Trans. E. L. Forbes, in *The Renaissance Philosophy of Man,* ed. Cassirer, Kristeller, and Randall (Chicago, 1948), pp. 224–26.

lead in the end to the same place: a masquerade in which something heavy and drossy is disguised and passed off as its opposite
by being "preposterously" placed above those things to which it is
by nature subordinate. The elevation of gold and playing are the
particular actions of dullness in *Volpone,* but behind this playing
we can still discern the recurrent actions of dullness. By means of
gold and acting each of the characters strives to magnify and
glorify himself—to turn his base metal into gold—and yet each
of their acts reduces life. In their eagerness for gold and pleasure,
each of the characters is turned into a mechanical puppet who can
be led and cozened in the most remarkable fashion; and the substitution of earthy gold for the fire of virtue is close to being a
definition of the reduction of spirit to matter. The result of these
actions is, of course, to drive a wedge between appearance and
reality and to create in the family and city monstrous disorders:
a man sells his wife for gold, another disinherits his son, a slave
becomes a magnifico while a magnifico becomes a slave, and a
court of law mistakes the snowiest innocents for deep-dyed villains
while it praises the most obvious villains for their civic virtue.
But in satire it is the nature of the pretense to reveal itself for what
it in fact is, and in *Volpone* this revelation takes the form of a
plot arranged in Swift's first pattern, the flight that soars so high
that it becomes a fall.[4]

To understand the way in which the plot is managed in *Volpone*
we shall have to look briefly at the physical and moral arrangement of the universe which E. M. W. Tillyard has called the
Elizabethan World Picture, and which was in one form or another
the central image of creation from the time of Aristotle until
the eighteenth century. Under one of its alternative names, the
Great Chain of Being, it is the organizing principle behind
Milton's *Paradise Lost,* Pope's *Essay on Man,* and Swift's *Gulliver's*

---

4. "What a rare punishment/ Is avarice to itself" (1.4.142–43) Volpone
comments on the ironic way Corbaccio's greed leads him to the loss of the
very gold he so desperately seeks. Jonson's method is simply to expand the
meaning of this conventional reversal by allowing greed not only to defeat itself
by its own efforts but to condemn itself from its own mouth.

Travels, as well as Jonson's plays and many other works of the
Renaissance. The Great Chain of Being is a way of ordering the
multiplicity and variety of existence into a meaningful whole.
The links in this chain, which binds all creation together, are the
various levels or categories of being beginning with God at the
top and moving downward through the angels, man, animals,
and plants, to the lowest link, inanimate objects. Inanimate objects simply *are,* they occupy space; the plants *are* and can feed
themselves and reproduce; animals do all this and in addition
have senses, mobility, and memory. Man possesses all these faculties and adds to them understanding, i.e. reason and will. The
higher beings, angels in the Christian system, are pure understanding; while God is above them as pure being. The Great
Chain is a ladder upward, with each category of life possessing
in addition to all the faculties of the categories below some unique
faculty which distinguishes it from its inferiors. Within each
category the various kinds are hierarchically arranged in the same
manner: among the animals the parasite has only mobility and
the sense of touch and is therefore lower on the scale than the
fox, who has all five senses plus memory.

Man is, of course, the link in the chain which most intrigued
the philosophers, and the one which concerns us here. Most frequently he is spoken of as a microcosm, a little world, because he
contained in himself all the faculties, though none pre-eminently,
of the remainder of creation. He had the ability of the plants to
grow and reproduce, the senses and mobility of the animals, and
the reason of the angels. But he could not grow as mighty as the
oak, he could not run with the speed of the antelope, nor was his
reason as pure as that of the angels, who could apprehend God
clearly and therefore obey him without question. Having all
these faculties, man was, as Pico shows, a series of possibilities
rather than an actuality, and since God had also given him freedom
of will, it followed that man was free to choose whether he
would realize his angelic nature by exercising his reason or his
animal nature by following the pull of his lower faculties: greed,
the perversion of the nutritive faculties; lust, the perversion of the

reproductive faculties; voluptuousness, the perversion of the sensory faculties. Pico in his "Oration" is, of course, working within the Great Chain, but he is wildly optimistic about the pleasure of free choice, the range of human possibility, and the inevitability of man choosing his angelic nature over his bestial. Certain other Renaissance thinkers—Machiavelli and John Calvin, for example —were equally pessimistic, believing as Calvin says, that "our nature is not only destitute of all good, but is so fertile in all evils that it cannot remain inactive . . . every thing in man, the understanding and will, the soul and body, is polluted and engrossed by concupiscence."[5]

But there was in the Renaissance, as always, a middle way, a balanced view of the possibility of man controlling the beast in himself and nurturing his reason. Sir John Hayward expresses this view (which would also seem to have been Jonson's) in terms which are so appropriate for *Volpone* that I shall quote at some length:

> Certainly of all the creatures under heaven, which have received being from God, none degenerate, none forsake their naturall dignitie and being, but onely man; Onely man, abandoning the dignitie of his proper nature, is changed like *Proteus,* into divers forms. And this is occasioned by reason of the libertie of his will: which is a facultie that transformeth men into so many things, as with violent appetite it doth pursue. Hence it proceeded, that in the creation of other things, God approved them, and saw that they were good; because hee gave them a stable and permanent nature. But of the goodnesse of man no mention at all. Mans goodnesse was left unapproved at the first because God gave him liberty of will; either to embrace vertue and bee like unto God, or to adhere to sensualitie and be like unto beasts.
>
> And as every kind of beast is principally inclined to one sensualitie more then to any other; so man transformeth

5. *Institutes of the Christian Religion,* II.1.8.

himselfe into that beast, to whose sensualitie he principallie
declines . . . This did the ancient wisemen shadow foorth
by their fables of certaine persons changed into such beasts,
whose crueltie, or sotterie, or other brutish nature they did
express.[6]

Hayward describes perfectly what happens in *Volpone*. The
beast fable which underlies the play and the names of the characters—the fox, the crow, the vulture, the parrot, the flesh fly—
make it clear that the men who bear these names have been
transformed by their cunning and greed into the beasts to whose
sensuality they "principallie decline." The animal imagery—wolf,
hyena, chameleon, crocodile, tortoise, swine, hog-louse—which
appears throughout the play also serves to remind us that we are
watching a spectacle of men turning into beasts. Mosca describes
them in terms which reduce them below the level even of animal
to that of dirt, mere gross matter:

> Merchants may talk of trade, and your great signors
> Of land that yields well; but if Italy
> Have any glebe more fruitful than these fellows,
> I am deceived.
>
> (V.2.29–32)

All the characters of the play, with the exception of Celia
and Bonario, move themselves downward on the scale of being.
By choosing their lower faculties over their higher, they succeed
in reducing themselves to animals and clods. But Jonson turns
a simple moral point into the plot of his play by use of dramatic
irony. Each of the gold seekers, from Volpone to Sir Politic,
thinks of himself as rising in both the social and the hierarchical
scale by his efforts. Voltore considers himself well on the way to
being the richest and most learned advocate in Venice; Corbaccio
thinks he will live forever like the angels; Lady Wouldbe with
her painting and her chatter thinks she has made a great lady
of herself; Sir Politic with his empty-headed schemes and his

6. *David's Tears* (London, 1623), pp. 251–52.

idle rumors feels that he has become a great statesman and a
mercantile wizard. What they actually are is always grossly apparent to all but themselves, and the great joke, for Mosca and
Volpone as well as the audience, is that purely by their own great
efforts and expense have they made themselves into vultures,
crows, and parrots.

The transformations of Volpone and Mosca are considerably
more intricate and more interesting, and an examination of their
degeneration reveals the extreme care with which Jonson constructed his play. Both of these master spirits of the play regard
all the other characters as fools and potential sources of profit.
But Volpone and Mosca are supremely unaware that they are
subject to the same irony as their victims. Elevating the gold
coin over the sun in the first lines of the play is, as I have said,
Volpone's crucial act, and like all other actions in the play it is
heavy with irony. What Volpone considers a raising, both of
gold and of himself, is in fact a lowering. Gold, a heavy, drossy,
inanimate metal has been placed above pure fire, a reversal of
the proper order of the elements which in the Great Chain properly ascend in purity, and in the arrangement of the cosmos
from water and earth through air to fire. And in choosing gold
over the heat of the true sun, i.e. inert matter over vital spirit,
Volpone is, by analogy, preferring the lower to the higher elements in the world and in himself. Therefore, what he regards
as a supreme triumph, in fact symbolizes disaster for him as a
man. Sir John Hayward again supplies an appropriate warning
to man in terms which suggest the full meaning of "sun": "You
are now in passage through a wide and wilde forrest; wherein
you may be easily lost, wherein easily you may lose the use of that
sunne, which should both enlighten and direct you to your
journeys end."[7]

Volpone and Mosca believe their genius is most fully expressed
in their ability to act, to play a part, to make of themselves what

7. *David's Tears*, p. 255.

they will. Each "act" raises them higher in the scale of being, they believe, until in Volpone's case he becomes nothing less than a god, Mars, Jove; while Mosca considers that he is able to transcend altogether the limitations of the flesh through a skill which enables him, like angels or other pure essences, "to be here, and there, and here, and yonder, all at once." But their progression is in fact a degeneration. In social terms this is immediately evident. Volpone begins as a *magnifico,* a noble of Venice occupying a place of dignity and responsibility in the state. In Act II he appears in the role of an itinerant mountebank, a mere quack living by his wits and without an accepted place in society. From this disguise he passes on to playing a clownish sergeant of the court, a minor hireling of the state subject to whipping. In the end he is reduced to the status of eternal prisoner confined in irons—but this is no role, it is the form which manifests finally and irrevocably the dangerous beast which Volpone has made of himself. Mosca's case proceeds somewhat differently, for as Volpone appears to degenerate socially, Mosca appears to rise. His proper place in society is that of servant. By his cunning acting he rises to the position of parasite, trusted confidant of a great man and the agent of other great men of the city. Ultimately he occupies Volpone's vacated place and becomes a *magnifico* about to marry into one of the city's great families. But this meteoric rise is all pretense, and it finally melts away to the reality of the galley slave, the sentence imposed upon him by the court.

"The way up is the way down," a reverse statement of the religious belief that humility raises a man spiritually, applies to Volpone on the physical and psychic levels as well as the social. His chief disguise throughout the play is that of a sick and dying man, and it requires no particular knowledge of Elizabethan lore or the Great Chain of Being to see that the physical pretense here is the spiritual reality. In his soul Volpone is as sick as he pretends to be in body, and so, ironically, each detail of sickness which Volpone and Mosca work out and act so artfully, instead of covering reality reveals the truth about the man who has sub-

stituted gold for his God and his soul.[8] But over and above this
general irony of disguise, Volpone is traced down the scale in
considerable detail; and to appreciate this degeneration we must
look more closely at the image of man as he was defined within
the Great Chain of Being. The lowest of human faculties were
believed to be those man shares with the vegetable world: the
ability to eat, to nourish the body, and to procreate. Next in
order came the faculties shared with the animals, mobility and
the five senses. The senses were also ordered hierarchically, and
in general, following Aristotle, sight was considered the highest
of the five and touch the lowest. Above the animal faculties were
ranged the rational faculties, which man shares with the angels,
and these were, in ascending order: common sense, fancy, memory,
and reason. Reason is further subdivided into the understanding,
or wit, and the will. The understanding permits man to know the
good, either inherently or by acquired knowledge, and the will
permits him to choose the good. The proper way of life for man is,
of course, to order his lower faculties with his higher, and to live,
to the degree possible for so mixed a creature, a life of reason.

In outline the theory is quite simple, and many of us still sub-
scribe to it to some degree, at least sufficiently to understand the
moral judgment of Volpone based on this psychology and ethic.
What Jonson has done in the play, in a general if not a perfectly
systematic manner, is to allow Volpone to drive himself, via his
disguises, down this hierarchy of human faculties. His understanding disappears in the opening lines, where he conceives of
good as residing in gold, the material world, rather than in the
soul and those institutions, religion and society, which express
man's spiritual nature. His will is immediately corrupted, for he
chooses gold as his soul and his god with all the fervor of a saint
choosing salvation. His higher faculties gone, it is inevitable that

8. The same technique is used to reveal the lawyer Voltore. In V.12, where
he pretends to be possessed by a devil "in shape of a blue toad with a bat's
wings," the pretense discloses the truth about a lawyer who pleads so eloquently
for falsehood and for gold.

he will further degenerate. Common sense disappears at once as
he becomes susceptible to the most outrageous flattery and forgets
that he is only a mortal man with severe limitations. The
remainder of the descent is accomplished by means of the disguise
of sickness. Memory soon goes:

> He knows no man,
> No face of friend, nor name of any servant,
> Who 't was that fed him last, or gave him drink;
> Not those he hath begotten, or brought up,
> Can he remember.
>
> (I.5.39–43)

His five senses disappear one by one—and while they may re-
appear if the situation requires it, the general movement is downward. Sight, the highest of the senses, goes first (I.3.17) and by
Act I, scene 5, he is described as retaining only touch, the lowest
of the senses: Mosca advises Corvino to place the pearl he has
brought into Volpone's hands because:

> 'tis only there
> He apprehends, he has his feeling yet.
> See how he grasps it!
>
> (I.5.18–20)

In Acts II and III, when Volpone resumes the disguise of sickness, his symptoms reveal even further degeneration. Act I has
brought him to the level of the lowest of the animals—the parasite is the usual example given of the animal who has only the
sense of touch—but now he falls below the vegetable level as his
reproductive and nutritive faculties disappear. Corvino is gulled
into believing that there is no danger in lending his beautiful wife
to a Volpone so far gone that his sexual powers have disappeared.
"A long forgetfulness hath seized that part," Mosca says, and
"nought can warm his blood . . . but a fever" (II.6.64–66). In
Act III Corvino assures his wife, Celia, that getting into bed with

Volpone involves no danger to her honor because the man is so weak that he can no longer even feed himself:

> An old, decrepit wretch,
> That has no sense, no sinew; takes his meat
> With others' fingers; only knows to gape
> When you do scald his gums; a voice, a shadow . . .
>
> (III.7.42–45)

Below the level of vegetable it would seem impossible for a man to go, but Volpone predicts his own end when he compares himself to a "stone" and to a "dead leaf." By Act IV, when he is brought into the court "as impotent," he has become simply an object to be carried about. The end is inevitable, and Volpone seeks it out with his usual pride in his genius for inventing roles. To instrument a final joke on the fortune hunters he pretends to be dead. His descent from man to mere corrupt matter is completed when Mosca asks what he is to say if anyone should ask what has become of the body:

> *Volpone.* Say it was corrupted.
> *Mosca.* I'll say it stunk, sir; and was fain t' have it
> Coffined up instantly and sent away.
>
> (V.2.77–79)

While Volpone's symptoms are pretenses, they do mirror genuine moral failings. The loss of sight and hearing suggests his moral blindness and deafness. The retention of only the sense of touch is a perfect image of his grossness and materialism: only if you can touch a thing is it real! The failure of reproductive powers reminds us that Volpone has cut himself off from society and from family. His children are those monstrous distortions of nature, the dwarf, the hermaphrodite, the eunuch, and other bastards begotten on "beggars, Gypsies, and Jews, and blackmoors when he was drunk." His inability to feed and nourish himself reflects the very real spiritual starvation which he is undergoing, which ends in the death of the soul and the corruption of the body. Greed, lust, selfish

individualism, and vulgar materialism are identified with the process of physical decay to mark the "progress" down the ladder of
being from man to corruption. And the man chose freely to trace
this path, thinking all the while that he was achieving godhead.

The greatness of Jonson's play comes from his ability to bring,
by means of irony, two great views of human nature into perfect
juxtaposition. On one hand we have a vivid depiction in Volpone
and Mosca of an exuberantly sensual delight in the physical world,
here symbolized by gold, and a bursting vitality which enables
man to believe that by himself he can remake world and man to
conform to his own desires—here symbolized by acting. These are
views which we take to be characteristic of the Renaissance, and
Jonson gives them shape and language which for sheer vitality
and evocative power have never been surpassed. The brilliance of
phrase and the urgency of rhythms in such speeches as Volpone's
praise of his gold and his temptation of Celia guarantee that Jonson
himself responded powerfully to this optimism; but he was at the
same time the greatest classicist of his age, profoundly committed
to the principles of order and tradition in religion, society, and
literature. And so he counterweights the joyful worldliness of his
characters with a rigid moral system and a vision of reality built
up and refined upon by pagan and Christian thinkers over two
thousand years. Volpone and the views he represents were, in
Jonson's time, only the latest of a long series of challenges to society and established order. They were as contemporary and shining new as a fresh-minted coin, and yet they were as old as Satan
himself. And the end was the same in both cases. With the pre-
dictable regularity of a machine, each step upward in defiance of
nature becomes a step downward. Mosca perfectly, though unintentionally, describes this specious progress of "your fine elegant
rascal," who, he says, "can rise and stoop almost together." And
by the end of *Volpone,* despite all attempts to cover truth and all
skill at playing, reality asserts itself once more as the impostors'
physical shapes are brought into conformity with their true natures. Their own greed unmasks them, and the court locks these
Proteans into the shapes they have wrought for themselves: Mosca

becomes a perpetual galley slave; Volpone is condemned to prison, where, as a moral incurable, his body will be cramped by irons to fit it to his spiritual diseases; Voltore is exiled from his profession and the state, condemned to wander outside society like the outlaw he truly is; Corbaccio is confined to a monastery and treated as a moral idiot who has forgotten that he has a soul which will be held to account; and Corvino is turned into a civic joke, made to wear a cap with asses ears and sit in the pillory.[9]

9. The subplot has the same pattern. Sir Politic, after pretending to be a clever statesman, is forced to confess his pretenses and, driven by his fears, to disguising (revealing) himself as a tortoise.

Running in Circles:
The Early Novels of Evelyn Waugh

In Evelyn Waugh's novel *Helena,* Constantius, father of the future Roman emperor Constantine, rides with his new bride Helena, later St. Helena the discoverer of the true cross, along the rough Roman wall which separates Gaul from Germany and forms the outermost defense of the City of Rome. He explains to Helena the meaning of the wall:

> Think of it, mile upon mile, from snow to desert, a single great girdle round the civilized world; inside, peace, decency, the law, the altars of the Gods, industry, the arts, order; outside, wild beasts and savages, forest and swamp, bloody mumbo-jumbo, men like wolf-packs; and along the wall the armed might of the Empire, sleepless, holding the line. Doesn't it make you see what The City means?   (Ch. III)[1]

On one side of a guarded wall, barbarism, on the other civilization; on one side animals, on the other social man; on one side the jungle, on the other The City; on one side chaos, on the other order.

This is a particularly clear geographical form of a master image of history, society, and human nature which underlies Waugh's satiric novels. But since in Waugh's hardheaded conservative view of life the powers of destruction are ineradicable, this scene represents an ideal situation. Here the opposing forces are distinctly separated, barbarism and chaos on the outside, civilization and order on the inside, with the ceaselessly manned wall in between.

1. All quotations from Waugh, unless otherwise stated, are from the Uniform Edition of his works published by Chapman and Hall, London.

But in the post-war England of the '20s and '30s, the principal setting of Waugh's first four satiric novels, *Decline and Fall* (1928), *Vile Bodies* (1930), *Black Mischief* (1932), and *A Handful of Dust* (1934)—which I propose to treat as a unit—the walls have already been breached and the jungle powers are at work within The City. *Decline and Fall* opens with a night scene in the quadrangle of Scone College, Oxford. High up in the walls of the college sit the present-day guardians of order, education, and tradition—the Junior Dean, Mr. Sniggs, and the Domestic Bursar, Mr. Postlethwaite. Their lights are extinguished for fear that they will be seen by the rioting members of the Bollinger Club holding their annual meeting in college. From below in the darkness comes the shrill sound of "the English county families baying for broken glass," and out into the quad, dressed in bottle-green evening coats, rush the members of the Boller, "epileptic royalty from their villas of exile; uncouth peers from crumbling country seats; smooth young men of uncertain tastes from embassies and legations; illiterate lairds from wet granite hovels in the Highlands; ambitious young barristers and Conservative candidates torn from the London season and the indelicate advances of debutantes." Savagely drunk, they break up a grand piano, smash a china collection, throw a Matisse into a waterjug, have "great fun" with the manuscript of a Newdigate prize poem found in an undergraduate's room, and round off their evening, before becoming sick and passing out, by debagging and throwing into the fountain a passing student who is unfortunate enough to be wearing a tie resembling the Boller's. Above, the two dons creep to the window, peer cautiously out, and rub their hands in anticipation of the huge fines, which will provide a week of Founder's port for the senior common room. The Junior Dean, hoping for even larger fines and more port, prays for the ultimate barbarism: "Oh, please God, make them attack the Chapel." Next day authority reasserts itself with all pomp and ceremony: in solemn assembly the officials of Scone fine the undergraduate members of the Bollinger Club, ensure Founder's port for the High Table, and send down the young man who was debagged for indecent behavior with the

awesome words, "That sort of young man does the College no good."

Nearly every scene in Waugh's satiric novels is built on the pattern of the Scone Côllege scene. When an actual wall appears, its form and history betray its inability to hold out the forces of barbarism. The machiolated, towered, and turreted wall—with workable portcullis—around Llanabba Castle in *Decline and Fall* was built by unemployed mill workers during the cotton famine of the 1860s. The ladies of the house were upset by the thought of the men starving and went so far as to hold a charity bazaar to raise money for relief; the husband, a Lancashire millowner influenced by the Liberal economists, was equally upset by the thought of giving the men money "without due return." Sentimentality and enlightened self-interest were both neatly satisfied by putting the men to work on the wall. "A great deal of work was done very cheaply," and the Victorian taste for the romantic was satisfied by the neo-Gothic character of the construction which transformed plain Llanabba House into Llanabba Castle. The shabby, self-satisfied, and self-glorifying attitudes which caused the wall to be built were merely the leached-out remnants of older, more meaningful values such as work and responsibility toward one's workers and fellow men. Already well along the way toward barbarism themselves, these Victorian attitudes offer no real resistance to the forces of destruction, and the wall they built is overwhelmed in the next century when the house becomes a boys' school which shelters every kind of greed, ignorance, and savagery.

While actual stone walls are not always present in Waugh's scenes, the immaterial walls of culture are. The traditions, the social institutions, the ancient rites, the buildings, the manners, the morals, the logic and grammar of English, the codes of service, the aesthetic values, "all that seemingly solid, patiently built, gorgeously ornamented structure of Western life,"[2] are for Waugh the walls protecting the ordered, meaningful life from riot and savagery. These defenses of value are omnipresent in Waugh's

2. From the Preface of Waugh's selection of his travel books, *When The Going Was Good* (Boston, 1947).

works, and one of the major effects of his novels comes from the
ceremonial fullness with which they are voiced and acted out.
His statesmen, financiers, peers, and educators carry such heroic
titles, fill out their robes so superbly, speak with such golden
tongues, and conduct themselves with such marvelous certainty
that the world seems as solid and substantial as ever. Dignified
judges speak with timeless authority of the right of society to
repress ruthlessly those "human vampires who prey upon the degradation of their species"; earnest, well-trained customs officials
meticulously sift all incoming books to exclude any writing which
might affect the moral welfare of the English people; ministers
of His Britannic Majesty are sent to savage lands to protect truth
and justice, and to show the more unfortunate peoples of the earth
the way to civilization; the children destined to rule the nation
study at ancient public schools where their minds and characters
are carefully moulded; and the inquiring minds of men of science
press forward to the discovery of new truths about the operations
of nature.

But Waugh is a vicious ironist, and he always places us where
we can look beneath the robes of the great. The judge who defends
society with such sonority is condemning an innocent, powerless
man and letting the real criminal go free. The careful customs
officials ferret out and burn Dante with a warning delivered in
official tones that, "if we can't stamp out literature in this country,
we can at least stop its being brought in from the outside." The
Envoy Extraordinary to Azania has forgotten how to speak all
foreign languages and spends his time at the Legation, located
ten miles outside the capital where the air is better, playing in the
bath with rubber animals. A new master at a public school who
asks what he should try to teach the boys is handed a heavy stick
and told, "Oh, I shouldn't try to *teach* them anything, not just yet,
anyway. Just keep them quiet." Scientific inquiry continues its
onward march with such inventions as the Huxdane-Halley bomb,
"for the dissemination of leprosy germs"; and the spirit of Mill
and Darwin descends to the sociologist Sir Wilfred Lucas-Dockery,
the warden of Blackstone Gaol, who when he hears that the hun-

gry prisoners working in the prison bindery have been eating paste, instructs his keepers to weigh them daily to find out if they are gaining or losing weight.

Waugh has frequently been accused of being a snob and a deadly conservative, but it should be noted that he finds as much dullness and savagery in the representatives of the old order as he does in the new barbarians. He defends tradition, not the status quo; social order, not the establishment. He chronicles life among the ruins of a magnificent civilization, and here, as in those older Central American cultures where "Man had deserted his post and the jungle was creeping back to its old strongholds,"[3] the invasion has taken place and is continuing from within, not without.

But no one who lives in this world sees the irony and takes Waugh's England for anything other than the familiar, secure old Empire. The realities of this strange half-world are caught perfectly, though unknowingly of course, by the Christmas Sermon delivered in an English church of an addled minister who somehow forgets that he is no longer the chaplain of a regiment on foreign service:

> How difficult it is for us . . . to realize that this is indeed Christmas. Instead of the glowing log fire and windows tight shuttered against the drifting snow, we have only the harsh glare of an alien sun; instead of the happy circle of loved faces, of home and family, we have the uncomprehending stares of the subjugated, though no doubt grateful, heathen. Instead of the placid ox and ass of Bethlehem . . . we have for companions the ravening tiger and the exotic camel, the furtive jackal and the ponderous elephant.
>
> (*A Handful of Dust,* Ch. II, 4)[4]

These lines describe exactly the peculiar quality of Waugh's England. It is at once the happy circle of loved faces and a strange

---

3. *When The Going Was Good,* Preface.

4. To one edition of *Vile Bodies,* Waugh adds this prefatory note for the enlightenment of his pagan readers, "Christmas is observed by the Western Church on December 25th."

wasteland burning under the harsh glare of an alien sun. It is peopled with all the familiar types of English comic fiction, and yet these people are ravening tigers and furtive jackals. The anarchic appetites of these animals are shown to be ineradicable human traits which at times break out into the open in cannibal feasts, jungle dances, savage riots, and great battlefields. Ordinarily this love of violence is muted, but it always throbs in the background, like the drums which continually beat in the hills just outside the city of Debra Dowa, where the Emperor Seth in *Black Mischief* attempts to create a modern state. It will appear only slightly disguised as an insane carpenter who has visions in which an Angel of the Lord commands him to smite the Philistines hip and thigh. Then it is the epileptic royalty, savage lairds, and opportunistic politicians of the Bollinger Club. Or it may take the form of the random sexual appetite of Brenda Last in *A Handful of Dust,* who abandons her family when she inexplicably becomes enamoured of the despicable John Beaver. Another time it will be the charming ruthlessness of a "howling cad" like Basil Seal, the eccentricity of "Lady ————, whose imitations of animal sounds are so lifelike that she can seldom be persuaded to converse in any other way," the brutality of a Colonel MacAdder or a General Strapper, the deviations of Miles Malpractice and Mrs. Panrast, or the far-flung operations of the efficiently run Latin American Entertainment Company, Ltd., Lady Metroland's chain of South American brothels.

But this more or less direct violence and depravity is less dangerous to civilization than emptyheaded vanity and mindless gravity, the exotic camel and the ponderous elephant. This emptiness of the mind and heart seems at first to be no more than traditional English reticence, but it is extended until great voids open up in the center of the characters and they are revealed as having no private minds, no intense feelings whatsoever. The novels are filled with automatons composed of readymade, fashionable phrases—"too sick making," "too, too bogus," "a top-hole little spot," "it doesn't tabulate"—of verbal formulas rattled off without the slightest comprehension—"If it's a choice between my moral

judgment and the nationalization of banking, I prefer nationalization"; "I've always maintained that success in this world depends on knowing exactly how little each job is worth." Such characters can be fully and adequately described by such newspaper clichés as "the lovely young daughter of Lord Chasm" or "the bright young things." Their names tell us all there is to know about them: Lady Circumference and her son little Lord Tangent, the Earl of Pastmaster, Paul Pennyfeather, Lord Maltravers the Minister of Transportation, Basil Seal, Agatha Runcible.

The use of type characters is, of course, common in satire, for the satirist is never interested in deep explorations of human nature. His characters are merely personifications of the particular form of dullness he wishes to give visible shape. But what in some other satirists is an artistic device for getting dullness out into the open by disentangling it from the complexities of real character, becomes in Waugh realism of sorts. He sings the rich, the powerful, the fashionable and the fortunate; and he shows them to be as stiff, empty, and mechanical as fictive abstractions. The rare occasions when there are hints that a character is feeling or thinking come as a great surprise. Who would have thought that the butterfly Agatha Runcible in *Vile Bodies* had any mind to go mad? Or that Simon Balcairn, the aristocrat turned gossip columnist in the same novel, could have felt enough despair to require suicide? Even when a rudimentary mind or heart is established by such actions, the thoughts and emotions which emerge have a primitive, childlike quality, as if the owners were completely unused to such functions as thinking and feeling.

This all-pervasive simplicity and mindlessness is one of the principal causes of the trouble in Waugh's satiric world. What hope for the future when the full exercise of intellect in one of the leading politicians of the country, Lord Metroland, results only in such "hand-to-mouth thinking"[5] as this? He has been told at a party that the mad antics of the younger generation result from a "radical instability" in the country. Somewhat

5. The phrase is Nigel Dennis', "Evelyn Waugh: The Pillar of Anchorage House," *Partisan Review, 10* (1943), p. 350.

puzzled and concerned because his sense of security is disturbed, Metroland returns to his mansion to find his drunken stepson, Peter Pastmaster, fumbling with the lock. To his greeting Peter's only answer, repeated several times, is "Oh, go to hell." Seeing a tall hat on the table by the door, Metroland concludes that it belongs to his wife's lover, Alastair Digby-Vaine-Trumpington, and goes into the study because "it would be awkward if he met young Trumpington on the stairs." Once in his study, he surveys the familiar details: the businesslike arrangement of the furniture, the solid green safe with the brass handle, and the rows of books which seem to guarantee the continuation of order and security, *Who's Who,* the *Encyclopaedia Brittanica, Debrett, The Dictionary of National Biography.* These reassure him greatly, and after he hears Trumpington leave, he exclaims, "radical instability indeed," and goes upstairs to his beautiful, aristocratic wife, whose wealth comes from the operation of a chain of South American brothels.

Such vacuity—and Metroland is a *thinker* compared to most of Waugh's characters—justifies Waugh's unstated but insistent argument that a meaningful society can only be one which follows and defends strenuously some traditional pattern of belief and value. If people cannot reason clearly or feel deeply—and there is no indication in Waugh's novels that the majority of them ever could—then their only hope of a full and valuable life is to follow the traditions evolved during the long course of trial and error which is human history. Leave man, individual man, to decide on his own values, throw him into a relativistic world in which nothing is certain, debase the traditional ways of doing things so that no honest man can believe in them, and the result will be, as Waugh regularly shows, confusion, self-defeat, the grotesque distortion of human nature, and frantic but meaningless activity.

Someone has said that a good satirist really loves his fools. They are, after all, such perfect specimens of their kind, so unalloyed with sense or virtue, that it is impossible not to be delighted with their purity. Waugh must love his fools very much, for they are

such perfect idiots that it is possible to take their actions as no more than happy bumbling, and a good many reviewers have read these satires as "hilarious tales of high society" or as "gay, comic adventures of the dazzling younger generation." That these novels are, however, savage indictments of a civilization in the last stages of its decline because the defenders have left the wall needs little argument. The consistent counterpoint of the old traditions and the new emptiness, the recurrent images of jungle chaos and animal madness, the futile activities of the characters, all these provide a bitter comment on the types of dullness Waugh chronicles so gaily.

It is, however, the arrangement of incidents and the over-all pattern of events—plot—which Waugh uses most effectively to show the emptiness in the lives of his representatives of twentieth-century progress and emancipation. Like most satires, these lack a conventional story, intricately contrived and carefully followed. The sporadic attempts of two young people to get married, a picaresque ramble through English society, occasional references to the decay of a marriage, these and other such devices loosely bind the incidents together. But the books are not constructed around these story lines, for they are referred to only sporadically. When the story does appear, the situation will often have changed considerably from what it was at last appearance, but no explanation is offered of how these changes came about. The effect is of something "just happening," of a discontinuity through which some unknown and unidentifiable power is working to force matters to a disastrous conclusion.

The major portion of the satires is composed of a series of brief and apparently unrelated—by cause and effect—episodes which flash on the pages in the manner of scenes from a newsreel. A scene in a fashionable London restaurant will be followed by a meal in the African or Brazilian jungles; a business journey will be interrupted by a long, carefully reported conversation between two women—neither of whom we have ever seen before or see again—about a recent scandal at Ten Downing Street. Varied events at a boys' school will give way to a discussion of modern

architecture by a Professor Otto Silenus. Even when Waugh follows for a considerable length of time the adventures of the same characters, they will move at random from watching a movie being made, to a party, to an automobile race, stopping along the way to have a number of drinks, look for a hotel room, drive through a slum in the industrial Midlands. Then the scene flickers to another setting and we are watching the ridiculous pretensions of a sister in a fashionable nursing home, listening to a gossip columnist telephone his editor, and hearing about a young boy who fell out of an airplane.

By some standards Waugh would appear to have put his novels together very badly, but he is, of course, reproducing in his arrangement of scenes and his handling of time the frenetic, disconnected movements of modern life. Only a true culture, not a disintegrating one, can have an Aristotelian plot in which one event follows inevitably from another and the whole is composed of a beginning, a middle, and an end. But randomness and disorganization are only surface effects. Each of the episodes is thematically related to the others with which it is in sequence. All show in different terms the assault of appetite and stupidity on the old beliefs and ways of life, and the consequent emptiness. The scenes are also carefully arranged to allow the events in one scene to define the events in the next: an episode of polite savagery in London will be juxtaposed to a scene of overt savagery in the jungle, or a description of an ultra-modern house built for machines to live in rather than men will border on a party scene in which fashionable men and women move with the predictability of machines or in a pattern of conditioned responses.

Satire regularly offers, not a still, quiet world, but a busy, bustling one in which crowds of men race furiously about pursuing some ignis fatuus. In Waugh's satires railway lines are thrown across great primitive wastes, huge business empires are in ceaseless movement searching for new markets, busy factories cover the landscape, and cars race madly about the roads. Solemn, serious politicians, educators, clergymen, financiers, and men of affairs move confidently forward on the path of change, progress, and

enlightened self-interest. The disillusioned younger generation rushes restlessly about in search of pleasure and something new in life. Amiable rogues move endlessly on looking for new amusements and more profitable deals. This is, on the surface, the humming, vigorous world of the twentieth century, the era of ceaseless change and inevitable progress. But all this movement is illusory, for in Waugh's world, as in Carroll's Wonderland, "it takes all the running you can do, to keep in the same place. If you want to get somewhere else, you must run at least twice as fast as that."[6]

What in fact happens in Waugh's novels is that all the running produces only circular movement—the second of the patterns Swift shows to result from self-delusive flights of fancy, which go "like one who travels the East into West; or like a strait line drawn by its own length into a Circle." The circle has been in the past a figure of perfection, but it has also been the figure of empty, meaningless movement, of eternal hunger which never finds satisfaction or rest:

> Here saw I people, more than elsewhere, many,
>   On one side and the other, with great howls,
>   Rolling weights forward by main-force of chest.
> They clashed together, and then at that point
>   Each one turned backward, rolling retrograde,
>   Crying, "Why keepest?" and, "Why squanderest thou?"
> Thus they returned along the lurid circle
>   On either hand unto the opposite point,
>   Shouting their shameful metre evermore.
> Then each, when he arrived there, wheeled about
>   Through his half-circle to another joust.[7]

6. Quoted by Waugh in the epigraph of *Vile Bodies*.

7. *The Inferno*, Canto VII, lines 25–35. *The Inferno* is a catalogue of the symbolic forms which appear regularly in satire. Of particular interest for my argument is the fact that, except for the downward progress of Dante and Vergil, all other movement in the infernal world is circular. The condemned ones are forced to do the same things again and again, and in many cases they move ceaselessly and restlessly around their particular level. This cir-

It is in this "infernal" sense that circularity appears in Waugh. It is the pattern of aimless, self-defeating life, the natural movement of the jungle and the savage:

> Dancing was resumed, faster this time and more clearly oblivious of fatigue. In emulation of the witch doctors, the tribesmen began slashing themselves on chest and arms with their hunting knives; blood and sweat mingled in shining rivulets over their dark skins. Now and then one of them would pitch forward onto his face and lie panting or roll stiff in a nervous seizure. Women joined in the dance, making another chain, circling in the reverse way to the men. They were dazed with drink, stamping themselves into ecstasy. The two chains jostled and combined. They shuffled together interlocked.
>
> (*Black Mischief*, Ch. VII)

The English spectator at this dance draws back dazed from the heat of the fire, the monotonous sound of the drums, and the mind-obliterating circular movement of the dance; but the man of the future, the hypercivilized Professor Otto Silenus, who looks forward to the day when men will be as functional as machines and houses as simple in design as factories, finds the circle the only true image of life:

> It's like the big wheel at Luna Park. . . . You pay five francs and go into a room with tiers of seats all round, and in the centre the floor is made of a great disc of polished wood that revolves quickly. At first you sit down and watch the others. They are all trying to sit in the wheel, and they

---

cul…rity is reflected in the shape of Hell as a narrowing set of concentric circles centering on Satan. This is the vortex which is the defining shape of the movement of dullness in *The Dunciad*:

> The gath'ring number, as it moves along,
> Involves a vast involuntary throng,
> Who gently drawn, and struggling less and less,
> Roll in her Vortex, and her pow'r confess. (IV, 81–84)

keep getting flung off, and that makes them laugh, and you laugh too . . . the nearer you can get to the hub of the wheel the slower it is moving and the easier it is to stay on. There's generally someone in the centre who stands up and sometimes does a sort of dance. Often he's paid by the management, though. . . . Of course at the very centre there's a point completely at rest, if one could only find it. . . . Lots of people just enjoy scrambling on and being whisked off and scrambling on again. . . . Then there are others . . . who sit as far out as they can and hold on for dear life . . . the scrambling and excitement and bumps and the effort to get to the middle, and when we do get to the middle, it's just as if we never started. It's so odd.

(Decline and Fall, Part III, Ch. 7)

The jungle dance and the wheel at Luna Park are the two extremes which meet, primitive past and primitive future, the blood-crazed wandering of the stone-age savage and the mechanical construction of a technologically advanced civilization without humane direction. These are the two great images of hopeless circles on which existence moves in Waugh's world, but the circular pattern appears everywhere in more attenuated forms. Politics is a circular game. The Right Honourable Walter Outrage M.P. is in one week as Prime Minister and out the next, and it is an attentive man who can tell at any given moment whether Outrage is in or out. The bright young things in search of amuse-ment go to an endless series of parties—parties in hospitals, parties in hotels, masked parties, savage parties, parties in stately old homes, parties in bed—but all parties turn out to be the same party where one hears the same talk and sees the same faces. Waugh's trick, picked up from Thackeray and Chesterton, of having the same people with the same ridiculous names pop up again and again in different books makes it appear that it is im-possible to break out of this circle of familiars. And when these people do pop up, they are always doing the same old things. Lady Metroland is always suggesting to attractive young girls

that if they are dissatisfied with their present situation, a position can be found for them as an entertainer in Buenos Aires. Lord Monomark is still surrounded by several perfect beauties and several sycophants listening to him talk about his latest fad diet. Peter Pastmaster is still drunk, Alastair Digby-Vaine-Trumpington is still drinking, and the mysterious Toby Crutwell—sometime cat burglar, war hero, and M.P.—has still left the party just before we arrived. *The Daily Excess* and *The Daily Beast* are still getting the news wrong, the older generation is still worried about the younger, Parsnip and Pimpernell are still writing left-wing poetry and issuing manifestoes, and Basil Seal is still managing to get money out of someone.

Round and round go the parts of the world, each setting up a centrifugal movement which contributes to the larger circular plot in each novel. *Decline and Fall* follows the adventures of a young innocent, Paul Pennyfeather, who is sent down from Scone College for running pantless across the quadrangle after being debagged by the Bollinger Club. In his search for a living he first takes a position as a master in a boys' school, Llanabba Castle, run as a private venture by Augustus Fagan, Ph.D. Falling in love with Margot Beste-Chetwynde, the mother of one of his students, he follows her into the fashionable world of wealthy London society. Just before they are to be married, she sends him on a business trip to Marseilles to clear up some difficulties about the transportation of several girls to her South American enterprise. Paul, completely unaware of the nature of this business, is shadowed by a League of Nations representative—and old college chum named Potts—and later arrested. Sentenced to a long term in jail, he is later rescued by Margot, who buys him out by agreeing to marry Metroland, the Home Secretary. A bogus death is arranged at a nursing home run by Dr. Fagan, and later Paul returns to Scone to resume his "education." He uses the same name, explaining that he is a cousin of the deceased Pennyfeather, and grows a moustache. As the book ends, Paul has just returned from listening to a paper on the Polish plebiscites, the subject of the paper he had listened to on the fateful evening when he was caught by the Boller. Outside there is "a confused roaring

and breaking of glass." The Bollinger Club is again holding its
annual meeting.

What starts as a linear progress, a picaresque journey, through
the various levels of English society gradually takes the shape
of a great circle, the wheel in Luna Park described by Professor
Silenus. Men and women scramble frantically over its surface,
dancing, cavorting, grimly seeking the center, or just spinning
dizzily for the ride. But they get nowhere. As the wheel turns
we see different aspects of English society—a college at Oxford,
the home of a well-to-do lawyer, an employment office in London,
a school in Wales, an old manor house, a fashionable week-end
party in a modern house in the country, a police court, a parson's
house, a prison, a nursing home, and again the college at Oxford.
As each new scene turns into view it becomes but a new version
of what we have already found elsewhere. These recurring forms
of dullness have sometimes different, sometimes the same names.
Augustus Fagan, Ph.D., first appears running a pretentious
school designed simply to make money, and he ends running a
shabby nursing home and arranging false death certificates to
make money. Prendergast will appear as the minister who while
sitting one day in his pleasant house with the chintz curtains put
up by his mother suddenly is unable to understand "why God
made the world at all." He is next a master at a school where he
is unable to discipline the boys and cannot teach them anything
because he has nothing to teach. Then he crops up as a Modern
Churchman—"who draws the full salary of a beneficed clergyman
and need not commit himself to any religious belief"—and the
Chaplain of the prison to which Paul is sent. Here he has the
same trouble with the prisoners that he had with the boys and
ends, appropriately enough, as the victim of the mad carpenter
who with true dissenting zeal dreams that he is commanded by
the Angel of the Lord to "Kill and Spare Not." This little parable
on the contemporary Church of England serves also to demon-
strate the disordering effects in church, school, and prison of loss
of belief. In every place, this and similar disordering powers—
savagery, greed, pomposity, ignorance, and idealism so simpleminded as to be criminal—crop up in the characters of Grimes,

Philbrick, Maltravers, Margot Beste-Chetwynde, and Peter Pastmaster, and their doubles; and their recurrence turns every scene into the same scene. College, school, prison, the Ritz are all the same places, governed by the same people, for the same purposes. Perhaps the only change in the novel occurs in Paul who, having died and been reborn, has lost his simpleminded beliefs about the inherent goodness of human nature and the perfectibility of man and come to share Waugh's view of the necessity of a rigidly enforced social order. Upon returning to Scone and hearing of a heretical second-century bishop who "denied the divinity of Christ, the immortality of the soul, the existence of good, the legality of marriage, and the validity of the Sacrament of Extreme Unction"—all the values denied in the giddy world through which he has passed—Paul can only reflect with satisfaction, "How right they had been to condemn him!"

Vile Bodies is a panorama of the life of the "bright young things" of the late '20s and their disapproving elders. The scenes of the novel are gathered loosely around the engagement of Adam Fenwick-Symes and Nina Blount, which is now on, now off, now on, as Adam seeks, finds, and then loses the money which would enable them to marry. As giddy as they are, their search for marriage represents the search for a traditional way of life and solid values, which in many ways all the younger people of the book restlessly seek. Money comes to represent the support offered by society and by the older generation to those who will share and perpetuate their values. Adam first tries to earn the necessary money, the emblematic support, by writing his autobiography, but officious, ignorant customs officials, acting in accordance with government policy, destroy his manuscript with the ominous words, "that's just downright dirt, and we burns that straight away, see." Adam turns then for money to the business world and is forced to sign a "very simple" contract with the publishers Rampole and Benfleet:

> No royalty on the first two thousand, then a royalty of two
> and a half per cent., rising to five per cent. on the tenth

thousand. We retain serial, cinema, dramatic, American, Colonial and translation rights, of course. And, of course, an option on your next twelve books on the same terms. It's a very straightforward arrangement really. Doesn't leave room for any of the disputes which embitter the relations of author and publisher. (Ch. II)

Still seeking support, Adam travels down to see Colonel Blount, Nina's father and the master of Doubting Hall—usually pronounced Doubting 'All by the natives—a halfwitted but cunning old eccentric who spends all his time sleeping and eating. Lately Colonel Blount has found a passion for the "silver screen" and in hopes of getting a bit part he has financed a fantastic horse-opera version of the life of John Wesley which has been filmed at his house.[8] When Adam asks him for money, the old man responds cheerfully with a check for a thousand pounds, signed "Charlie Chaplin."

His identity rejected with his autobiography, his hope of making a living by writing turned to economic slavery, and all possibility of support from the older generation and traditional social arrangements obliterated, Adam and Nina can only trust themselves to Fortune and its turning wheel. They begin a joyless little affair, and Fortune then arrives in the person of a drunk Major to whom Adam entrusts a thousand pounds he has just won in an idiotic bet. The money is to be placed on a horse named Indian Runner. The horse wins, but for the remainder of the book Adam and the drunk Major chase one another around trying to collect or give away 35,000 pounds, though it is never quite certain whether the Major really has the money or whether he has simply bilked Adam. Each time the fortune seems within Adam's grasp, the marriage to Nina is on; each time he loses sight of the Major, it is off. No Juliet, Nina finally marries a wealthy young boor named Ginger Littlejohn but immediately recommences the affair

8. Waugh regularly makes remarkably fine economic use of such small details as this. Wesley and the whole tradition of dissent are here connected by association with the vulgarity of the movies and the disintegration of English social values consequent on the loss of firm belief in anything—Doubting 'All.

with Adam, even passing him off as her husband on a Christmas visit to Doubting 'All. When Adam and the Major finally do complete their transaction, it is on the enormous wasteland of the greatest battlefield in history, where the book ends; but the 35,000 devalued pounds are only worth a couple of drinks and a newspaper. Nina, still married to Ginger, is about to bear Adam's child, and all the other nincompoops of the book are carrying on in their usual way.

Most of the scenes in *Vile Bodies* deal with the varied activities of the other "bright young things," Miles Malpractice, Agatha Runcible, Archie Schwert, and Mary Mouse. They have, like Adam and Nina, committed themselves to fortune because everything else in their world is, in their language, "too, too bogus." They reel from party to party, body to body, and binge to binge, racing faster and faster after an elusive something which always escapes them. And because they have lost their bearings, they travel in endless circles. The dizzying circularity of their movements is objectified in the motor races, the great scene of the book. These dirt-track races are held in the Midlands near a grimy industrial city where a vast crowd, fascinated with speed and hoping for bloodshed, gathers to watch the "Speed Kings" go round and round. But the real Speed Kings are the bright, young people whose mad races are reported daily to the sensation-hungry readers of the press, and it is inevitable that one of them will find his way into the race. Dead drunk and mistakenly wearing a spare driver's brassard, Agatha Runcible ends up behind the wheel of the Plunkett-Bowse. After a few magnificent whirls around the course, she speeds off into the countryside until, losing control of the car, she runs head on into a market cross. She later dies in a delirium still shouting, "faster, faster."

Black Mischief is essentially the story of the arch-rogue Basil Seal and Seth, "Emperor of Azania, Chief of Chiefs of the Sakuyu, Lord of the Wanda and Tyrant of the Seas, Bachelor of the Arts of Oxford University." Azania is a thinly disguised version of Abyssinia, which Waugh visited as a reporter twice during the 1930s. The book turns around Seth's random attempts to make

of Azania a model state and to impose on his savage people those modern ways of thought, institutions, and hard goods which romantic liberals at one time or another believed would bring about the reform of society and the perfection of man: paper money, birth control, boots for the imperial guards, woman suffrage, atheism, a bicameral legislature, kindness to animals, modern architecture, and esperanto. The local population offers considerable resistance to such innovations—the guardsmen eat the boots—and when they do accept the new ideas, they somehow get them all wrong. They think, for example, that birth control and its apparatus—which is known as "the Emperor's juju"—will provide them with immense numbers of children, and so they march proudly in the Place Marie Stopes under the brave banner, "Through Sterility to Culture." Most readers have considered, wrongly, that *Black Mischief* is a brutal and unjustified satire on the stupidity of the black races and their comical mangling of Western ideas and institutions. Some elements of racial chauvinism can undoubtedly be found, but the main thrust of the satire is against Western liberals who believe that life can be utterly reformed, anywhere, by increased control over nature and the change of social institutions. Waugh makes this point very cleverly, and very consistently, by juxtaposing similar scenes in Africa and England, showing the same forces at work in both places, and by the cunning use of various kinds of imagery and inversions. When we see a gigantic savage with the unlikely title of the Earl of Ngumo roaring for raw camel meat in a local restaurant, do we laugh at his pretensions to the title of Earl or do we laugh at the pretensions of certain members of the English aristocracy to be something more than illiterate savages? And when an Azanian noble at a banquet for two English ladies who have come to his savage land to insure that no animals are being mistreated remarks humbly that, though the Azanians have much to learn from the white races, they too are in their "small way . . . cruel to animals" and sweeps on grandly to declaiming, "Ladies and Gentlemen we must be Modern, we must be refined in our Cruelty to Animals," where is the satire directed?

Black Mischief is not a caricature of a savage and ludicrous African kingdom but a grotesque image of Western civilization in the twentieth century. Where in Waugh's earlier books he sends his characters into only the figurative jungles of English society to encounter metaphoric snakes, tigers, and ponderous elephants, he now sends Seth and Basil Seal into an actual jungle where cannibalism becomes a reality and the barbarians file their teeth, not just their tongues and wits. The apostles of progress, the defenders of the old order, and the jungle savages of Azania are extensions of attitudes and people who appear in more usual clothes and speak in more familiar accents in the novels set in England.

Here as in England life runs in great meaningless circles. At the center deep in the Azanian jungle Basil Seal buries the murdered Emperor and Bachelor of the Arts of Oxford University who had thought to abolish savagery and darkness by fiat, technology, education, and Swedish exercises. The drums throb in the funeral ceremony, round and round goes the maddened dance until it at last distintegrates into grunting couples on the ground in the darkness. Out of the stewpot and into Basil's stomach comes the unrecognized flesh of Prudence Courteney, his mistress and the silly daughter of the even sillier English envoy to Azania, who because he believed that all the threats of trouble would "no doubt blow over," tended to his knitting, literally, and never concerned himself with politics or his official duties. Out beyond these circles there are others which look less insane only because they are more familiar. *Black Mischief* begins with a description of early Portuguese attempts to colonize Azania and the later invasion of the Arabs, and then deals with, in succession, the rise to power of a Wanda chief, Seth's progressive administration, and the establishment of a protectorate by the French and English. This latter looks like what is called progress: paved roads, neat administrative bungalows, clean water supply, lighted and policed streets. But it is in fact only another form of the old power game, and back in the jungle the drums still beat and the tribesmen still tear up the railroad irons for spearheads and rip

down telegraph lines to make copper bracelets for their women. In the middle of the main thoroughfare of town a family that no government has been able to move, still squats in a wrecked car, while in the market place, the age-old racket of selling junk to the government goes on. Plus ça change, plus c'est la même chose. After his cannibal feast Basil Seal returns to the savages of London and finds them still doing the' same things they were doing when he left. Azania fades from sight with the comforting music of Gilbert and Sullivan floating out over the waters which lap continuously at the sea wall,

> "Is it weakness of intellect, birdie?" I cried,
> "Or a rather tough worm in your little inside?"

A question to which Waugh's satires give the most un-Victorian answer, "Both."

A Handful of Dust gives the illusion of a developing plot. It begins with another of Waugh's havens of innocence, Hetton, a huge Victorian Gothic house which is the family home of the Lasts. Tony Last, the present owner, is an English gentleman raised in the humane tradition. He loves his home, cares for the tenantry long after it has ceased to be economical to do so, is seriously concerned with new farming methods and improving the land, loves his wife and only son, has charming manners, and goes to church every week, though he has no religious beliefs. Tony Last is, as Waugh once pointed out, a "humanist,"[9] and his old-fashioned, nineteenth-century dream of a City of Man held together by good sense and warm hearts finds its architectural expression in the grotesquely attractive Victorian-Gothic Hetton, which is, significantly, a reconstruction of an older, more beautiful Hetton Abbey. The present Hetton's heavy battlements, clock tower, armorial stained glass, huge brass and wrought iron

9. Tony Last has often been taken as the unqualified, though unlucky, hero of this novel, and he is certainly the most attractive person in it. But Waugh made Tony's inadequacies quite clear when he wrote of *A Handful of Dust*, "It was humanist and contained all I had to say about humanism." *Life*, April 8, 1946, p. 60.

gasolier, and pitch-pine minstrels' gallery, whatever their peculiar interest, were no more than a dream of chivalry and ancient values when they were put together in the 1860s with money earned from the cotton mills, collieries, and furnaces of Coketown. The impracticality of Hetton in the twentieth century is apparent in the impossibility of keeping it in repair, staffing it, or heating it after paying death duties and estate taxes. The naiveté of the social values it expresses in glazed brick and encaustic tile is apparent in the names given its bedrooms—Yseult, Elaine, Mordred, Gawain, Lancelot, and Guinevere—by men who read Tennyson rather than Malory.

In Waugh's world such a dream, no matter how attractive it may appear, is doomed, for it provides no defenses against the inevitable attacks of savagery and brutality. Tony Last's amusing and beautiful wife, Brenda, bored with life at Hetton, conceives an inexplicable and uncontrolled passion for a bloodless, self-centered young man, John Beaver, and leaves Hetton to plunge into the polite cruelty of London social life. Each week end she returns and looses a new group of savages on Hetton: interior decorators, spiritualists, international fancy women, young gigolos, and fashionable sponges. Each week she drains more money from Hetton to support her young man and pay for her pleasures. There is no planned malice in this, only a kind of mindless cruelty, which is echoed in nature by a highly bred and poorly trained horse who kicks Tony's only child, John Andrew, to death at a hunt.

This accident brings the marriage to an end, and Brenda demands a divorce and all the money needed to run Hetton. Tony refuses, but even after all this he cannot give up his humanistic dream of a City of Man:

> The Shining, the Many Watered, the Bright Feathered, the Aromatic Jam. He had a clear picture of it in his mind. It was Gothic in character, all vanes and pinnacles, gargoyles, battlements, groining and tracery, pavilions and terraces, a transfigured Hetton, pennons and banners floating on the

sweet breeze, everything luminous and translucent; a coral
citadel crowning a green hill top sown with daisies, among
groves and streams; a tapestry landscape filled with heraldic
and fabulous animals and symmetrical, disproportionate
blossom. (Ch. V, 1)

Led on by tales of a lost city, Tony plunges into the Brazilian
jungle, still in search of his dream. But the fabled city turns out
also to be an illusion, and, with his guide dead, Tony wanders
feverishly through the jungle to fall at last into the hands of an
unquestionable madman, the illiterate half-caste Todd. Todd's
father has left him a complete set of Dickens which he loves to
have read to him. He holds Tony prisoner, forcing him to read
again and again those sentimental stories—which, like Hetton,
express the Victorian, humane vision of life—in which villains
always die and intelligent little boys and pure young women after
periods of trial and suffering win through at last to peace, prosperity, and the discovery of their rightful names and heritages.
    The wheel has come full circle once again, with the difference
that Tony is now condemned to live forever reading over and
over his dream of life in a setting which makes clear that it is
nothing but a dream. At the opening of *A Handful of Dust* the
fiction embodied in the architecture of Hetton, Brenda's familiar
face and kind voice, and the peaceful round of daily life concealed
from Tony the fact that he lived not among the "happy circle of
loved faces," but under "the harsh glare of an alien sun" among
the "ravening tiger and the exotic camel, the furtive jackal and the
ponderous elephant." At the end he can stare into the mad eyes
of Mr. Todd and look at the tangled jungle and empty waste
around him and see the truth. But on and on he must go, reading
again and again of how all turns out well because the human heart
is good and kind.
    But back in England the pretense of The City continues un-
troubled. Brenda, after a period of difficulties, finally marries a
rising young politician, Jock Grant-Menzies, whom everyone had
expected her to marry before she met Tony. At Hetton, inherited

dream persists

by a cousin, more rooms are closed off, more servants let go, but the old dream hangs on. A noble statue of Tony is set up with the inscription, "Anthony Last of Hetton, Explorer," and the new owner turns the estate into a silver fox farm. Once again animals are penned in ingenious cages and carefully tended. Richard Last innocently hopes to restore the ancient glory of Hetton with these animals, but they, like the previous animals, cannot be relied on. More than one of the keepers has been badly bitten.

In Waugh's first novel, *Decline and Fall,* there is a remarkably fine comic description of the Annual School Sports at Llanabba Castle. The stated purpose of the meet is, of course, to encourage and test the endurance, courage, and physical skills of the young gentlemen being educated at Llanabba. The actual purpose is to impress and gratify, by allowing their sons to win, several important visiting parents. Since the parsimonious daughter of the headmaster has burned the high and low hurdles for firewood during the winter—and the spiked iron railings provided as substitutes are at length declared unsuitable—the major events of the meet are the foot races. Dr. Fagan, the headmaster, has stated firmly that he is not interested in the details of the races but in "style," and very stylish the fête is, with champagne cup, masses of flowers, a pavilion, elaborately printed programs, and the Llandudno Silver Band ceaselessly playing "Men of Harlech." But there is no track, no distance markers are set out, and no decision is made about the distance of the races. The boys chosen to race for the delight of their parents are simply lined up and told to run to a clump of trees and back again. They are to go on racing "until it is time for tea." Mr. Prendergast, the master serving as starter, is dead drunk and fires his first shot from an enormous pistol loaned by Philbrick the butler into one of the boys, little Lord Tangent. Tangent is carried off, and around and around go the boys to the encouraging shouts of "Well run, Percy!" and "Jolly good race," and the unceasing noise of the Llandudno Silver Band. One boy, young Clutterbuck the son of the local brewer, simply omits a lap by hiding behind the trees, and when at last the race is brought to a conclusion by the arrival of the most important guest and

the beginning of tea, he "breasts the tape" well ahead of the others. When the win is disputed, Dr. Fagan easily settles the matter by declaring Clutterbuck the winner of the five-furlong race, "a very exacting length," while the other boys are called the winner and runners-up in the three-mile, another "exacting length." The prizes for the winners in these remarkable games are, fittingly enough, awarded by Lady Circumference.

It is, I believe, impossible to discover in Waugh's early novels any specific social arrangements or absolute set of values which he espouses and uses as a standard for measuring the failure of modern life. The pomposity of the old regime is always as ridiculous and self-defeating as the grotesque antics of the new men, and the bits of more ancient history which appear here and there suggest that in Waugh's view human beings have seldom been more gifted or capable of handling things much better than they do in the twentieth century. What Waugh seems to value is order in social and personal life—not any particular order, but order. In his description of the revolutionary government in Mexico in the 1930s, *Robbery Under Law,* Waugh remarks that he does not believe that there is any one God-given form of government, but that a govenment consistent in its principles and dedicated to keeping order is necessary because "the anarchic elements in society are so strong that it is a wholetime task to keep the peace." Failure to keep the peace results in those meaningless, endless circles around which the characters run in his novels. Once the boundaries, the rules, and the markers are destroyed, as they are at the Llanabba races, then the rational judgment no longer has a framework within which to locate and identify things, and the purpose of human effort is lost. Cupidity, pride, stupidity, and cunning are loosed to complete the wreckage of order and obliterate the meaning of any dimly remembered purpose. However, running round and round until tea time and the arrival of the most important guest is no doubt the best possible training for boys about to enter the giddy whirl of Waugh's world, where all rules are off, all the markers gone, all races shams because there is no longer any sense of being a "creature with a defined purpose."[10]

10. Waugh, *Life,* April 8, 1946, p. 56.

IV

THE PERSPECTIVE OF SATIRE

> *Lastly,* I shall place the Cumbrous, which moves heavily under
> a Load of Metaphors, and draws after it a long Train of Words.
> And the Buskin, or *Stately,* frequently and with great Felicity
> mix'd with the Former. For as the first is the proper Engine to
> depress what is High, so is the second to raise what is Base and
> Low to a ridiculous Visibility: When both these can be done
> at once, then is the *Bathos* in Perfection; as when a Man is set
> with his Head downward, and his Breech upright, his Degrada-
> tion is compleat: One End of him is as high as ever, only that
> End is the wrong one. (*Peri Bathous,* Ch. XII)

This is Pope's statement, in ironic terms, of one of the critical
problems of the author of satire. He must contrive to show in
some manner that the mad world he constructs is truly mad, that
it is the breech which is up, not the head. The major actions of
dullness—degrading, magnifying, and jumbling—are, after all,
relative movements which can be seen for what they are only in
relation to certain fixed points.

The easiest way of establishing the necessary reference points
is to provide a spokesman for the truth, as in formal verse satire,
who breaks into the narrative to tell us what is wrong with his
world and what should be done to change it. But this tactic fails
to validate the standard it offers. The spokesman tells us that the
world has gone to the dogs and that men should use common
sense or return to the good old ways of their ancestors, but we
have only his word for the value of these approaches to life. The
method of the direct moralizer has been considerably improved
upon by those authors of formal satire who distance themselves
from their satirists and attempt to support his standards by showing him leading a reasonable life and reflecting in his person the

advantages of his approach to existence. Horace's calmness, urbanity, and simple tastes act out that measured life which condemns as frenzied and meaningless the busy activity of the Romans he satirizes.

But the most successful methods for showing that the satiric world is askew have developed from more oblique approaches to the problem. The most common of these techniques has been to build into the satiric world and parallel with the satiric plot suggestions, images, of more normative and time-tested modes of conduct and systems of value, which are validated once again by showing the disastrous consequences of failing to observe them. Jonson inserts into *Volpone* continuing references to the Great Chain of Being, that image of an orderly and hierarchical nature, which his dunces continually attempt to violate but which reasserts its reality in the end. Pope in *The Dunciad* constructs parallels with *The Aeneid, Paradise Lost,* and Christian myth to establish his norms. In the hands of such masters, the gap, often so perceptible in weaker satire, between the moral norm and the dramatization of dullness is closed, for the statements of the norm and the dramatizations of dullness become one. In any skillful mock-epic, the pretensions of dullness lead it to seek out epic dress and expression, which at once establish the norm and thereby convict the dunces for what they are.

But the satires we have looked at suggest that, at least in the greatest satiric works, dullness is ultimately measured and found wanting by standards which underlie any local code of ethics and manners which may be invoked, directly or ironically. Jonson may ask us to judge Volpone a dunce for defying the conservative Renaissance view of the possibilities of human nature, and Pope may present his scribblers as dunces because they fall so ludicrously short of the classics they dully imitate. But dullness is finally located and proven—the breech shown to be higher than the head—by the nature of the repetitive actions of the dunces and the cumulative plot of these satires. Whatever we may think of Jonson's view of Nature or Pope's view of the classics, we can all agree that making the small large, or the large small, and jumbling

things until the real can no longer be distinguished from the unreal are the actions of dullness, not of wit. And, beyond this, we can
further agree, no matter what our persuasion, that any furious
activity which achieves the very opposite of its intentions is both
laughable and dangerous, particularly when the perpetrators stand
blindly pointing with pride to the mess they have made. Older
satirists were more willing than the modern to try their dunces
by specific standards. Juvenal would condemn a Roman aristocrat
for driving his own chariot, while West and Waugh, whose conservatism is really extremely general, will only finally condemn
their dunces for their self-defeating movements, for following
courses of action that can do no more than intensify their already
desperate situations. But, no matter what standards he may invoke
at the first level of his writing, a great satirist ultimately allows
dullness to define itself by encouraging his dunces to follow their
nature and seek out those jumbles and frustrations, in action and
plot, which deny the ends they so busily and painfully seek. It is
then, finally, the plot of satire which defines dullness.

I wish to turn now to a poem, Byron's *Don Juan,* which reveals
this self-defeating, blind quality of dullness in an unusual and
distinct way, and which, at the same time, will help us to place
satire, and further define it, in relation to the other major literary
genres.

I

A rich confusion formed a disarray
    In such sort, that the eye along it cast
Could hardly carry anything away,
    Object on object flashed so bright and fast;
A dazzling mass of gems, and gold, and glitter,
Magnificently mingled in a litter.

(V, 93)[1]

1. References to *Don Juan* give canto and stanza numbers. The text used
is that in "Poetry," Volume 6 of *The Works of Lord Byron,* ed. E. H. Coleridge (London, 1903).

This description of the Sultan's palace is also a perfect image of Byron's sprawling, wandering tale of the travels of Don Juan. The poem is like a new world seen for the first time in which the richness, plenitude, and variety of creation have not yet been named and catalogued. The events of the primary story, the adventures of Don Juan, take place over all Europe: Spain, Greece, Turkey, Russia, England. These countries are peopled by an enormous range of humanity: pirates, empresses, opera singers, grandees, slaves, lawyers, English peers, sailors, harem girls, poachers, educated women. This "ferment" is "in full activity," and the *dramatis personae* rush here and there into duels, love affairs, shipwrecks, slave trading, fox hunts, wars, commercial speculations, formal banquets, and divorce courts—only to come to rest at last in death, old age, or the tedium of daily life. Whatever of the fullness and variety of creation is not encountered by Don Juan in his wanderings is introduced from the side by a garrulous narrator who breaks in on the story at will to talk about such diverse matters as his own marriage, the fall of Troy, the latest styles of dress, idealist philosophy, contemporary politics, poetry ancient and modern, and the best cure for hangovers. The substance of the poem is, then, composed in part of the objective persons and events of the Don Juan fable, in part of the narrator's personal memories, and in part of historical events and the memories of the race, which the narrator introduces in his digressions.

This crammed, various creation renders the Romantic view of a world too large in all directions and too complex in its workings to be captured and arranged in any neat system of thought or formal pattern. Throughout *Don Juan,* traditional forms and systems are reduced to nonsense by showing their inability to take the measure of man and his world. Plato's philosophy becomes no more than "confounded fantasies" which have paved the way to immoral conduct by deluding men into thinking that they can exercise some control over their "controlless core." The grave philosopher himself becomes a "bore, a charlatan, a coxcomb . . . a go-between." In dealing with the attack on Ismail, the narrator informs us that "History can only take things in the gross," and

that the chronicle of the glories of conquest and the sweep of empire which makes up history is nothing but the childish sound of "Murder's rattles," which leaves out the infinite number of human actions and sufferings which are the truth of life. Science fares no better. Newton's "calculations" of the principles of nature—which the narrator begs leave to doubt—"I'll not answer above ground / For any sage's creed or calculation"—have led only to mechanical contrivances which balance one another out: rockets and vaccination, guillotines and surgery, artillery and artificial respiration. Religion, metaphysics, psychology, social custom, law, all received systems of thought, are sieves through which existence pours in the fluid, shifting world of *Don Juan*. Even poetry is mocked for its pretensions to tell the truth about the strange creature man. After testing many systems against the reality of life as his poem presents it, the narrator can only exclaim,

> Oh! ye immortal Gods! what is Theogony?
> Oh! thou, too, mortal man! what is Philanthropy?
> Oh! World, which was and is, what is Cosmogony?
>
> (IX, 20)

Since all systems and forms are by their nature inadequate to life, then only by being unsystematic can the poet hope to describe things as they are, for

> if a writer should be quite consistent,
> How could he possibly show things existent?
>
> (XV, 87)

Don Juan, by and large, fulfills the implicit prescription for a poetry which wishes to "show things existent," and the result is a baffling mixture of changes and shifting points of view.[2] Noth-

---

2. Ernest J. Lovell, Jr., "Irony and Image in *Don Juan,*" in *The Major English Romantic Poets,* eds. Thorpe, Baker, and Weaver (Carbondale, Ill., 1957), pp. 129–48, discusses the complexity of tone at various levels of the poem. Though my argument diverges considerably from Lovell's, I am greatly indebted to his insights, and particularly to such statements as, "The satire may merge so successfully with comedy or at other times with tragedy that it is often hardly recognizable as 'serious' satire."

ing, or almost nothing, remains constant: a love which at one moment seems the source of the greatest good becomes a painful trap; spirit and vitality which make their possessor in one incident attractive lead him in the next to brutal and destructive actions; pleasure turns pain and pain turns pleasure; what is now comic becomes in an instant tragic, and what was tragic with a sudden shift of perspective becomes meaningless.

Yet, in this heterocosm, despite the poet's warnings about the futility of systems, the parts are arranged and related to one another in a loosely systematic manner. It will not do to call this arrangement "structure," for this metaphor suggests rigidity, a series of modular units, of arrested, still *situations*. This is precisely not the state of affairs in *Don Juan,* where nothing—man, woman, society, nature, or poem—can "hold this visible shape"[3] for more than an instant. Instead, the poem develops a recurring rhythm, flows again and again through a particular movement, which imitates the essential movement of life as Byron sensed it. This central rhythm comprehends and is made up of the movements of all the component parts, characters, events, metaphors, settings, stanza form, rhythms, and rhymes.

We can begin our discussion of this rhythm on the most obvious level of the poem, the Don Juan plot, which gives a loose continuity to the rambling collection of stories and digressions. The most striking quality of this primary plot is its "but then" movement. Juan's father and mother are apparently happily wed, but then Don José begins to stray, the marriage is dissolved, and José dies. Donna Inez plans to make of her son Juan a paragon of learning and virtue, but then he falls in love with Donna Julia, is discovered by her husband, fights and wounds him, and is forced to flee Spain. He sets out for Italy, but then he is shipwrecked, cast ashore on a Greek island, and falls in love with Haidée. Their

---

3. *Antony and Cleopatra,* IV.10.14. The sense of life as endless movement and change which is central to *Don Juan* is also the basic fact of existence in *Antony and Cleopatra,* where Shakespeare catches it perfectly in such terms as "the varying shore o' the world," and in the character of Cleopatra, the woman of "infinite variety."

love seems perfect and enduring, but then Haidée's papa, the pirate Lambro, returns. Juan is wounded and sold into slavery, and Haidée dies. Juan, unaware of Haidée's death (he never learns of it, nor does he ever seek to return to her), is heartbroken and feels that he can never live or love again, but then he finds himself by strange accident in bed in a Turkish harem with the luscious Dudù, is thrown in the Bosporus, saved by some unmentioned good chance, and fights with the Russian army at the siege of Ismail. Bravery and fortune cause him to be chosen to carry dispatches to the Russian empress, Catherine, who is vastly pleased with the young man. They fall in "love"—at least Juan is flattered by the attentions of a Queen—but then he falls sick and is forced to leave Russia and travel as an emissary across Europe to England. Here he is accepted by the best society and accompanies the Amundevilles to their country estate. He seems destined to fall in love once more, with either Lady Adeline Amundeville or the young beauty Aurora Raby, but finds himself alone at night with "her frolic Grace," the Duchess of FitzFulke, dressed as a monk who haunts the castle. But then the poem ends, for Byron went to Greece to die there in the spring of 1824.

Don Juan is an unfinished poem, but then it seems doubtful that it ever could have been finished, for what conclusion could there have been to this sequence of events in which man settles for only a moment in one condition and identity, to be swept inevitably onward into further change?[4] In a curious way, the sudden transformation of the bored but resigned lover of the Countess Guiccioli into the martyr of liberty dying of fever at Missilonghi illustrates perfectly the vision of life his poem embodies—just as the death of the poet provides the final comment on the pilgrimage to Canterbury in the other most famous unfinished poem in English.

4. The accident of Byron's death was not the sole cause of the "unfinished" state of the poem. In I, 200, he states, though perhaps ironically, that *Don Juan* will have twelve books and three episodes. Considering his extension of the poem far beyond these limits, it seems certain that Byron himself felt or knew that an ending would be false to the action he was imitating.

This particular rhythm of existence, eternally in movement like the ceaselessly changing waters of ocean, is the controlling concept of the poem, its basic action. It can be heard in the primary plot, and it remains audible in all the movements of the various world. It originates in that "indecent sun" which

> cannot leave alone our helpless clay,
> But will keep baking, broiling, burning on.
>
> (I, 63)

It sounds loudly and fiercely in the attack on Ismail:

> But on they marched, dead bodies trampling o'er,
> Firing, and thrusting, slashing, sweating, glowing.
>
> (VIII, 19)

It sounds softly, but just as insistently, in the description of poetry as the "shadow which the onward Soul behind throws," or in the sad description of the ladies in the harem who move "with stately march and slow, / Like water-lilies floating down a rill." It is present in the primeval forest where Daniel Boone and his men live as "fresh as is a torrent or a tree" with "motion . . . in their days"; and it is equally present in great cities "that boil over with their scum," where life is one great swirling movement,

> coaches, drays, choked turnpikes, and a whirl
> Of wheels, and roar of voices and confusion;
> Here taverns wooing to a pint of "purl,"
> There mails fast flying off like a delusion.
>
> (XI, 22)

The onward movement of life is not, however, uncomplicated. Like the waves to which it is frequently compared, the individual life and the life of civilizations sweep forward and upward to a crest, pause there for an illusory moment of certainty in love, identity, and glory, and then plunge downward and onward into the great sweep of eternity. We can hear this characteristic rhythm in the "but then" pattern of the Juan story, and it is compressed

into a single line in which a young wife struggles not to give herself to a lover, "And whispering 'I will ne'er consent'—consented." It sounds again in the metamorphosis of the Greek pirate Lambro, who had once been an idealist and a patriot:

> His Country's wrongs and his despair to save her
> Had stung him from a slave to an enslaver.
>
> (III, 53)

It receives full orchestration in this description of the passing of life and empires:

> The eternal surge
> Of Time and Tide rolls on and bears afar
>   Our bubbles; as the old burst, new emerge,
> Lashed from the foam of ages; while the graves
> Of Empires heave but like some passing waves.
>
> (XV, 99)

But this movement, upward to a pause, and then a sweep away, is most consistently present in the stanza form, *ottava rima,* which Byron found so suitable. The first six lines stagger forward, like the life they contain, toward the resting place of the concluding couplet and the security of its rhyme—and a very shaky resting place it most often is. Since the majority of these couplets are end-stopped, it is possible to pause for an instant, but only an instant, before pressing on to the inevitable next stanza, where the process is repeated once more. The length of the poem intensifies this onward effect, for there seems always another stanza or another canto to sweep forward and destroy every momentary conclusion.

However much the rising to pauses and falling away from them may complicate the rhythm of the poem, the over-all movement is one of change passing on to change. The pressure is in man's very blood which "flows on too fast . . . as the torrent widens toward the ocean," which "beats" in his heart, "moves" him to action, and "bursts forth" from his veins as "the Simoom sweeps the blasted plain" if his free movement is restrained. The same

pressure is in nature: in the ever-present ocean which foams and surges ever onward, in the "showering grapes" which

> In Bacchanal profusion reel to earth,
> Purple and gushing.
>
> (I, 124)

It is the power which forces great poetry,

> As on the beach the waves at last are broke,
>   Thus to their extreme verge the passions brought
> Dash into poetry.
>
> (IV, 106)

It is the force of time which drives history onward and buries the past in oblivion:

> The very generations of the dead
>   Are swept away, and tomb inherits tomb,
> Until the memory of an Age is fled,
>   And, buried, sinks beneath its offspring's doom.
>
> (IV, 102)

No more can be done than to suggest the omnipresence of this onward rush in *Don Juan,* but it is quite obviously, whether Byron employed it consciously or unconsciously, the governing concept, the central action of life which the poem imitates. Even the slighter instances of imagery, conventional though they may appear to be, keep this idea of a vital, forceful onward movement playing through the poem. A family grows like a springing branch, the veins of a beautiful woman run lightning, the blood of a woman in love rushes to where her spirit's set, the blood pours on like a headlong torrent overpowering a river's rush, glances dart out, water ripples onto a beach as champagne brims over a glass, two lovers' senses dash on and their hearts beat against one another's bosom, revenge springs like the tiger, life is the current of years, fury is like the yeasty ocean, hair flows like an Alpine torrent, looks swim, two hearts pour into one another, blood runs like a

brook, Fate puts from the shore, bosoms beat for love as a caged bird for free air, a girl in love expands into life, men are killed as gales sweep foam away.

Ultimately, all these various movements are included in the two master symbols of the poem, fire and ocean. Fire is the vital spirit, the Promethean flame, the mysterious, motivating energy which urges all life on to seek its full expression in love, war, pleasure, poetry. No explanation is offered for the sources of this fire, it simply is the vital power which "will keep baking, broiling, burning on." Ocean is the visible form of history, and is specifically identified as the, "Watery Outline of Eternity, / Or miniature, at least."

The poem reveals that Byron thought of "our nautical existence" as a process and that he consistently used a particular type of imagery to identify each stage of life. Early life is identified with the fresh-water stream flowing from high mountains, tumbling impetuously over rocks and down mountainsides; as youth passes and disillusionments come, the fresh stream is dammed up or flows into a lake, and then joins a river which broadens and deepens toward the sea; finally, when joy and illusion are gone, the waters flow into the salt "sea of ocean" to become mingled with and indistinguishable from all the other waters which have flowed there through all time. No reference is made in *Don Juan* to the other part of the natural cycle in which salt water is evaporated by the sun and returned sweet to the mountain tops once more.

II

Whene'er I have expressed
Opinions two, which at first sight may look
Twin opposites, the second is the best.
Perhaps I have a third too, in a nook,
Or none at all—which seems a sorry jest:
But if a writer should be quite consistent,
How could he possibly show things existent?

(XV, 87)

The constant flow of life leading on from change to change is the essential reality of the world of *Don Juan,* the basic action running through the poem and shaping life. The nominal hero, the young Spaniard Don Juan, lives this action but is not aware that he does so, for he is, as the narrator frequently reminds us, "thoughtless." He feels passionately, acts directly, moves with grace and ease through the flux of existence, but he does not know what he is or does.

Juan's lack of consciousness is constantly thrown into relief by the restless, probing, analytic quality of the narrator's mind; but though the two represent different aspects of being—Juan all body and passion, the narrator only a voice and mind—their different existences still follow the basic rhythm of life. If Juan lives change, the narrator thinks it. The stanza quoted above is an explicit recognition on his part that his thoughts on any subject are no more than opinions, and that these opinions shift as frequently and violently as do Juan's loves and fortunes. The instability of the narrator's thought has always been the most interesting part of the poem, and critics have long recognized that he makes startlingly contradictory statements about life and people. To take a simple example, in Stanza 31 of Canto V we are told that the enjoyment of food is piggish indulgence which always reminds us that we are gross animals, not pure spirits; but then in Stanza 47 food is cheerfully presented as man's restorer, an unalloyed benefit. To follow the narrator's views on food and drink through the entire poem is to be treated to a display of nearly every possible attitude toward this subject, and his position is further complicated by his endlessly ambiguous handling of the subject of food in such scenes as the feast on Haidée's island celebrating the marriage of Haidée and Juan, the cannibal feast in the open boat, and the elaborate formal banquet at Norman Abbey. The variety of opinions on food gives only a slight indication of the endless shifts of perspective on more complicated matters such as women, love, glory, society, or pleasure.

If, as is first suggested in the stanza quoted above, we could regard the narrator's second opinion as always better than the

first, there would be little difficulty in following him on his journey toward wisdom. Since, as he frequently tells us, he was once a young man very like Juan who entered life with the same expectations and passed through the same experiences, we would account for his two opinions as a simple irony expressing the views of an old hand at life on the simplemindedness of youth and the ridiculous pretensions of the righteous. But one opinion never does cancel out its opposite in *Don Juan,* for the first opinion always comes back to haunt the second, and a third appears to qualify its predecessors. What we are faced with is not a simple irony, which involves only two points, what seems and what is, but an endlessly complicating ambiguity, a series of perspectives, each one of which is as true as any other. In the end, the narrator recognizes that all these opposites tend to cancel one another out, and we are left with the possibility that rather than having one, or two or three opinions, he actually may have "none at all."

But before we come to the nihilistic possibility, it is, I believe, possible to organize to some degree the variety of views expressed through the voice of the narrator and the events of the plot. Kenneth Burke in his *Attitudes Toward History*[5] has called the various literary categories, or genres, "strategies for living." Tragedy, epic, comedy, and satire cease in his view to be *merely* literary forms and become fundamental ways of thinking about, organizing, and managing the vast, confusing swirl of life. Thus, in Burke's view, a theology, a psychology, a form of government, a philosophical system, or a game, as well as a work of literature, may be termed comic or tragic—though Burke's literary orientation suggests that he still believes that literature provides the most complete and subtle statements of the different "strategies." Northrop Frye in *Anatomy of Criticism* supports Burke's position by designating the major genres as *mythoi* and arguing that they are not imitations of life but organizational forms imposed on experience which express man's deepest hopes and fears. The more cheerful literary kinds, comedy and romance, are described in the

5. Rev. ed. (Los Altos, Cal., 1959).

terms of William Blake, as "the forms of human desire," and the more somber kinds, tragedy and satire, "the world that desire totally rejects." No single genre, in the view of these critics, has any absolute validity as an image of the world; each is a fundamental pattern of thought which can be used to give shape and form to any group of experiences, historical events, or perceptions.

Don Juan puts this critical view in dramatic terms, for the bewildering number of contradictory opinions which the poem offers through the voice of the narrator and the actions of its *dramatis personae* resolve ultimately into three senses of life, comic, satiric, and tragic. The fact of life in the poem, the reality of the world, is the constant flux, the onward flow of all things under the pressure of the mysterious Promethean fire to their disappearance in the great sea of ocean. This is existence, and man willy-nilly participates in this flow, is one with it. He may swim on with it joyfully and vigorously, as Juan most often does, or he may resist it and seek to maintain the status quo, as the various political and social reactionaries in the poem do, but in the end everything is swept on in time to become as "indistinct as water is in water."[6] But man, as the poem often notes, is a curious creature who has a mind as well as a body and feelings; and while the body and feelings cannot escape being subject to mutability, the mind can reflect upon this experience and evaluate it in different ways. It is this aspect of man which is dramatized in the person of the narrator. As a result, we get a series of perspectives on the various, plentiful, turbulent world of the poem, and these perspectives, correspond, as I have said, to the major literary genres.

It is clear that the poet it also aware of the possibility of organizing life in an epic pattern, since he speaks regularly of the traditional devices of the heroic poem. There are even some remnants of true epic: the vast sweep of the world portrayed and the occasional serious uses of the grand style to describe some heroic act or the great powers that move through all being. But on the whole, the epic is invoked only for purposes of mockery.

6. *Antony and Cleopatra*, IV.9.10–11.

And while Byron occasionally uses the mock-epic technique as Pope and Dryden did to provide a standard of life and manners against which the shabbiness of the present can be measured, he ordinarily realizes a tendency always latent in the mock-epic to mock not only the unheroic present but the pretentiousness of the epic form itself. If its elevated view of man and its orderly view of the world define by contrast the self-seeking, stupidity, and confusion of the contemporary, then these latter-day realities raise inevitably the question of whether man and his world were not always so; and when the insights into reality are extended to cover the past in such a way that the ancient heroes and the gods become brutes and tyrants, then the epic form is itself discredited.

Let us look first at the comic parts of the poem, since it is necessary to understand the true nature of comedy in order to separate it from satire in a meaningful way.

III

COMEDY

The terms "comedy" and "satire" are often used interchangeably, and many critics regard satire as simply a darker form of comedy. If fools begin to shade into villains, if idiocy begins to assume monstrous proportions, and if the poet's wit becomes acid, then according to this view we have satire. The belief that satire is only a more somber form of comedy derives from a negative approach to comedy which was stabilized in such works as Meredith's *Essay on Comedy* and Bergson's *De Rire.* Both of these works, particularly Bergson's, are extremely useful for understanding comedy, but they do not deal with the comic; they treat the anticomic. That is, instead of exploring those positive values which comedy celebrates, these works deal almost entirely with those characters, actions, and ways of speaking which comic writers use to define the beliefs and manners which hinder the realization of the values of comedy. It is as if a definition of tragedy were based on a study of Creon or Iago.

Only in recent years have critics begun to seek out and define the positive values which are embodied in the heroes of comedy, which control the comic world, and which eventually triumph over foolishness and misfortune. Susanne Langer calls the comic sense of life a "realization in direct feeling of what sets organic nature apart from inorganic: self-preservation, self-restoration, functional tendency, purpose. Life is teleological, the rest of nature is, apparently, mechanical."[7] This drive toward life is clever in defending itself, in accommodating changed circumstances, in seizing opportunities, and in "maintaining a vital balance amid the alien and impartial chances of the world."

Where Langer sees the essence of the comic residing in the individual living thing's successful struggle with its chancy environment, Helen Gardner offers a longer perspective and thereby enlarges the scene of comedy to include more than the single hero and his immediate world:

> The great symbol of pure comedy is marriage by which the world is renewed, and its endings are always instinct with a sense of fresh beginnings. Its rhythm is the rhythm of the life of mankind, which goes on and renews itself as the life of nature does. The rhythm of tragedy, on the other hand, is the rhythm of the individual life which comes to a close, and its great symbol is death. . . . A comedy, which contrives an end which is not implicit in its beginning, and which is, in itself, a fresh beginning, is an image of the flow of human life. The young wed, so that they may become in turn the older generation, whose children will wed, and so on, as long as the world lasts. Comedy pictures what Rosalind calls "the full stream of the world."[8]

Miss Gardner goes on to remark that the world of comedy is not always the hostile, challenging place Miss Langer pictures. It is a

---

7. *Feeling and Form* (New York, 1953), pp. 327–28.
8. *"As You Like It,"* in *More Talking of Shakespeare,* ed. John Garrett (London, 1959), p. 21.

world of surprises and unplanned coincidences, but these "changes, chances, and surprises" present "fresh opportunities for happiness and laughter," and since life is filled with good chance, events are not irreversible, which means that foolish mortals are often "mercifully saved from being as wicked as they meant to be."

Where Langer and Gardner concentrate on the sense of life, the action, which underlies comedy, Northrop Frye defines the symbols, characters, and plot arrangements which give concrete form to the comic sense of life in literary comedy. He shows that the regular movement of comedy is from "a society controlled by habit, ritual bondage, arbitrary law and the older characters to a society controlled by youth and pragmatic freedom."[9] He also describes in detail those staples of comedy which realize both the comic and anticomic values: the young lovers, the rich and adamant old father, the "blocking forces" or fools who oppose the realization of the vital forces, the twist in the plot which brings unexpected success, and the party, feast, or dance which celebrates the final triumph of life.

These modern theories of comedy allow us to see the relationship of comedies as diverse as those of Aristophanes, the Italian street farces, the polished comedy of Molière and Congreve, Shakespeare's romantic comedies, the talky comedy of Shaw, and even the grotesquely comic theater of the absurd. They direct our attention not to Witwoud and Petulant, but to Mirabell and Millamant; not to Mr. Shandy and Slawkenbergius, but to Uncle Toby and that disconcerted Tristram who can never make any sense of his life or write fast enough to keep up with it.

Rosalind's "full stream of life" is a happy description of the ceaseless flow of all existence which is at the center of *Don Juan,* and the comic view of life dictates plunging into the current and moving vigorously with it, enjoying the surge of life, meeting whatever mischances occur with that "brainy opportunism" of which Langer speaks, enjoying the immediate pleasures which life offers, and merging at last, without regret, into the great

9. *Anatomy of Criticism,* p. 169.

cycles through which all nature passes. The fact that the poem is unfinished saves Don Juan from the difficult test of merging with life, but otherwise his is, in the main, a comical existence, and his adventures, with frequent encouraging remarks from the narrator, carry the comic theme of the poem.

Byron deliberately chose to narrate the youthful adventures of his hero before he arrived at the cynicism and hardened depravity which qualify his zest for life in the older legend and the versions of Tirso de Molina, Molière, and Mozart. Byron's Juan is the pure embodiment of all those virtues which comedy shows as the key to successful life. These virtues are in origin natural, innate in man, though they are refined and improved upon in some varieties of comedy—principally Shakespeare's—by the order, still natural in origin, of society. Juan is the very essence of the natural, as the Romantics understood that term. He is lively and vital,

> A little curly-headed, good-for-nothing,
>   And mischief-making monkey from his birth.
> (I, 25)

As a youth he is tall, slim, lithe, and handsome—the human form of the beautiful and well-proportioned world of comedy. He possesses all the natural virtues—courage, quick wit, passionate feelings, uprightness, frankness, warmth—and all the natural appetites for love, food, and pleasure. These instincts are not destructive in him but lead to beneficent actions, to enjoyment, pity, love, concern for others.

Juan's heart is sound enough, and he does have sense enough to come in out of the rain, but by academic standards his mind is somewhat deficient. This is perfectly proper in the world of comedy where, since truth is obvious and value apparent, the analytic intellect can lead only to confusion and loss.[10] Occasionally, Juan does attempt deep thought, but his nature always saves

10. There are comedies in which intelligence is one of the dominant qualities of the hero—Shaw's plays, for example, or Congreve's—but even in this kind of comedy the quality of mind celebrated is natural and immediate, an

him, as in this effort to probe the cosmos and construct a meta-physic:

> He thought about himself, and the whole earth,
>   Of man the wonderful, and of the stars,
> And how the deuce they ever could have birth;
>   And then he thought of earthquakes, and of wars,
> How many miles the moon might have in girth,
>   Of air-balloons, and of the many bars
> To perfect knowledge of the boundless skies;—
> And then he thought of Donna Julia's eyes.
>
> (I, 92)

Juan's instincts are too clear and direct to allow him to lose himself in useless theoretical speculation and to forget the real and meaningful, a woman's beautiful eyes. The healthy limitations of his mind are realized by his speech, or more precisely, his failure to speak very often. His usual silence is emphasized by the loquaciousness of those around him, particularly the garrulous narrator who can never stop talking. Without question Juan is at his best when he neither tries to think or speak, for thinking always involves him in ludicrous tangles, and his few speeches are either commonplace or hopelessly romantic.

Nor does Juan learn very much from his experiences. By the end of the poem he has become a suave young diplomat, more courteous and formal than he was as a boy, but no more profound and still oblivious of those sad realities of life with which the narrator, who has traveled Juan's path before him, is forced to live. It is not only that Juan lacks the ability to organize and schematize life, but chiefly that he lacks that mental function which is the source of so much of the narrator's suffering: memory. Where the narrator cannot forget his loves, his youth, and his images of men who are now only dust and names, Juan's regrets

---

extended common sense, rather than the profound and brooding thought of tragedy.

for yesterday last only one intense moment and then are gone as yesterday ceases to be. He suffers horribly when first separated from Donna Julia and vows,

> Sooner shall Earth resolve itself to sea,
> Than I resign thine image, oh, my fair!
>   (II, 19)

But the image fades quickly enough as he becomes sea-sick, struggles for survival in an open boat, and then finds another love. He never returns to Julia, and in fact never mentions her again. Even more curious is his relinquishment of his most intense love, the Greek girl, Haidée. Since Juan is wounded and carried off to slavery before Haidée dies, he never knows of her death. Yet despite his unusual grief for this loss—it lasts a week or so— he never tries to return to Lambro's island again, but drifts onward to further adventures and new loves.[11] Juan is a comic hero of the romantic variety, a Ferdinand rather than a Falstaff, but his virtues still enable him to live that life of immediacy which can always be described in somewhat cruder terms by a more earthy comic approach to life. When Juan and an Englishman named Acres are chained together in a Turkish slave market, Juan announces in his inflated style: not for the

> present doom
> I mourn, but for the past;—I loved a maid.
>   (V, 18)

To which Acres replies that he understands, for he too cried when his first wife died, and again when the second ran away, but that he had run away from the third.

While Juan continues to take himself quite seriously, never quite seeing the wonderfully efficient way he manages to stay alive and happy in a constantly changing world, he is constantly

---

11. In XV, 58, there is a comparison of Aurora Raby as a gem with Haidée as a flower, to the latter's advantage, but it is not clear whether the comparison is made in Juan's mind or that of the narrator. At any rate, we are not aware in reading the poem of Juan cherishing the memory of Haidée.

being undercut by a comic sense of life more basic and honest than his own. The narrator and characters like Acres know that, since all things pass, there is no point in worrying or of taking yourself and your passions too seriously. At the same time, of course, Juan's delicacy and refinement in taking his pleasures call into question the lower comic values, and in this way the tone is complicated even within the comic portions of the poem. But whatever form the comic values may take—pure love or pure pleasure—the comic way of life remains a natural, unthinking instinct for what is good and a freedom in moving with the full stream of life.

For this way of life to be workable, it is necessary that the comic hero live in a world friendly to him and suitable to his virtues. The stream of life to which he commits himself cannot carry him to disaster but must cast him in the way of pleasure and joy. Viewed from one angle, Juan does live in a beneficent world. He often lands in temporary trouble, but bad luck is only momentary and usually turns out to be good luck in disguise. If he is wrecked at sea by a ferocious storm, he is thrown up on an island and into the arms of a beautiful princess. Sold into slavery, his good looks immediately attract the attention of the Sultan's wife, and in no time he finds himself in a harem with a multitude of beautiful women and in bed with a lovely harem girl. Tied in a sack and thrown into the Bosporus, he miraculously turns up in the Russian army and soon becomes the lover of Catherine the Great. While Juan's natural virtues, his courage and his physical attractiveness, contribute to his good fortune, such virtues would be of little use in a world which did not favor those who give themselves to it.

Furthermore, if lack of introspection, a poor memory, and a mind which has very limited analytical powers are to be valuable assets, they must be located in a world which is not only good enough to be trusted but of such a nature that any attempt to understand its operations through reason be futile and ludicrous. The relativism characteristic of *Don Juan* creates just such a world. Variety, plenitude, and mutability combine to make ridiculous

all received philosophies and religions, to destroy any belief in history and progress, and to make laughable any attempts to speculate on and systematize the workings of the universe. And why worry about it, says comedy. Everything may change, but nothing can be done about it; and the world as immediately sensed is full of joy and pleasure. Women's eyes flash beauty, wine excites wonderfully, the pulse beats, torrents crash down mountainsides, and the whole spectacle of nature is a satisfying display of the richness, power, and springing vitality of the world. The over-all somberness of *Don Juan* often obscures this romantic and comic joy in life, man, and nature; but it is regularly present, and it validates both Juan's trust in the life known to his senses and feelings and his thoughtless commitment of himself to whatever chances the world offers.

But though the comic world is essentially good, it always allows for forces which attempt to pervert this good. The way of the world is inevitable, however, and these anti-life forces have no real chance of success. Foolishness, not evil, constitutes the opposition in comedy. Since in *Don Juan* the comic way is to give oneself to life and move with it through change, foolishness is necessarily any attempt to stay life, to deny its pleasures, and to cramp it into any rigid, permanent form, a philosophical system or a marriage bed. The poem is filled with characters who attempt to do just this: Donna Inez and her efforts to educate Juan by means of sermons and homilies which try to stifle his natural impulses and curb his passions; the stiff, placid, aristocratic ladies and gentlemen who gather at Norman Abbey, scarcely able to breathe within their stays and their rigid sense of propriety; the Turkish sultan who buys, locks away, and guards elaborately the numerous but unused beauties of his harem. The narrator, in his digressions, provides a host of parallels: the art of the Lake poets, which imposes ludicrous boundaries on human nature; Coleridge's metaphysics, which pretends to enfold the mysteries of the universe; Plato's philosophy of the ideal, which insists that the physical is unreal and that the passions can be controlled; the ridiculous attempts of tyranny through the ages to enslave men and contain

their drive toward political freedom; the laughable pretensions of polite society to order and bottle up man's natural appetites. But restraint and enfolding are also treated as inescapable realities of life which take such forms as physical ageing which stiffens and binds the once-free body, the tendency of the mind to remember what once was and therefore to suffer in the painful grasp of memory, the inevitable movement of time toward decay and death, that ultimate form of containment and stillness which contains all other forms of enslavement.[12]

The attempts to impose bonds on life and the hero's successful escapes from each of the snares constitute the comic plot of *Don Juan.* Juan's pedantic tutors try to eradicate his passions, and Donna Julia's careful parents try to lock her into a marriage with a wealthy old man; but when the two young people meet, their love flares and destroys all barriers to pleasure. Caught in her bedroom, muffled under the bedclothes, his exit barred by an

---

12. One difficulty with most criticism of comedy is that it approaches the genre on only one of its many levels and assumes that the values celebrated at this level are the absolute values of comedy. In recent years, for example, the most familiar argument has been that comedy is "social," and that it always shows the triumph of society over the individual. In one way this is true, for in comedy at the same time that the necessity of individual pleasure and immediate enjoyment of life are stressed, the value of the particular individual is reduced in numerous ways. What finally counts, however, is the continuity of *life,* and if the individual and his society serve that value, as they do in many forms of comedy, then they are championed; but if they hinder the continuity of life, then they are the enemies of the comic spirit and their destruction is inevitable. Most English comedy, particularly Shakespearean, has shown social arrangements as the best way of funneling man's natural energies into ways which further life and bring him into working agreement with those forces which make for prosperity and continuity. But there are other kinds of comedy—the typical *commedia dell'arte* type of farce, for example—which show all social forms, particularly marriage, as hindrances to the life spirit. The stories in Boccaccio's *Decameron* provide a catalogue of the many levels on which the fundamental comic values can be expressed, ranging from bawdy treatments of the joys and rewards of illicit love and roguery, through stories in which it is shown that man's raw energies are self-destructive if not controlled by society, to serene, *Tempest*-like acquiescences to the great stream of life and time which transcend immediate pleasure and social order.

enraged husband, Juan, naked, nearly murders the old man and his servants to break free. Finding the garden gate, the last barrier to freedom, locked, Juan opens it and then relocks it from the outside, leaving the prisoners of society inside. Becalmed on the sea in an open boat, most of the survivors of a shipwreck turn cannibals and perish as a result, but Juan plunges into the sea and, aided by the current, swims to an island where he finds Haidée and the full enjoyment of natural love. But even on this Edenic island, restraints exist, and Haidée's papa, to give him his comic epithet, returns suddenly, has Juan bound, and ships him off to a Turkish slave market. From here on Juan's life is a continued series of escapes from a variety of bonds, political, physical, social, and amorous which the world attempts to impose upon him.

While the comic plot requires that its hero have certain virtues for success, he is never as responsible as the tragic hero is for his fate. Helen Gardner notes that,

> Comic plots are made up of changes, chances, and surprises. Coincidences can destroy tragic feeling: they heighten comic feeling. It is absurd to complain in poetic comedy of improbable encounters and characters arriving pat on their cue, of sudden changes of mind and mood by which an enemy becomes a friend. Puck who creates and presides over the central comedy of *A Midsummer Night's Dream,* speaks for all comic writers and lovers of true comedy when he says:
>
> > And those things do best please me
> > That befall preposterously.
>
> ... There are no "events" in comedy; there are only "happenings." Events are irreversible and comedy is not concerned with the irreversible, which is why it must always shun the presentation of death.[13]

This is to say that comedy envisions a world which is not only good, or at least potentially so if men only have the sense to recognize it,

13. *"As You Like It,"* p. 22.

but one which works unsystematically, in which there is no traceable chain of cause and effect. Furthermore, it is a world which quite surprisingly moves men without their volition toward their destiny. If character makes plot in tragedy, the world often manages it in comedy, and the *deus ex machina,* coincidence, sudden reversals—a fortunate shift of the wind or the chance discovery of a lost will—are the devices by which its workings are manifested. To express this chancy working of nature in comedy, we often say that the comic hero is lucky, and certainly Juan is lucky in every way. Even his personal virtues are the unsought gifts of nature, and throughout the poem good chance plays a crucial part in his life. If his luck runs out in Spain, the sea carries him to a magical island; if he is sold to the Turks, he just happens to find his way into a harem. Perhaps nothing in the poem makes clearer the role that fortune plays in shaping Juan's plot than the absence of any explanation of how he gets out of trouble at the end of Canto VI. Gulbeyaz, the Sultan's favorite wife, has discovered that her pleasures with Juan have been anticipated by one of the ladies of the harem, Dudù, and wild with rage she calls all the guilty parties before her. The usual punishment, we are told, for such malefactors is to tie them in bags—another form of containment—and throw them into the Bosporus. But we are never told what actually happens. The narrator turns to a description of the siege of Ismail, "trusting Juan will escape the fishes." When next seen, however, Juan and his party are coming up to join the Russians. Good fortune has become such a commonplace in his life that the details of its workings no longer need to be described.

Where tragedy has usually been limited in critical theory and in practice to the portrayal of narrow spaces and short periods of time[14]—to dramatize the tragic limitation of "world enough

---

14. The neoclassic unities of time and place prescribed for tragedy were in their strict application little more than the rules of pedants, but they do contain the shadows of genuine perception about the nature of the tragic vision: the warriors of the *Iliad* trapped on their limited battlefield before Troy and forced into "the narrow place between the ships," Prometheus

and time"—comedy often chooses for its scene larger spaces and longer periods of time in order to realize its long-range view of human affairs. Despite early trials, life turns out well in the end for individuals in comedy, and if some individuals are unluckily sacrificed, their children survive and life goes on. There are exceptions, of course, but where tragedy usually contains a sense of the shortness of life and the confinement of choice, comedy manages to convey, most often, a sense of openness in space and time. In *The Winter's Tale* sixteen years pass as Time speaks; in *The Skin of Our Teeth,* the Ice Age, the Great Deluge, and life in suburban New Jersey are collapsed into the same scenes in order to bring on stage the full range of human history; and in *Tristram Shandy,* search as he will, poor Tristram can find no beginning and no end to his biography. The movement of comedy is characteristically from "Once upon a time" to "and they lived happily ever after"; and even if the actual story is quite short, its outline is so traditional—after the first scene we know roughly what will happen —that it takes on a timeless quality. In the end, as always before,

> Jack shall have Jill,
> Naught shall go ill,
> The man shall have his mare again, and all shall be well.[15]

The mere length of *Don Juan* and the multitude of adventures it contains create this long-range view. Juan rambles over all Europe, going from love to shipwreck to prison to war to court and back to love again. As he moves through his spacious world, time takes no toll of him. He grows less impulsive, but at the end of the poem he is still young and passionate and ready for further adventures. In himself, like a figure of myth rather than a mere man, he contains the timeless energy and appetite of the human

chained to his rock by Force and Violence, Lear bound upon his wheel of fire. These images of limited physical space express the limits of choice and freedom imposed by life and his own mind on tragic man.

15. *A Midsummer Night's Dream,* III.2.461–63.

race.[16] Byron suggests in several places that he plans to reduce Juan to marriage, disillusionment, and old age, but he can never bring himself to do it. Juan's ultimate escape from the poet's plans may be a result of the accident of Byron's death, but the adventure on which the poem ends is a climactic comic image of all the tests Juan has earlier endured, and once again his vitality and felt sense of life triumph. The scene is Norman Abbey, the country house of the Amundeville family, where Juan has gone as the member of a house party. Here, all is restraint and confinement. The water of the artificial lake is still, the skies overcast and gray, the landscape autumnal and dreary, the castle—a "Gothic Babel"—heavy and earthbound because its many dissimilar parts and styles lack any soaring quality and life-giving unity. The upper-class English men and women of the party are equally lifeless. Their clothes and manners are stiff and smooth, their vitality smothered in a fashionable ennui, their moral spots varnished over, and their only interests dinner and sleep. Beauty here is completely self-possessed, and Byron describes the great beauties of the party as locked in ice or buried deep within the polished surfaces of a gem. Whenever life does burst forth in this society it is destroyed by gossip and ostracism—as Byron had once been destroyed—or is brutally restrained. Two poachers are caught in huge steel traps and then imprisoned; a young unmarried girl with child, a "poacher upon Nature's manor," is made to wear a scarlet coat and hauled for sentencing before a Justice of the Peace.

This concentration of confinement and tyranny is further focused in the ghost of a Monk who has haunted the castle since Henry VIII dissolved the monastery and gave the lands to the Amundevilles. Juan and the ghostly Monk are worthy antagonists,

---

16. The gap between the attributes necessary for the completely comic existence and those possessed by real men is stressed at the beginning of Canto I, where Byron finds real heroes, living and dead, unable to stand the test of time. They live, fight, suffer, are disgraced and then forgotten; so the poet is forced to turn to romance for his hero and "take our ancient friend Don Juan."

and their combat raises to the mythic level the comic struggle which has heretofore been presented realistically. On one side we have the ultimate comic hero whose blazing vitality cannot weaken or be entrapped; on the other side the ultimate comic antagonist, the very spirit of the anti-vital. The ghostly form of the Monk makes him completely bodiless, and his monkishness is the absolute form of asceticism and a strict, religious ordering of life. His ceaseless search for revenge on those who have robbed him is the final extension of that perversion of life to a sterile emptiness which overtakes those characters in *Don Juan* who cramp their natural instincts too severely. He walks ordinarily in the portrait gallery where those other ghosts, The Amundeville ancestors, stiff and hypocritical enough in their own lifetimes, have been finally frozen in rigid, respectable, lifeless positions by the painter's art. The Monk haunts and curses the marriage beds of the Amundevilles, he attends their childbirths and tries to blight the children, he appears gloating at their deaths. He is, in short, the very spirit of death, and it is with death in some of its less obvious forms that Juan has struggled since childhood.

Juan's encounters with the Ghost are handled in the manner of a Gothic Tale, and it is impossible to consider the Ghost as a real threat to Juan's life. But on the symbolic level the struggle is to the death. The full force of the danger is carried by the language and imagery: when Juan sees the Ghost he is "petrified," and he gazes

> upon it with a stare,
> Yet could not speak or move; but, on its base
> As stands a statue, stood: he felt his hair
> Twine like a knot of snakes around his face.
> (XVI, 23)

After several appearances, the "sable Friar in his solemn hood" comes to fetch Juan from his bed. The door creaks on his entrance and seems to say, "Lasciate ogni speranza, voi, ch'entrate!" and the words over the entrance to Dante's Hell sum up all the many forms of damnation in *Don Juan*. Though terrified of this "dark-

ening darkness," Juan moves to fight once more, and as he advances, the Monk retreats until pressed against a courtyard wall.
Juan's hand reaches forward and presses a "hard but glowing
bust." The sable frock and dreary cowl fall away to reveal,

> In full, voluptuous, but *not o'er*grown bulk,
> The phantom of her frolic Grace—Fitz-Fulke!

These are the last lines of the poem, though Byron may have
written a few stanzas more, and while they have a realistic explanation—the Duchess of Fitz-Fulke is a rather forward beauty
who has been eyeing Juan for some time and has taken advantage
of the story of the ghost to get to his chamber unobserved—they
are at the same time a climactic image of the comic triumph of
life over death. The illusion of a pale, bloodless world moving
toward sterility and death is transformed by courage, vitality, and
good chance into a living, breathing, and satisfying immediacy.

Unfortunately, the majority of readers do not go past the Haidée
episode or Juan's Turkish captivity, and for that reason overesti-
mate the pessimistic qualities of the poem. But *Don Juan* as
Byron left it ends on an affirmation of the goodness of life, and
the entire poem is thus framed by a comic view of experience.

IV

SATIRE

The constant juxtaposition of Juan the comic hero and the
older, more cynical narrator dramatizes the fact that, however
attractive and even necessary the nature of reality makes the
comic acceptance of a mysterious, varying, onward-flowing world,
it is finally impossible for *man* to live and accept existence in
this fashion. To do so requires youth, good digestion, a certain
innocent trust, and perhaps even a legendary status such as Don
Juan's; and the older, very human narrator, worn out in body
and feelings, keeps the fact of human degeneration and mortality
constantly on stage with the ageless Juan. Furthermore, comic
existence eliminates another very human faculty, that of rational,

analytic thought. The word frequently applied to Juan, "thought-less," is, taken in its best sense, the crucial term of comedy, which is finally an acceptance of one's own nature and the world without undue puzzling over complex moral problems or trying to under-stand fully the mystery of life and nature.

Satire, on the other hand, is intensely, persistently rational in its approach to life—which may go a long way toward accounting for the characteristic distrust of the form. Its consistent, uncon-cealed use of rhetoric, its overt contriving of effects, its regular use of such poetic devices and schemes as mock-epic or beast fable establish the presence behind even the most impersonal or the most passionate satire—Juvenal or Swift in their more titanic moments—of a shrewd, icy mind, carefully calculating poetic strategy, selecting details, and manipulating materials for a de-sired end. The emphasis on rationality is increased by satire's claim to deal only with literal reality,

> to show things really as they are,
> Not as they ought to be.
>
> (XIII, 40)

This claim to objectivity is usually supported by avoidance of poetic diction in favor of ordinary speech—even slang at times— by references to contemporary customs, places, and objects, and by direct discussion of living rather than fictitious personalities. The satirist's first occupation is the revelation of the opposition between what seems to be and what is, the perception and ex-posure of the sadist underneath the solemn manner and scarlet robes of the hanging judge, the animal underneath the silk gown, paint, and refined manner of the lady of fashion. Satire is composed of a series of these perceptions and demonstrations of the gap be-tween appearance and reality, each one a flash of the probing intellect. The ultimate rational method for summing up and understanding the totality of existence is statistics, and satire pro-vides a statistical image of the world. It does not present a few characters and a few events, as do comedy and tragedy, but ranges over a vast number of persons, objects, and actions. If you don't

believe that the world is a mess, says the satirist, look at the next
ten people who come down this street we just happen to be standing on, look at the fantastic jumble of styles and buildings crowded
together in this city, look at the corruption in the courts, the
venality in government, the stupidity in the schools—and he
provides us with a brief glimpse of each.

Don Juan is not, of course, witless or amoral, but his wit is of
the commonsense variety, and his morals, which have their source
in his nature, are instinctive and uncodified. His life is spontaneous,
and mind does not intervene between his perceptions of the world
and his understanding of it. But the older, disillusioned narrator
knows that the "sweetness" of life does not reside in life itself
but in the spirit of the young man who perceives it.

> No more—no more—Oh! never more on me
>   The freshness of the heart can fall like dew,
> Which out of all the lovely things we see
>   Extracts emotions beautiful and new,
> Hived in our bosoms like the bag o' the bee.
>   Think'st thou the honey with those objects grew?
> Alas! 't was not in them, but in thy power
> To double even the sweetness of a flower.
>
>   (I, 214)

The narrator's heart can no longer be his "sole world," his "universe"; and his head, his acquired "deal of judgment," reveals
that the comic view of a world in which things always turn out
for the best in the long run doesn't square with reality. Juan
himself is not heavily attacked, but when he is viewed objectively
and analytically, some most uncomic facts appear. He is often a
ridiculous poseur, an ever-faithful lover who forgets the woman
once she is out of sight, a fiery creature of spirit who cannot bear
to miss a meal, and a lucky booby who has not the simple sense
to see the dreadful realities around him or to realize that his life
is saved again and again not by his own virtue but by the most
miraculous, and ultimately ludicrous, chance. The criticism of
Juan deepens when the narrator reminds us that greathearted

and greatly loving though Juan may be, he, without the slightest awareness that he does so, leaves a trail of bodies behind him in his comic adventures. Commenting on the carnage Juan's blazing spirit creates at the siege of Ismail, the narrator remarks wryly

> But Juan was quite "a broth of a boy,"
>   A thing of impulse and a child of song;
> Now swimming in the sentiment of joy,
>   Or the *sensation* (if that phrase seem wrong),
> And afterward, if he must needs destroy,
>   In such good company as always throng
> To battles, sieges, and that kind of pleasure,
> No less delighted to employ his leisure.
>
> (VIII, 24)

The attacks on Juan are just heavy and frequent enough to call into question his way of life, but behind him the narrator opens up not the bubbling, racing, opportunity-filled world of comedy Juan thinks he lives in, but the heavy, hypocritical, confused world of satire where men seem determined to destroy themselves. Byron's contemporaries, shocked by his savage attacks on such living personalities as Lady Byron, Castlereagh, and the poet Southey, considered this "filthy and impious poem" nothing but a satire:

> Impiously railing against his God—madly and meanly disloyal to his Sovereign and his country—and abruptly outraging all the best feelings of female honour, affection, and confidence—how small a part of chivalry is that which remains to the descendant of the Byrons—a gloomy vizor and a deadly weapon! [17]

The *Blackwood's* reviewer goes on to put his finger on the immediate source of satire in the poem when he describes Byron as a "cool, unconcerned fiend, laughing with a detestable glee over the whole of the better and worse elements of which human life

17. "Remarks on *Don Juan*," *Blackwood's*, August 1819.

is composed—treating well nigh with equal derision the most pure of virtues, and the most odious of vices—dead alike to the beauty of the one, and the deformity of the other—a mere heartless despiser of that frail but noble humanity . . ." The impossibility of discriminating between what the world styles vice and what it styles virtue is Byron's immediate satiric subject, and the reviewer's impossible smugness, his calm assurance that, despite a few frailties, all legal governments are worthy respect, all religions religious, all ladies honest and chaste, all gentlemen honorable and noble, is a perfect instance of just what Byron was immediately attacking.

Byron admits in Canto II, Stanza 119, that "One should not rail without a decent cause," and in words which seem to recall the *Blackwood's* review he explicitly states his own decent cause:

> How differently the World would men behold!
> How oft would Vice and Virtue places change!
> The new world would be nothing to the old,
> If some Columbus of the moral seas
> Would show mankind their Souls' antipodes.
>
> What "antres vast and deserts idle" then,
> Would be discovered in the human soul!
> What icebergs in the hearts of mighty men,
> With self-love in the centre as their Pole!
> What Anthropophagi are nine of ten
> Of those who hold the kingdoms in control!
> Were things but only called by their right name,
> Caesar himself would be ashamed of Fame.
>
> (XIV, 101–02)

Byron was, as satirist, that "Columbus of the moral seas" sailing to the underside of his social world to reveal the shabby truths underlying the pretenses with which men cover themselves. His rhetoric and the events of the story are shaped to "call by their right name" the perfect lovers who in fact seek only to control one another, the learned doctors who practice only for their fees, the

grave politicians who rule for profit and because they fear those beneath them, the eloquent poets who write out of confusion of mind and to increase their sense of self-importance. Byron's keen sight sees that men who profess to love one another will resort to cannibalism to live another day, and that the more beautiful ideals which man so prides himself on yield always to such physical realities as seasickness, hunger, fear, and lust. Man is, after all,

> a carnivorous production,
> And must have meals, at least one meal a day;
> He cannot live, like woodcocks, upon suction,
> But, like the shark and tiger, must have prey.
>
> (II, 67)

The point of these attacks is not that man is "a carnivorous production," but that he tries so ridiculously to pretend that he is not. In the Preface to Cantos VI, VII, and VIII, Byron quotes with approval Voltaire's remark, "Plus les mœurs sont dépravés, plus les expressions deviennent mesurées; on croit regagner en langage ce qu'on a perdu en vertu." This compulsive hypocrisy is the most evident quality of the world which satire constructs, and the first activity of the satirist is exposing it. The rhetoric and events of *Don Juan,* while they allow Byron to develop the comic progression of his hero, are at the same time perfectly suited for revealing the sham of civilized life. The staggering rhythms, the jingling rhymes, the savage irony, the dreadful concluding couplet of the ottava-rima stanza which so regularly deflates the pretenses built up in the preceding six lines, the devices of mock epic and mock romance, all these open up the disguises of respectability and show men their "souls' antipodes." The events of the poem are constructed, as is usually the case in satire, to permit the satirist to reveal the truth not only about individual man but about his crucial institutions and social arrangements. We are given a close look at conventional marriage, at the activities of lawyers and the working of their law, at the education of a young man, at romantic love, at heroic war, at politics, and at upper-class social life. In every case the elaborate dressings are stripped

away and revealed as only pretty covers for more basic and less attractive passions, lust, fear, hatred, envy, the desire for power.

But the perception, no matter how perfectly executed, that man and his institutions are shams is really so rudimentary that it would not by itself constitute that "decent cause" which Byron makes the condition for railing. Great satires have at their center not merely some observation about stupidity or pride, but some profound, though not necessarily complex, grasp of the nature of reality, things as they truly are. The dunces of satire are those who, knowingly or unknowingly, pervert this natural bent of life. We have already seen that at the center of *Don Juan* is a realized sense of life as constant flow and change in which all things, man, society, civilization, and nature are swept forward by their own pressure into new conditions of being and ultimately to oblivion. This is an unusual view of reality for a satirist to hold—Byron is one of the very few romantic satirists—but it is finally the key to his satire. In every case, what he holds up to ridicule is some attempt to restrain life, to bind and force it into some narrow, permanent form. This is the burden of the attack on the Lake Poets, who, however unjust the charge, are treated as dunces not because they traffic in mystifying metaphysics and seek jobs in the Excise, but because they are *lake* poets, because they are inlanders who try to contain man in their poems while knowing nothing of man's "fiery dust" and never having seen the "sea of ocean," that "vast, salt, dread, eternal deep."[18] Castlereagh and the legitimists who controlled Europe after the Congress of Vienna are attacked not just because they are self-seeking frauds, but because they try to restrain on the political level that urgent movement toward freedom which is natural to man. These politicians have

> just enough of talent, and no more,
> To lengthen fetters by another fixed,
> And offer poison long already mixed.
> (Dedication, 12)

18. Byron develops the limitations of the Lake Poets in III, 98 ff. and in VIII, 10.

Older forms of tyranny in the Sultan's Turkey and Catherine's Russia are attacked for the same reason. Beliefs in material progress, philosophy, all forms of poetry, theories of history, religions, and monumental statuary come in for their share of ridicule because they seek to contain the uncontainable, to give fixed shape and deadly order to what is always shifting and changing.

The kind of bondage which is ridiculed in these institutions and activities also appears in the lives of the characters of the story. Young women are bound into marriage with older men against their desires; children are forbidden the exercise of their natural instincts and interests by a religious and scholastic training which seeks to make them "still and steady" by means of instruction in the "dead languages"; females formed by nature for life and love are turned into narrow prudes and bluestockings; men are imprisoned and chained together in slave gangs and on galley benches; women are denied free choice and locked in carefully guarded harems; subjects are treated as personal possessions by rulers; and imperious lovers tyrannize over one another. Hypocrisy, the first object of attack, is but a special, though most virulent form of unnatural restraint which buries man's real nature under layers of pretense.

The action of binding is also woven deep into the poem's imagery and details. Wherever life flows men attempt to dam it up and control it: Juan as a young boy is forbidden to read anything "loose" which hints at the "continuation of the species"; a proud, aristocratic family achieves its lifelessness by breeding "in and in"; a handsome young woman's eye "supresses half its fire" and her soul is "chasten'd down"; when she struggles against illicit longings she vows she will never "disgrace the ring she wore"; a passive life leaves the blood "dull in motion"; an outraged husband finding a lover with his wife, grapples "to detain the foe." Byron had a genius for finding and effectively placing words closely associated with traditional social and ethical values which suggest restraint or stillness: lawful wedlock, conjugal love, self-control, calmness, polished manners, smooth management, and self-possession. He made good use too of common objects suggesting restraint: stays,

wedding bands, rings, clasps, and chambers. The restraint carried by the language opens out into the scenes of the poem: overly elaborate and heavy banquets, stiff clothing, substantial wealth manifested in overly decorated and furnished rooms, becalmment on the ocean, prisons, harems. Nowhere does life seem more close and stifling than in England. The rich and well-born, stiff in their garments and manners, go dully through their daily routines trying to control "that awful yawn that sleep cannot abate," and longing only for dinner and retirement. All the rough, high spots of personality have been ground away, and now

> Society is smoothed to that excess,
> That manners hardly differ more than dress.
>
> (XIII, 94)

And though the English upper classes are still barbarians, their crudeness has become so homogenous that they can be described as

> one polished horde
> Formed of two mighty tribes, the *Bores* and *Bored.*
>
> (XIII, 95)

What I have said so far might suggest that Byron as satirist is championing libertinism, and this is, of course, how his contemporaries understood him, despite his protests that *Don Juan* was a moral poem.[19] But Byron had no illusions about the ultimate goodness of human nature or about the effects of the unlimited free exercise of instinct. Juan, for example, is praised for restraining his appetites and fears in the shipwreck scene in Canto II. But Byron did understand, however, that the human instincts are inescapable realities, dynamic forces surging toward satisfaction, and that to dam them up and deny them altogether is to intensify

19. *"Don Juan* will be known, *by and by,* for what it is intended—a *satire* on *abuses* in the present states of society, and not an eulogy of vice. It may be now and then voluptuous:—I can't help that. Ariosto is worse. Smollett ten times worse; and Fielding no better." Letter to John Murray, December 22, 1822, in *The Works of Lord Byron, Letters and Journals,* ed. R. E. Prothero (London, 1901), V, 242.

their explosive power when they inevitably detonate. He knew, furthermore, that when left free to realize themselves, these passions achieve a certain grandeur, but when restrained they corrupt and taint the character. The untrammeled love of Juan and Haidée has a quality of magnificence which is lacking in the covert liaison of Juan and Donna Julia; and when denied even illicit, hidden expression, the power of love sours to lust, sex hatred, and leering prudishness. What is true of love is equally true of the other passions. The courage of legitimists and tyrants like Castlereagh "stagnates to a vice," slavery turns the freedom-loving Lambro to an enslaver, social propriety makes walking dead of once vital men and women. The attempt to contain the passions and stop the flow of life always defeats itself in some manner. This is the particular form which the standard satiric plot takes in *Don Juan*.

The satiric elements of *Don Juan* are not arranged in so consistent a pattern as the comic plot built on the adventures of Don Juan. The satiric plot is made up of a great number of attenuated scenes, descriptions, and references which all show the same movement of life—in England, Spain, or Turkey, in the present or in the past—through containment to disaster. We can see this plot in little in the description of the textbooks given to young Juan. He is to be educated in the classics, of course, but the "filthy loves of gods and goddesses" and the "grosser parts" are removed from his texts, lest Juan "should grow vicious." The expurgation is done by pedants who are themselves such slaves to their training that, fearing "to deface . . . their modest bard," they cannot bring themselves to present an incomplete text. So they collect all the indecent passages in an appendix ("Which saves, in fact, the trouble of an index") where they stand like "garden gods—and not so decent either," easily accessible to "the ingenuous youth of future ages." These learned men no doubt congratulate themselves on their piety and their professional skill as educators, never knowing that they have achieved just the opposite of the intended effect. And this is the pattern of the satiric plot as we have seen it elsewhere, for dullness always manages to contrive the opposite of

its intention, though it is always too stupid to realize what it has actually done.

But the satiric episodes do not always end so gaily in *Don Juan* as does the textbook incident. The city of Seville pictured in Canto I is a remarkably moral place, sternly dedicated to the control of those unruly passions which corrupt the young, create unpleasant scandal, and destroy sane and sensibly arranged marriages. But somehow it all works out contrarily. Donna Inez, Juan's mother, is learned, efficient, and virtuous, the perfect spouse; but her husband, Don José, "a mortal of the careless kind," does not appreciate this paragon sufficiently, and their marriage turns into a prison which intensifies and corrupts the very passions it is intended to control:

> Don José and the Donna Inez led
>   For some time an unhappy sort of life,
> Wishing each other, not divorced, but dead;
>   They lived respectably as man and wife,
> Their conduct was exceedingly well-bred,
>   And gave no outward signs of inward strife,
> Until at length the smothered fire broke out,
> And put the business past all kind of doubt.
>
> (I, 26)

Don José follows his fancy, takes a mistress or two, and soon the lawyers are busy for their fees, friends intrude with unwanted advice, and the city buzzes with gossip. The matter is at last settled amicably: Don José dies. It turns out, however, that Donna Inez herself probably had a lover, Don Alfonso, who for reasons of prudence had married a woman thirty years younger than himself, the Donna Julia. But she and Don Juan, who had been so carefully restrained by his mother and trained to the path of virtue by so moral an education, fall desperately in love and begin an affair which ends in a rousing bedroom scene where Juan and Alfonso nearly kill one another. Julia is buried in a convent for the remainder of her life, the families' names are on every tongue

and in every paper, and Juan is forced to leave home. The result of too strict restraint and moral dishonesty has been two broken families, two deaths—one literal and one figurative—several ruined lives, and the advertisement of the fact that the best families of Seville are not what they are supposed to be. When last seen, Donna Inez, encouraged by "the great success of Juan's education," has set up "a Sunday school for naughty children," where she, according to a cancelled passage,

> Their manners helping and their morals curing
> Taught them to suppress their vice and urine.
>
> (II, 10)[20]

While Juan the comic hero always escapes this destructive pattern of restraint leading to explosion and perversion of what is best in man, the world he moves in does not. In Spain, in Greece, in Turkey, in Russia, and in England most of all, wherever Juan travels, the clothes and customs may differ, but the rich and powerful and virtuous are everywhere busily engaged in trying to dam up vitality, to bring social and political life to a standstill, to control the giddy fluctuations and powerful passions of their own and other natures by means of education, religion, philosophic systems, manners, and, if all else fails, brute force. The actions of the establishment are sometimes ludicrous, as in Seville, and sometimes deadly serious, as in England, but they always create the characteristic world of satire and produce the same plot. The world grows false and hypocritical; spirit is rejected for a gross, crammed materialism; the vital turns mechanical; direct, graceful bearing and style turn to heavy conglomerations. In this world the poorer spirits languish and corrupt, while the natural pressure of the bolder spirits is intensified until it rips apart the containing bonds. The narrator universalizes the pattern which his characters act out by tracing similar plots in history: tyranny leading again and again to bloody revolution, the search for reputation and fame

20. This couplet is printed in *Byron's Don Juan, A Variorum Edition*, eds. Steffan and Pratt (Austin, Texas, 1957), 2, 162.

leading to oblivion, the proud attempts to sum up the world in a single philosophy or to order life with a moral system making only more clear that life escapes any system and man any morality, the technology intended to produce a better world providing more efficient means for killing and turning life into hell.

The most powerful statement of the corrupting effect of calm and restraint on man occurs in Canto II of *Don Juan,* where after their ship has been sunk in a great storm, Juan and a number of sailors are becalmed in a small boat without food or oars. The sun burns down, the sea is stagnant, the men lie like carcasses, and then "the longings of the cannibal arise." Lots are made—from the touching farewell letter Julia wrote to Juan, *"Elle vous suit partout"*—the victim chosen and killed, the surgeon's fee paid by giving him first choice of the parts, the body divided and eaten, and the offal thrown to those sharks outside the boat. Juan, who as comic hero is not subject to the effects of repression, does not join the feast, and fortunately, for the results are ghastly. The cannibals

> Went raging mad—Lord! how they did blaspheme!
> And foam, and roll, with strange convulsions racked,
>   Drinking salt-water like a mountain stream,
> Tearing, and grinning, howling, screeching, swearing,
> And, with hyæna-laughter, died despairing.
>
> (II, 79)

The satiric plot which is presented in more conventional terms and scenes elsewhere is offered here undisguised. When life is stilled, the natural appetites unsatisfied, and free movement denied man, then his powers take perverted forms, and he changes to a mad animal and dies in despair. The food he seeks to sustain life drives him insane, and he mistakes salt water for fresh. The perversions of natural appetites and the movement toward self-destruction are not so spectacular in a polite household in Seville, in an aristocratic English country house, in a Turkish court, or in the nations of Europe controlled by the Holy Alliance, but they are of the same order and they move to the completion of the same plot.

IV

TRAGEDY

In comedy life flows excitingly, bubbling, a surge into which the youthful comic hero flings himself to enjoy the invigoration of being a part of the world's rushing power. The older comic hero—a Prospero or Leontes—glimpsing the endless sea of time into which all life flows, gives himself to the broadening current and finds satisfaction in becoming one with a bountiful world taken on trust. Satire expresses no particular joy in the way of the world, but it does assume that the nature of reality can be known by reason and that life can therefore be lived in reasonable conformity with what is, even if the majority of men are too senseless to accept the givens of existence. But the same world can be seen from another, a tragic, perspective, in which the isolated individual faces but cannot accept the oblivion to which the world dooms him as a man. "The rhythm of tragedy . . . is the rhythm of the individual life which comes to a close, and its great symbol is death. The one inescapable fact about every human being is that he must die. No skill in living, no sense of life, no inborn grace or acquired wisdom can avert this individual doom."[21] This is the root perception of the tragic, and all the more complex forms of the tragic vision which make up the history of literary tragedy from Homer to the present have grown directly from it. The form has developed in many ways, as the tragic sense of life has shifted in response to other beliefs such as Christianity, naturalistic philosophy, and Freudian psychology, but it has continued to draw its power from the terror of death, the isolation of the individual, and the inevitability of time. These realities account for some of the most permanent characteristics of the tragic form: the typical loneliness of the tragic hero, whose closest friends always answer his most pressing questions with Horatio's " 'Twere to consider too curiously, to consider so"; the constricted space within which

21. Helen Gardner, "As You Like It," p. 22.

the hero is confined—Prometheus chained to his rock, Raskolnikov sensing himself on a ledge so narrow that a deep breath will hurl him into the depths, Macbeth "cabined, cribbed, confined"—and the deliberate, fated movement of the plot, whether it be the mechanical revolution of Fortune's Wheel or the inevitable chain of Aristotelian consequence following on some action.

When viewed from the angle of the solitary man, the movement of life which flows through *Don Juan* darkens to a tragic setting in which while Life rolls on, the individual is fated to stillness and obliteration. The life principle continues, but tragic man is unable to maintain his oneness with the great energy which has briefly expressed itself in him. As the tragic situation begins to constrict, it becomes clear that while the essence of life is movement and change, every attempt to remain free and express the elemental passions becomes in itself a trap. The narrator is painfully familiar with this pattern, for his life as lover, romantic hero, sensualist, and poet has continually brought him face to face with paradox. Love, which begins so passionately and vitally, seeks marriage to express itself, but

> There's doubtless something in domestic doings
> Which forms, in fact, true Love's antithesis.
> (III, 8)

Even when not consolidated in marriage, love wears itself out in sameness and becomes a prison. Art which seeks to express the fullness and excitement of life's movement and variety deadens the reality and reduces it to such icy forms as *The Laocoön* and *The Dying Gaul,* where

> energy like life forms all their fame,
> Yet looks not life, for they are still the same.
> (IV, 61)

The search for pleasure, the gusto for all that life has to offer through the senses, ends in surfeit and sameness as the distinguishing taste is lost. Man's body, the instrument of his vitality, ages

and drags the spirit down with it. Joy in the objective world involves man in a deadening materialism. Even before man's great feeling for the free life entangles itself, it destroys the freedom in other great spirits: lover tyrannizes over lover, heroism feeds on the death of other heroes, passion extinguishes the passion which aroused it. All manifestations of vitality become the means of destroying the vital in individual man.

In words which suggest the essential quality of the tragic spirit large enough to meet the tragic situation, Wallace Stevens once defined imagination and nobility as a "violence from within that protects us from a violence without."[22] But very few people in the world of *Don Juan* have the violence necessary to resist the bondage which tragic life forces violently on them. They bend their knees to tyrants, stand submissively on slave blocks, go quietly off to convents, and grow old without protest. Only the pirate's daughter, Haidée, her human clay kindled from the sun and "full of power for good and evil," has the tragic strength and violence to know and maintain her kinship with the only god of Byron's universe, the onward surge of being. Like all tragic heroes, she is fated for her struggle. Life burns within her with more force than in other mortals, and her entire being is a flashing movement: her blood runs headlong like a torrent, her heart dashes on to beat against Juan's bosom, her spirit springs from her burning eyes, her hair flows downward like an Alpine stream, her kisses focus the rays of the sun, and her glances dart out like the swiftest arrow, or like

> the snake late coiled, who pours his length,
> And hurls at once his venom and his strength.
>
> (II, 117)

Haidée gives herself to love and life completely, and even as she does so, she encounters her fate. It comes in a number of forms. The narrator tells us that the act of love commits her to the loss

22. "The Noble Rider and the Sound of Words," *The Necessary Angel* (New York, 1951), p. 36.

of that love, for in time Juan can only grow weary of her and pass
on to new loves:

> Oh, Love! what is it in this world of ours
>   Which makes it fatal to be loved? Ah why
> With cypress branches hast thou wreathed thy bowers,
>   And made thy best interpreter a sigh?
> As those who dote on odours pluck the flowers,
>   And place them on their breast—but place to die—
> Thus the frail beings we would fondly cherish
> Are laid within our bosoms but to perish.
>
> (III, 2)

While Haidée does not consciously know the dangers to which
she has given herself, knowledge of her fate is deep within her,
and it presents itself in a dream—"the mystical usurper of the
mind"—in which she is bound immobile and forced to endure
whatever the world, in the form of ocean, may do to her:

> She dreamed of being alone on the sea-shore,
>   Chained to a rock; she knew not how, but stir
> She could not from the spot, and the loud roar
>   Grew, and each wave rose roughly, threatening her;
> And o'er her upper lip they seemed to pour,
>   Until she sobbed for breath, and soon they were
> Foaming o'er her lone head, so fierce and high—
> Each broke to drown her, yet she could not die.
>
> (IV, 31)

Here are all the elements of tragedy in little: the isolation of the
hero, the Promethean chaining to a single spot, the necessity for
enduring like Gloster who is "tied to th' stake and . . . must stand
the course," the proud refusal to yield even while longing for
death to escape the wheel of fire.

As is usual in the tragic world, the destructive forces are external
as well as internal. The setting is a sea-surrounded Greek island, a
Greece where the ancient spirit of freedom—recalled in the song,
"The Isles of Greece"—has been destroyed by the savage, oppres-

sive rule of the Turk. While Haidée's father, to give him his tragic epithet, the pirate Lambro, maintains his own island kingdom and rejects the Turkish rule and any law of man, he is in turn a tyrant who captures and sells men, an absolute ruler in his own small domain, and a loving but stern father who regards his daughter as a possession. The wealth Lambro has collected by piracy becomes a chain on Haidée's freedom in the form of the binding ornaments she wears: the "silken fillet" which "curbs" her flowing hair; the golden bracelet which "clasps" her arm, "clinging as if loath to lose its hold"; the rich, heavy garments which cover her and beneath which "her breast heaved like a little billow."

Juan and Haidée further tighten the bonds around themselves in realizing their love, though unaware of what they are doing:

> that which destroys
> Most love—possession—unto them appeared
> A thing which each endearment more endeared.
>   (IV, 16)

As their love ripens, its setting changes from the clear beach under the broad sky and in view of the pounding surf to an interior scene, heavy, ornate and grossly material. The rugs are crimson satin, the velvet cushions stiff with gold brocade; "crystal and marble, plate and porcelain" fill the room; heavy objects of ebony, mother of pearl, ivory, rare woods, gold, and silver cover the walls and press in on the lovers. Their entertainment and their service is provided by dwarfs and black slaves, who "gain their bread . . . by degradation." From the free, naked state in which they first loved, they have passed on to rich, intricate, confining clothing and circumstances.

Though they are tragically unable to escape the bondage they defy, the lovers do not ultimately chain themselves. But early death is the price that Haidée at least must pay for her escape— "whom the gods love die young." The final struggle comes with her father Lambro, who focuses all of the binding powers in the poem. He returns to find his daughter in a stranger's arms, has him bound, and ships him off to the slave market at Constantinople. The key words gathered around Lambro are "calm," "still,"

"fixed," and "hard." And, as always in *Don Juan,* a placid outer surface, a rigid control of feelings, guarantees that the fires within are dangerously compressed:

> High and inscrutable the old man stood,
>   Calm in his voice, and calm within his eye—
> Not always signs with him of calmest mood.
>
> (IV, 39)

Lambro, though a rebel himself against political and social authority, and though intensely fond of his daughter, in this moment acts like the most conventional father and invokes the sacred word "duty." Since his honor and his daughter's virtue have been marred, he feels that he must do his duty, and each of his duteous acts is identified as a binding. He *fixes* the lovers with a deadly look, he stands in the "fix'd ferocity" of relentless anger, he "compresses" his daughter "within his clasp," his followers wound Juan, bind him, carry him to a ship and chain him "so that he cannot move."

Juan is not fated to be a tragic hero, and he is carried away to new adventures, but Haidée is left with the tragic choice. Having asserted her freedom and then come against the inevitable countermovement, she can now either submit or die to maintain that freedom which in the tragic world can be asserted in no other way. Earlier in the poem Donna Julia in a similar situation allowed herself to be buried alive in a convent, but life in Haidée is so powerful that it cannot be restrained. Caught within her father's arms, helpless against physical force,

> The fire burst forth from her Numidian veins,
> Even as the Simoom sweeps the blasted plains.
>
> (IV, 57)

Writhing and turning in confinement, she is unable to release her body, but a vein bursts and her free blood runs on. "She had so much of soul / Earth could not claim the whole." And though reduced now in body to a statue—"fixed as marble's unchanged aspect"—when she hears a poet sing of the freedom of "ancient days, ere tyranny grew strong," and then of love, that "fierce name," Haidée's tears break forth in a "gushing stream," and the

"spirit from her passed." She was "One life could not hold, nor death destroy."

This is romantic tragedy. In its brief span it contains not only the isolation, the terror of death, and the narrowing movement which are characteristic of all tragedy, but also the fierce struggle of man with his paradoxical nature and world to win that freedom without which he feels he cannot truly live. And by her courage and tenacity, at enormous expense, Haidée achieves something like victory. But even as Byron writes of her, she and her lover fade back into some distant world:

> They were not made in the real world to fill
>   A busy character in the dull scene,
> But like two beings born from out a rill,
>   A Nymph and her beloved, all unseen
> To pass their lives in fountains and on flowers,
> And never know the weight of human hours.
>
> (IV, 15)

The narrator of *Don Juan,* who knows very well the weight of human hours, presses on beyond Haidée's tragedy to a darker tragic vision of an eternal ocean of time to which man, full and complete man, cannot possibly accommodate himself, and over which no victory, however qualified, is possible. In this vision men are born only to feed worms, the brazen head of the world tells no more than "Time is, Time was, Time's past," the only cry heard in the gray waste is the "solitary shriek . . . of some strong swimmer in his agony," "great names are nothing more than nominal," and the narrator who has "stood upon Achilles' tomb / And heard Troy doubted" knows that "time will doubt of Rome." This bleak view is fully revealed in the water imagery of one of the most moving stanzas of the poem:

> Between two worlds Life hovers like a star,
>   'Twixt Night and Morn, upon the horizon's verge.
> How little do we know that which we are!
>   How less what we may be! The eternal surge

Of Time and Tide rolls on and bears afar
  Our bubbles; as the old burst, new emerge,
Lashed from the foam of ages; while the graves
Of Empires heave but like some passing waves.
(XV, 99)

This "vast, salt, dread, eternal deep," is but one version of the
world which always opens up to the tragic hero. It is the same
mysterious darkness into which Hamlet peers beyond the battlements of Elsinore and sees in the skull of Yorick, it is the terror
which Oedipus hears in the voice of the oracle at Delphi and in
the riddle of the Sphinx outside Thebes, it is the malevolent waves
breaking over Haidée in her dream. But the tragic situation of the
narrator is more desperate than that of older tragic figures. He is
completely disembodied, for while he is the major character of
the poem, we never see him. His reality is not material but entirely
mental, and it is in his mind, endlessly reflecting on the scenes he
creates before him, speculating on past and present, relating what
he has seen to what he knows, and searching for meaning without
finding any truth other than provisional, that we meet the tragic
individual—late romantic or ironic type—and come to know the
full loneliness of existence emptied of pure feeling and passion,
estranged from nature, rejected by and rejecting society and history.

To this point the narrator's experience of his world is simply an
intensification and self-conscious formulation of the situation in
which Haidée and all tragic heroes find themselves. But where
they in some manner validate their positive assertions about themselves and life, the narrator has no hope of meaningful action because he finds the universe itself ultimately meaningless. The rest
is silence after Haidée's as well as Hamlet's death, but in *Don Juan*
that silence no longer suggests a perfect though mysterious com-
pleteness in human life lived greatly. The poet's gaze travels over
Lambro's island after the death of Haidée and the child she
carried:

That isle is now all desolate and bare,
  Its dwellings down, its tenants passed away;

None but her own and Father's grave is there,
  And nothing outward tells of human clay;
Ye could not know where lies a thing so fair,
  No stone is there to show, no tongue to say,
What was; no dirge, except the hollow sea's,
Mourns o'er the beauty of the Cyclades.

                                    (IV, 72)

Haidée gave her life to maintain the vital principle of her being, free movement in life. Having eluded stagnation and bondage, she achieves tragic stature and passes on to become an undiminished part of that ever-flowing power of the universe with which she identified herself. But the narrator has come to understand that movement and change, uncontrasted and infinite, become sameness: "Change grows too changeable, without being new." This being the case, tragic action, like comic and satiric, becomes meaningless, for in the end all things pass on to the *hollow* sea, where endless movement becomes only endless stasis, and the infinity of time and space become mere pinpoints. Man cannot accept such a world, nor can he deny it, so all action becomes equally meaningful and meaningless. "He who doubts all things nothing can deny."

Don Juan makes a crucial point about the nature and relationship of literary genres. The true subject of the poem, I take it, is freedom and the onward flow of all life. This ultimate view of the nature of reality is common to the comic, satiric, and tragic portions of the poem; so it would appear that the major literary genres may, but need not, differ in their view of the fundamental movements of life and the ultimate order of nature. The major genres differ, however, in the perspectives they take on that ultimate order of the world, and in the way in which their major characters attempt to deal with that world. In comedy, the focus is on the excitement and goodness of the long sweep of life; and the hero is the man who naturally knows the way of the world and commits himself to the zestful experience, while avoiding the traps laid for him by the fools who attempt to deny nature.

In satire, nature is viewed in a more neutral manner, simply as the way things are; and the plot follows the workings of the dunces who for one reason or another attempt to deny nature but succeed only in perverting life. In tragedy, nature is viewed from the perspective of the isolated, solitary individual who grows old and dies; and the plot traces his fearful struggles with a nature toward which he feels kinship and revulsion simultaneously.

Every literary work with real power is a battleground of these various perspectives on and attitudes toward reality, as it is defined by the work. *Lear,* for example, moves toward satire in such speeches as Lear's "change places, and, handy-dandy, which is the justice, which is the thief?" and in such scenes as the end of II.iv where the King's daughters primly decide that he is himself entirely responsible for being thrust out onto the heath. But the play also has pronounced comic tendencies: latent in the exact parallelism of the plots involving two sons and three daughters, more explicit in the Fool's speeches, in Gloucester's supposed fall over Dover Cliff, and in the great reconciliation scene between Lear and Cordelia. But throughout the play, and particularly in Act V, the tragic momentum overwhelms the comic and satiric impulses. Because the plot consistently takes a tragic direction, because the tragic perspective persistently blots out the comic and satiric, we call *Lear* a tragedy. But we should not think that a genre designation is an airtight category which excludes all traces of other genres. Every great work has a tendency to become epic, comedy, tragedy, and satire; and the degree to which the author allows these tendencies to develop is a principal ingredient of the particular tone of his writing, a prime constituent of his unique style. Ben Jonson, for example, worked at one time or another in comedy, satire, and tragedy—*The Alchemist, Volpone, Sejanus* —but his tragedies and comedies always have such a strong satiric quality that there is considerable uneasiness about their correct genre designation. Vergil's *Aeneid* is obviously an epic celebrating the world triumph of Roman values as defined by Augustus, but at the same time Aeneas' painful loss of his personal identity and the destruction of his emotional life are so powerfully presented

that the epic exists in a most uneasy balance with tragic tendencies. Horace's good-humored acceptance of life and his easy tolerance nearly conquer the satiric energies of his *Sermones;* while Swift's terrifying vision of human dullness always threatens to conquer his satiric perspective, and becomes so intense and agonizing at times that it topples his writings into tragedy.

Concluding Remarks

Criticism is a reductive activity, and the end result of any critical description of a work of art, no matter how finely drawn and sensitive, inevitably involves dismemberment of organic wholes and the obliteration of delicate tones and shadings. When criticism is extended beyond the description of a single work to the study of entire genres, as it is in this book, then the process of abstraction and the resultant coarseness of reading is intensified—so much so that many critics have thought that such large-scale criticism leads away from the literary work rather than toward it, and blocks rather than sharpens our vision.

If anyone were to take the terms and the scheme of satire offered in these pages as a sufficient way of describing any particular satire—contenting himself with pointing out that the characters in, say, *Jonathan Wild* or *1984* were engaged in magnifying their own importance and reducing the vital to the mechanical— then this book will have done a disservice to criticism, and my own worst fears will be realized. What I have tried to do is to offer sight lines which lead not away from particular satiric works toward some cold abstraction or some heavenly form but toward the particular qualities and shapes of specific satires. I have used the general name "dullness" in order to talk about the blundering energies which drive the world along in satire, and the name as used by Pope seemed more apt than such alternatives as vice or folly. But dullness has a unique style in Juvenal, in Jonson, in Pope, in Waugh and in every satire of any importance; and in each satire the particular form of dullness spins out its own special world and plot. To describe this uniqueness is the business of criticism, but I know no better way of coming at it than to look first for what the varieties of dullness have in common. Once we

really understand what plot is in the abstract, then the way is cleared to understanding even such strange forms of plot as those found in satire, and once we see the over-all pattern of the type of work we call satire, then we are in a position to say with some surety whether a particular work is a satire and to see more clearly the nature of particular satires.

In hope of demonstrating this relation between genre theory and criticism of specific works, I have moved back and forth from general statements about the nature of satire to the discussion of specific satires. In this way the theory is abstracted from particular works and the works illuminated in turn by the theory, but the intention of the examination has been, hopefully, to bring us closer to particular works of art.

Index

Shinagel